"*An Analytical Exploration of Intimacy* provides an excellen[t]... [narcis]sism so relevant in today's wo[rld]... narcissism, and by giving the character Echo a well-deserved larger role than she has been given so far, Susan Schwartz provides a rich and inspiring addition to previous Jungian studies on narcissism – not least because of her cross-disciplinary focus. I find the book most interesting and highly commendable."

Misser Berg, *Jungian Analyst, Denmark, President of the IAAP*

"In her compelling new book, Susan Schwartz engages a depth exploration of the myth of Narcissus and Echo, bringing new insights to our understanding of the despair residing beneath the false self of the narcissist. She invites the reader into a compassionate perspective for the vulnerabilities of an ego disconnected from the Self, and clarifies the courage required for both therapist and patient to walk together through the intimate, tumultuous struggle that awaits the patient, caught between the longing wish to be seen, and the terrifying fear of that very thing."

Carolyn Bates, *PhD, Jungian Analyst, co-editor of The Journal of Analytical Psychology*

"This book is an essential reference for everyone who wants to understand narcissism, a fundamental issue in our contemporary society. Susan Schwartz is an experienced analyst and articulates Jungian concepts in a brilliant way!"

Alvaro Ancona de Faria, *MD, psychiatrist, Jungian Analyst, President of SBrPA in Brazil, and former member of the IAAP Executive Committee*

An Analytical Exploration of Love and Narcissism

This book reflects the psychic wounds of narcissism from the perspective of Jungian analytical psychology. Oriented towards the richness and plurality of the psyche, it sheds light on clinical practice as well as the common and intricate issues of this personality type.

Narcissism is described as a grandiose sense of self, exhibitionistic, needing reassurance, but suffering in disturbed relationships. The perspective of Jungian analytical psychology expands the symbolism within narcissism. Clinical examples, dreams, the myth of Narcissus and Echo, and basic Jungian concepts move us further into the psyche. Topics covered are: what narcissism is and why it's misunderstood, and if narcissists are capable of love and their perfectionist burden. It explores how to forge knowledge and emotional transformation with a narcissist in clinical treatment and all relationships.

Exploring this complex and intriguing phenomenon, the book will appeal to readers and therapists from various fields including psychoanalysis, general psychology, gender studies, culture and sociology.

Susan E. Schwartz, PhD, trained in Switzerland as a Jungian analyst. A member of the International Association of Analytical Psychology (IAAP) and a presenter at conferences, workshops and on YouTube channels, she has authored numerous journal articles and book chapters. Her previous books include *A Jungian Exploration of the Puella Archetype: Girl Unfolding*; *Imposter Syndrome and the 'As-If' Personality in Analytical Psychology: The Fragility of Self*; and *The Absent Father Effect on Daughters: Father Desire, Father Wounds*. Her website is www.susanschwartzphd.com

An Analytical Exploration of Love and Narcissism

The Tragedy of Isolation and Intimacy

Susan E. Schwartz

Routledge
Taylor & Francis Group
LONDON AND NEW YORK

Designed cover image: Barbara Aliza

First published 2025
by Routledge
4 Park Square, Milton Park, Abingdon, Oxon OX14 4RN

and by Routledge
605 Third Avenue, New York, NY 10158

Routledge is an imprint of the Taylor & Francis Group, an informa business

© 2025 Susan E. Schwartz

The right of Susan E. Schwartz to be identified as author of this work has been asserted in accordance with sections 77 and 78 of the Copyright, Designs and Patents Act 1988.

All rights reserved. No part of this book may be reprinted or reproduced or utilised in any form or by any electronic, mechanical, or other means, now known or hereafter invented, including photocopying and recording, or in any information storage or retrieval system, without permission in writing from the publishers.

Trademark notice: Product or corporate names may be trademarks or registered trademarks, and are used only for identification and explanation without intent to infringe.

British Library Cataloguing-in-Publication Data
A catalogue record for this book is available from the British Library

ISBN: 978-1-032-73252-7 (hbk)
ISBN: 978-1-032-73251-0 (pbk)
ISBN: 978-1-003-46329-0 (ebk)

DOI: 10.4324/9781003463290

Typeset in Times New Roman
by codeMantra

I'm nobody! Who are you?
Are you nobody, too?

Emily Dickinson

> (Emily Dickinson, *The Project Gutenberg eBook of Poems by Emily Dickinson, Series One*, edited by Thomas Wentworth Higginson and Mabel Loomis Todd, originally published 1890)

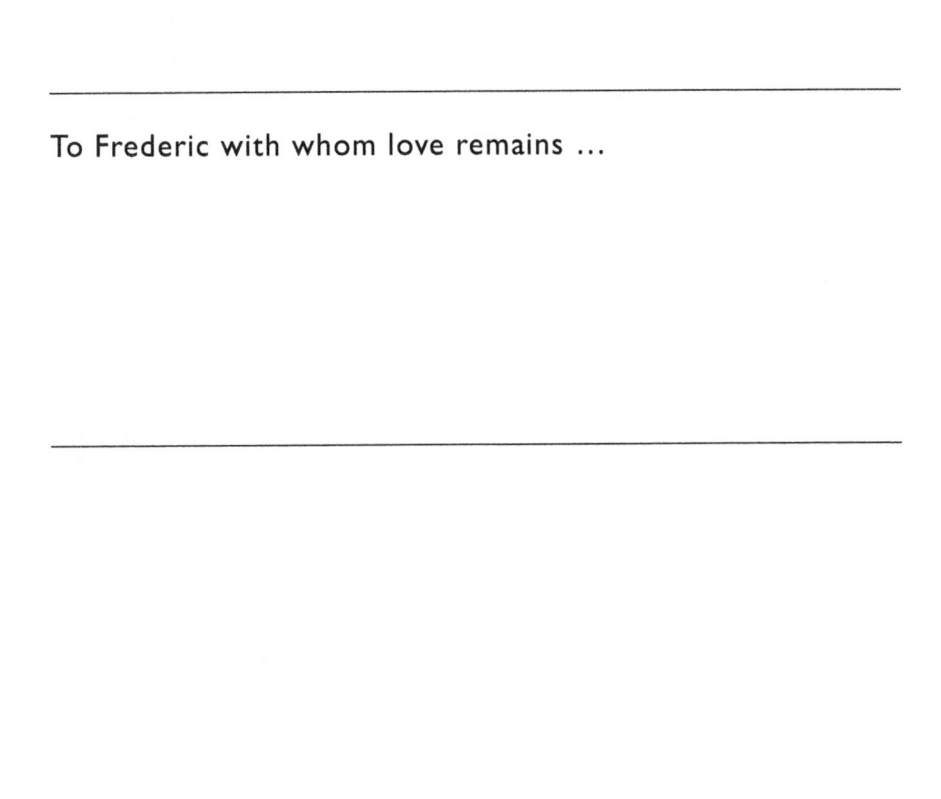

To Frederic with whom love remains ...

Contents

Acknowledgements		*xiii*
Introduction		1
1	The mythological beginnings	3
2	The vagaries of narcissism	17
3	Emotion and desire obstructed by envy	34
4	Emptiness and boredom	50
5	The body talks – does a narcissist listen?	68
6	Echo's tragedy – narcissistic isolation from intimacy	82
7	Psychoanalysis and André Green's life and death narcissism	97
8	Narcissism in Jungian thought	117
9	The shadows of love in relationship	131
10	The analytical bridge to Self through cultural diversity	146
11	The nigredo of now	165
12	Where do we go from here? Can Narcissus and Echo bloom into love?	181
Index		*189*

Acknowledgements

The acknowledgements are never ending as the years of relating with analysands, colleagues and friends all pile up, each in a memorable and unique way. The interest and support of friends during this time has been invaluable. And, of course, I wish to deeply thank those people who agreed for their material and dreams to be noted here.

I also want to acknowledge the continual enthusiasm of Katie Randall at Routledge to support my proposals.

LeeAnn Pickrell edits beautifully and sensitively.

Barbara Aliza creates amazing covers.

Daniela Roher continues to read and convey discerning commentary on chapters of the book and exude confidence in my work.

Introduction

This book is written from the need to understand more about the easily bantered around label of narcissism. Who really comprehends the suffering, loneliness and isolation of a person so trapped within themselves? It is least of all the narcissist who cannot assess the ramifications of their self-imposed limitations. My emphasis here is on the 'I am solitary' aspect of narcissism, indicating a profound early relational and empathic failure.

For the narcissist to be able to help or understand themselves takes time. Narcissism as a personality type and trait is currently prevalent in the Western-oriented world. This book is written to light a path towards a fuller life and conscious awareness of the disasters and opportunities afforded by narcissism. The focus is the perspective of Jungian analytical psychology and my own orientation and belief in the richness of the psyche. My exploration reaches into the valuable depths and breadths of being. Although there are some mysteries we may never comprehend, the process of self-discovery and the coming together of the personality on conscious and unconscious planes is the exciting prospect of this journey.

'The past is a series of opportunities and repair from the disappointments, missed chances revealing a pattern and logic to our life trajectory' (Greenblatt & Phillips, 2024, pp. 250–251). By reflecting and analysing, seeing if these patterns fit, a person can begin to act with more awareness. This attitude is central to the Jungian analytical approach and requires both sober seriousness and a search for joy. The process opens the question of what it is to be known and changed enough to move out from the narcissistic cavern of singularity. This movement requires an emulsification of psychological elements flowing together rather than remaining inert, distant or unconscious.

This perspective arises from my work with various people of all orientations, backgrounds, social classes and personal strivings. It is from the analytical work that these words and thoughts originate. The quest for meaning and making sense out of suffering is the point of any analytical thought as it enables a greater understanding of humanity. We all encounter narcissism in some form and can benefit from delving into the significance of Narcissus and Echo, the protagonists in the Greek mythology called the *Metamorphosis*, written by Ovid in 30 BCE.

Although the central themes appear somewhat altered in each culture, the essence of human enactments and the search for knowledge are similar.

Narcissism is a knotty prospect and untangling its strands is the aim of this work. The narcissistic struggle is reflected through myriad interpretations. These reflect the way we organise our experience of self and world, allowing us to recognise and identify narcissistic strategies for coping. The narcissist has been encased in the singular, with a resistance and refusal that keep growth from occurring. Yet, the Self continually searches for its origins and the renewal encountered in the opportunity to explore ambitions, desires, experiences and affections. The more aware we become, the more hope for Self and other coming together, not to meld but to meet, not to become one but to respect and honour both the same and the different.

The Jungian process of individuation is about becoming and continuing to become all we are but do not yet recognise. The unfolding of this mystery never ceases to amaze. For example, a woman with a narcissistic bent and a tendency to singularity hidden behind a successful persona, found herself in the midst of a life crisis. *She dreamt it was raining outside and she had no umbrella. She went out but did not get wet, although she did slip a bit on the wet surface. In slipping she did not fall; however, and when she looked up saw a rainbow.* To her, the rainbow was a special symbol and a reminder of change. She realised she could use her energy and instincts to save the day, to recover what seemed to have been almost lost. She recognised the self-destructive parts within, the isolating bits, and resisted her old pattern of closing down alternatives. Now she had to amass her strength and defy the internal persecutors. Rather than self-negation, she heeded the warning and the promise of the rainbow as an omen to attend to her value and look to a wider horizon.

All the examples in this book are composites, disguised combinations from my analytical experience, colleagues, narratives from literature and common to those engaged in the psychological search. In the following pages, narcissism, its traits and personality aspects are described and perceived as both an obstacle and pathway to the Self in all of its manifestations. As Marcel Proust wrote in *Time Regained*:

> Every reader, as he reads, is actually the reader of himself. The writer's work is only a kind of optical instrument he provides the reader so he can discern what he might never have seen in himself without this book. The reader's recognition in himself of what the book says is the proof of the book's truth.

References

Greenblatt, S., & Phillips, A. (2024). *Second chances: Shakespeare and Freud*. Yale University Press.

Proust, M. (1927). *Le temps retrouvé* (Vol. 7). https://www.gutenberg.org/ebooks/74091

Chapter 1

The mythological beginnings

The concept of narcissism originates from the story in *Metamorphosis,* written by the poet Ovid (1922) in 30 BCE:

> Avert your gaze and you will lose your love,
> for this that holds your eyes is nothing save
> the image of yourself reflected back to you.

Is it possible this passage refers to you or to people whom you love?

'You are a narcissist' is a common accusation these days, increasingly appearing not only in the psychological and analytical jargon but also in mainstream communication. But what does narcissism really mean? Being referred to as a narcissist is more than just an accusation; it is complex and many layered. When labelled as such, it is often taken as an insult, and the person is interpreted to be self-centred, self-absorbed, grandstanding and impossible relationally. The accuser is usually someone hurt by a narcissist, a person like the narcissist who is damaged by not receiving the promised love and who, from early in life, was unable to garner the correct attention.

There is within the narcissist, and unknown to most, intense insecurity and profound disappointment, including shame. These all create the reactions of hiding in singularity, discomfort with intimacy, obscuring misery and needing shields and walls to protect their fragility. Nothing creates security and nothing quells the desire for more as each achievement only opens the door to the next to avoid the gaping abyss. Too often the narcissist stops at conscious and behavioural adaptations but does not plumb the richness of the plurality of the psyche. In the myth itself, unable to accept the changes necessary for development, Narcissus died. He was not prepared to go into the unconscious, and he got lost in all he could not recognise that was himself.

However, the journey into narcissism can also lead to more complete knowledge of the psyche, including the unconscious and its wealth of material. If nothing opens to the unconscious, nothing comes back, and the narcissist cannot be fully desired or satisfied. They cannot grow as they need to love more than themselves to come alive.

Many books focus on how to cope with narcissism as a problem to solve more than providing a staircase to deeper understanding of the psyche. They lack the symbolism, mutuality of psychological transferences and the intricacy gained through exploration of the multifaceted nature of narcissism. In addition, the narcissistic mother is more prevalently noted than the narcissistic father, a lacuna that is also striking.

This exploration into narcissism is oriented to be empathic and widen the scope beyond the usual pathology and dictums to avoid narcissism and narcissists. That perspective limits and narrows. It denies the reality of healthy narcissism and avoids sensitively exploring the many nuances of the convoluted and often-misunderstood trials and pathos of narcissism. This exploration adds to the concept of narcissism with openness to the mystery of the psyche.

The stories encountered here have meaning for our lives, although the details differ. We are not alone with an empty self; instead, we become enriched ourselves and communications with others are enhanced. Learning more about narcissism uncovers its roots, estrangements and the personal and collective restraints to growth and finding love of self and others.

The narcissists given as examples are not all overt, apparent or offensive. Many are quiet, withdrawn, suffering silently. They are singular, wrapped away from others, not seeing themselves being seen in any appreciative, talented, competent or joyful ways. They are not easy to know or unite with in analytical treatment as much is hidden within, and they do not reveal easily due to vulnerability, tenderness and shame. Trust is not a given; it takes time. Early hurt leads to patterns that are tenacious against being open, attached and self-accepting. Narcissists are performers and often uneasy, but this is not readily acknowledged by them or others. Their circle of protection remains a barrier to intimacy. They share many of the traits of the overt narcissist who is busy, defended, but in a louder way. Neither type has an easy time being alive and present.

Narcissism is a desire for life and preservation of self. We all want to live, to access ways of reaching out and communicating our stories. Julia Kristeva, French Lacanian psychoanalyst, said, 'Self-love is perhaps the most enigmatic expression and experience there is' (1983; quoted in DeArmitt, 2014, p. 53). These words bring forward the knotty question surrounding narcissism and plaguing the psychological world since its beginnings. It means sharing what it is like to be alive within our cycle of life and inhabiting a particular perspective and style within our allotted fractions of time.

Narcissism contains a world of infinite complexity, of infinite possibility. The healthy narcissist has an adequate and balanced portion of self-love to be able to share, trust and express their creativity, meaning and purpose. All these are of interest in Jungian analytical psychology, for tracing this interpretation of narcissism through various case examples, including their dreams, illustrates the narcissist's charm, impenetrability, vulnerability, frustration and lack of awareness.

The narcissist is driven by an urge propelling the search for their own significance. James Hillman, archetypal psychologist, commented about narcissism as

> described by Freud in 1922 as an absence or disturbance of 'object libido', that desire reaching into the world 'out there'. Instead, desire flows inward, activating one's isolated subjectivity. The beauty of the world holds no allure, no echo that draws our noticing. Because the world's beauty does not call, I seek and find that beauty in a self-concentrated gaze. This is narcissism and, as the word itself betrays from its origin in the Ovid tale, narcissism is a beauty disorder, the face of the world unattended, the libido objectless, turned toward the narcissistic subject, disordering his character. Narcissus was captivated not by himself, not by reflection, but by beauty.
>
> (1998, p. 265)

In following the myth, we find Narcissus was not flamboyant or grandiose to others. In fact, for him, others did not exist. Likewise, here the narcissistic depiction is not on the showy or the star, but the one involved with their inner self, preoccupied, and for many reasons unable to love or be loved as they wish. Life is limited while desire is heightened. Too often they are stopped by themselves. This exploration seeks to discover some of those reasons.

The narcissist is run by a passion for self-definition but one confused with adulation, obscuring the search for Self. The solipsistic view of the narcissist entails sorrows, grief and mourning, melancholia; the symptoms of their suffering cause illusion, façade, egoism, paranoia and grandiosity, with masking behaviours a necessity. The narcissist can be like the petulant child, highly sensitive and easily injured. The sufferings arise from the unknown and yet to be discovered psychological material.

For the narcissist the experience of emotional abyss and bewilderment is an inescapable torment. Aspects of the self are frail, and self-regulation is rendered dysfunctional because it is undeveloped. Identity is fragmented and the absence of the self-as-object unable to be accessed. This means reflection and introspection are impaired, affecting the ability to access self-knowledge.

In a comment Édouard Glissant, 20th-century poet and writer, wrote, 'But imagination changes mentalities, however slowly it may go about this' (Munro, 2024, p. 183). However, the narcissist, although often quite imaginative, is derailed by narrow ego preoccupations. Self-value is contingent on the approval of others. Self-esteem and confidence are missing, although outwardly it seems otherwise.

The ego wants and wants and is never filled up because it remains disconnected from the Self. As we delve into the outer and grandiose performance of the narcissist, we find a merger of the ego with the Self rather than a relationship with the Self. To explain this further, the concept and definition of the Self in Jungian approaches can be easily misconstrued, partially because it was variously described by Jung. The Self, as opposed to the self, means all the knowable and unknowable aspects of living. It contains a mystery not to solve, a pluralism not to simplify, but offers, instead, a psychological response to our times and ultimately a way of integrating the hidden, fragmented personality needing to be more completely known and put together. The concept of the Self includes what is absent and yet to evolve into the future we make from what we are lacking. Lack in the present can lead to fulfilment in the future. As Hannah Arendt wrote in *Love and Saint Augustine*, 'Fearlessness is what love seeks … Such fearlessness exists only in the complete calm that can no longer be shaken by events expected of the future … Hence the only valid tense is the present, the Now' (1998). However, to accomplish this, we must feel the lack, and paradoxically, this is what the narcissist tries to avoid. The individuation process leads to more individual and expanded definitions that form the uniqueness of each person. It is not accomplished alone, but blossoms in the relational world with others. And here is where the narcissist has become stuck.

Narcissism is a multifaceted experience that can reveal what obstructs self-love and love with others. To broaden one's perspective aligns with the Jungian process of individuation, a transformative process of reshaping and accepting with consciousness the new, different and formerly unconscious material. The knowledge thus gained ploughs through the layers of distancing, disdain, misunderstandings, the psyche fearful of intimacy with self and others. By dividing the world into us versus them, me versus you, the entirety of person and world is disjointed. This is the stumbling block faced by the narcissist who cannot imagine any altered image of themselves and what such a transformation would imply. The narcissist avoids the paradoxes and possibilities and unfortunately promotes rigidity and resistance to the natural processes of living.

To all outer appearances these people are successful performers and high achievers but are overlaid with coldness and superficiality. There is a barrier around them. They find false safety in their aloofness, untouchability, and avoid hurt by taking the spotlight as much as possible. Although sparkling and appealing outwardly, their inner life remains hidden and split, tumultuous. A combination of self-love fights with self-hate. These co-exist in their conflicting emotions, feelings, desires, loves and the various versions and contradictions of self. Change and the narcissistic resistance to change are part of their psychological make-up. It can be frightening to step out of the familiar into the unknown as it means bringing in other knowledge.

The narcissist resists and refuses but simultaneously longs for what they think they cannot have or are not yet living. 'We share our lives with the people we have failed to be' (Phillips, 2013, p. xii). This is what the narcissist cannot tolerate, grieve or accept. The option they take is to ossify in sameness, sacrificing the willingness to look outside themself to discover other perspectives. Doing so means altering course, finding another option, turning from the same, allowing loss, the passing of time and the inherent revisions required.

All this brings the crash of ego-ideals, the unmet fantasies, the comfort in certainties. It means bearing the frustration of not knowing and letting in the authentic and its imperfections. Recognising lack precedes actualising its fulfilment. The narcissist is unmoored by being hampered from fulfilment by their narrow views bounded by self-absorption, fear and insecurity; they are separated from the totality of their personality.

This signifies narcissistic immaturity and a backing away from intimacy or genuineness. Wanting to be most special keeps this person out of touch with *mater/materia* as psyche and soma are dissociated. They feel empty at their core, without connection to the natural instincts, and are emotionally deprived.

So why do we love them so much? Or try to love them? Or get caught in their desire for more as nothing is ever enough? How are we narcissistic personally and culturally and is this healthy or not? These and other questions are part of the complexity involved in the pursuit of understanding narcissism.

Circumambulation

This writing is a *circumambulation*, an alchemical term for moving in circles around the issue and thereby gaining ever more insight and comprehension. By doing so, I collect aspects of the dilemma of narcissism particular to our era. The descriptors of these qualities reveal the stories people tell about themselves and hopefully bring light onto a subject intriguing and affecting others, our culture and our collective lives.

We all have some form of narcissism, and the conundrum is how to understand and use this personality aspect consciously. Therefore, magnifying the details of life means comprehending this form of human reaction, where it is derived from and where to go from here. It is not to pathologise but rather to unwrap and understand this texture of the human experience. This personality gripping our era is pervasive but rarely comprehended – especially by those caught within the narcissistic embrace and its psychic entanglement.

Narcissism is convoluted, complex, a mixture of theories, elusive, defined, upsetting. There is much sorrow and loss as it touches our hearts, and we realise what has been lost but may not recognise how much can be gained. The study of narcissism also elicits the enactment of conscious awareness. It is more than an intellectual endeavour; it stretches into uncomfortable emotions and reactions of frustration, insecurity, envy, shame and so on. It is a slice of what it means to be human. And how difficult this deep dive into the psyche and body, personal and cultural, is in the pursuit of the relational and inclusive rather than the solitary and excluding.

The narcissist's fascination with themselves and others with them will remain superficial and self-serving if it does not sufficiently confront the unconscious complexes composed of disassociated psychic pain. Narcissism is complex, a difficult and trying place from which to exist. It can signify the sad and lonely. It requires working with the non-rational, with psychic imagery and going deeply into the complex unconscious processes. Narcissism is anything but superficial.

Mythology of living

The concept of narcissism is based on the ancient Greek myth of Narcissus and Echo. Yet, this is a pertinent story about a psychological conflict relevant to the modern-day narcissist who, like Narcissus, lets no one else in. Mythology tells stories of people and their struggles in daily life, love and relationships, addressing both psyche and body for transformation. The myths are enactments of how to transform energy or libido and tell our life story. The beauty of mythology is it unfolds the ageless conflicts, challenges and unifications possible in the psyche. The road to self-knowledge is not easy but walking it enriches life and adds to a collective way of being. As we come to know ourselves, we are more open to understanding others. All the information lies within if we access it. Jung called this the collective unconscious, which contains the mysteries and quandaries of human life.

We each have a myth we are to live out and part of the psychological search is to do so. As Jung said,

> We are confronted, at every new stage in the differentiation of consciousness to which civilisation attains, with the task of finding a new interpretation appropriate to this stage to connect the life of the past that still exists in us with the life of the present, which threatens to slip away from it.
>
> (1968, CW 9i, para. 267)

Jung believed myths were expressions of the collective unconscious and human nature. He claimed myths are ubiquitous and found in diverse cultures with similar themes. They express the archetypes as common patterns in the psyche. They connect us to the collective unconscious, bringing into fuller awareness how much there is beyond our own world. 'By penetrating into the blocked subterranean passages of our own psyches we grasp the living meaning of classical civilisation and at the same time ... gain an objective understanding of our own foundations' (Jung, 1967, CW 5, para. 2). Mythology compels and unites the personal and archetypal, and their symbolic meanings refer to timeless conscious and unconscious processes. These stories are not always happy, and learning usually entails facing and surmounting various trials, pitfalls, unsavoury characters and ultimately becoming oneself.

In the Greek myth of Narcissus and Echo, the author Ovid depicts the nature of their encounter as being composed of loss, mourning, longing, desire. The tragedy of their unrequited love and eventual deaths depicts the transformations in psyche and body. The story relates the mystery of human relationships while addressing the paucity of the personality. The myth of Narcissus and Echo lays out the story of narcissism from its origins of tragic singularity, allowing for no differences, no others to be close and no consummation of love. Understanding narcissism requires a walkabout as we look at different angles, a process foreign to narcissistic make-up as the narcissist is dismayed by anything different.

Case example: Lucius

Lucius says he is bored. As he recounts his early life, it seems that, although home was intact, he did not learn about openness in relationships. He did, however, learn hiding and avoiding. He has had many affairs currently and over the years. He views each as being the same as the previous one; no one penetrates or stirs him. The affairs are interspersed with visits to prostitutes. I wonder if this enacts some sort of defiance and greed to grab all he was told he could not have. Do the affairs represent emptiness in love? Is love known by him and where is his warmth to himself and others? He seems to want, but the idea of what will penetrate seems vague, and he expects to get little intimate attention.

The same scenario happens with food, as he does not know when he should attend to or feel hunger. It is a constant battle for him. His internal world contains defensive and aggressive qualities that are unseen externally. Lucius has no good self-image, ever. He is in conflict and punishes himself with periodic excess, seems restless and does not know when or why he becomes lost. Weight plagues him, and his body image is poor, yet he continues to eat to excess, drink as well, and sex always occupies his mind. From childhood he learned he was wrong in his religious thoughts. He did not believe in the family community church and began to feel low self-worth because of this. He internalised the disconnect as his insufficiency, so he had to pretend he agreed when he did not. Lucius was rewarded for the lie against himself.

Lucius has an absence of inner containing spaces where his emotional experiences can be mediated. He does not self-reflect and makes everything rational. Otherwise, it all feels potentially overwhelming, and he cannot stand the sense of a self so fragile in the face of anxiety and feelings of annihilation. These all must be denied and isolated from, so he is then walled off from others, inhabiting an emotionally removed and cold place. In the absence of adequate internal and external containers Lucius describes being hollow inside, numb and unfeeling. It is as if he were a robot and cannot find his own direction or impetus.

Encounter with the other is crucial for overcoming narcissistic defences and their character structures. But Lucius feels fraudulent, flawed without knowing why. He just knows he does not measure up. However, when a person feels so deeply flawed, they cannot imagine fitting into human society and one solution is to attempt to rise above it all. This is the grandiose narcissistic escape from the painful place of shame: 'If I am not lovable for who I am, I will have to make people admire me for what I can do.' Like Lucius, narcissists often develop a false self (Winnicott, 1960) to deal with the outside world. The creation of the false self can serve in one way to protect, but in another way, it is a trap – a painful split between the private and public self. Feelings of being fake, unseen and worthless are tangled up with a sense of entitlement and fury. Like Lucius, narcissists grow up suffering from extreme loneliness and a confusing sense of despair. To avoid all this, they are always longing for stimulation. The question 'Where is love?' remains unanswered.

In the myth of Narcissus, it is the hunger to be seen and to see oneself that ultimately brings about his tragic end. One might argue that having never known adequate mirroring, Narcissus would rather stay with the comfort of his own image than seek a relationship with an external other. This is the dangerous power the sole mirror of self-reflection holds for some people. They cannot leave off looking for themselves, but they are never sufficiently found in the unconscious swirl away from deeper emotional relationships with another person.

Lucius dreamt he was on a precarious bicycle, balancing a water glass and going through snow to his hometown. He has 40 miles to go and decides to get an Uber a mile before the destination. He is conscious he will get spattered by the cars on the road, and he wants to appear clean, without mud, when he enters his hometown. He must be outwardly neat and composed. If the persona is in place, people will not negatively judge him as he expects them to. The dream reveals the need for persona cleanliness to avoid the anticipated rejection from the hometown ways, ideas and religious orientation he could not stomach.

The night before a therapy session, *Lucius dreamt he was in therapy, and I cut through what he was saying and asked the name of the second woman he had sex with. He gets chills as I say it was Mrs K. It was, and how did I know, he asked? Who is Mrs K.? She is the wife of the presidential supporter he does not like as he described the man as spineless, denigrating women and unscrupulous. Mrs K. is the nameless women he has been with.* As we talk, he says dreams are like guardrails for him to stay in line. Lucius identifies with the political candidate in his treatment of women and people in general to be controlled, bought and subject to his whims. The dream shows a mirror to the self he does not want to admit is him. He is trapped in his own maltreatment of himself and always trying to escape from it, hence the need for his addictive thoughts and behaviours.

Lucius has a voice inside he calls evil. It criticises all the time. It is so powerful he goes unconscious and often does not realise what has happened. *He dreamt of D. who is large in the dream. She says let's get married; he agrees and says let's do it now. It is night. He recalls he has been dating another woman, but oh well.* He decides not to tell his wife the dream. Lucius says D., a former sexual playmate, is changed and no threat any longer to him or his thoughts. However, why, in the dream, is he going to get married fast, lie to his wife and in effect abandon his life? The tricky female figure who is large still exists and can lure him away when he feels unaccepted or left out, vulnerable to any hint of abandonment. In a defensive reaction, he abandons himself and gets lost in his sexual fantasies to soothe the anxieties. This strategy only serves to separate him from himself and re-create the very dissociations he learned as a child. Then he could not be honest about his feelings and outwardly succumbed to being controlled for approval. The whole scenario has twisted him away from who he is, and the sexual thoughts function the same as the religious dogma. Lucius remains separated from himself.

Lucius comments he could accommodate others too much but equally can be very controlling. When not getting his way, he retaliates towards himself, simultaneously and sadistically punishing and gratifying with sex, food, drink, going unconscious. He denies hurt and does not get angry outwardly but directs the aggression inwards. In each dream he wants to appear good and without flaws but is repressive and unconscious to himself, consciously trying to correct it all by instituting stringent rules about exercise, body and weight loss for image and control.

I can hear Lucius's confusion, the ego dominant but not connected to the core self. His inner world persecutes, and his outer is devious. No one is allowed close enough to figure out what is going on and Lucius maintains his cover of being a compliant good guy. The problem is he cannot stop or understand any of his destructive habits. He is barricaded from himself and bombarded with destructive thoughts and actions. He lives in an internal dictatorship, restricted and unable to be spontaneous in any healthy way. This narcissist is sorely limited by himself.

Narcissistic intrigue

We must admit, narcissism intrigues us and draws us to the pond into which we also tend to gaze. This act is a falling into oneself and seeking recognition. To be fascinated is to be associated with excitement and enthusiasm and have access to the energy needed to persist on the journey. However, the journey also entails death to the old. Transformation means meeting the other parts of the personality assessed as difficult and strange. The singularity and defence of narcissism is marked by ignoring others and oneself. Too insecure and needing to cover this, narcissism is a self-absorption that eliminates any difference, surrounding itself by a false yet seemingly safe circle of sameness. The paradox of narcissism is how it can both harm and benefit in the emergence of self-discovery.

The absolute singularity of the narcissist is a painful isolated space where they are hidden from others but mostly from themself. This is based on an internal division beginning early and unconsciously, a defensive sorrow originating from the lack of sufficient love or being adequately seen. The narcissist often exists on gossamer wings, limpid, disenchanted and desperately trying to deny all distress, past and present. Narcissism stuck in ego and self-aggrandisement serves to lock the person inside themselves, withdrawn from the eros of relationships or intimacy with self and others.

The narcissistic lack of curiosity about any other erects walls of separation, shutting out other spaces; the narcissist is divided from the world through fragmented, polarised and conflictual positions. They compromise the survival, maturation and healthy striving that depends on the capacity to engage with and accept diversity and otherness. The resistance is to the mutuality and adaptation to change, so necessary for growth and expansion. For growth one becomes appropriately self-conscious and reflective, listening outside themselves, rather than being immersed in the chatter of self-aggrandisement and the damaging one-sidedness of unhealthy narcissism. We need healthy narcissism to feel good about ourselves and to be imbued with the self-esteem needed to advance but not crush or obliterate others with envy and cold, disconnected and projected rage.

However, the narcissist feels contempt for others, stuck in a haughty, prideful position. The matrix of the sense of self has become interrupted with narratives arrested and broken, preventing full development. The damage can go unnoticed as the narcissist dances fast to keep the whirling actions of competence and ability enclosed in a façade of persona charm. These actions keep them untouchable. To recover will take focus and time devoted to self-reflection; the narcissist must pause to examine and escape the frantic need to prove the elusive something.

Cultural impact

Narcissism is a marker of our current era and simultaneously seduces us to uncover the intricacies of this aspect of the psyche. It is integral to the culture of many Western countries. Christopher Lasch was an American historian and social critic who more than 70 years ago noted the cultural effects of narcissism as entitlement and decadence. He conceptualised 'the culture of narcissism', delineating the vanity, exhibitionism, arrogance and ingratitude apparent in American culture (Lasch, 1979, p. 33).

In defence and avoidance against being known, narcissism can disappear into the oversimplified rather than address the needs and understanding of the cultural complexes and social realities affecting people's lives. Christopher Lasch's pivotal work went beyond the Freudian psychoanalytic perspective on individual narcissism to place the cultural significance on personal outlook and lifestyle. He described our era as composed of fragile bonds, insecurities culturally and worldwide, and self-definition compromised. 'The stories we live by are cultural texts' (Jones, 2003, p. 620), and these are woven into the fabric of life. The point is to use them consciously and be aware of their effect on us.

Lasch contended the growing dependence on technologies had given rise to feelings of powerlessness and loss of cohesive identity. As time has gone on, we find it more and more difficult to achieve a sense of continuity, permanence or connection with the real world. We rely on apps to regulate emotions, talk for and to us, and orchestrate our lives. Relationships with others are notably fragile; goods are made for obsolescence and discarded; reality is experienced as an unstable environment of flickering images. Everything conspires to encourage escapist solutions to the psychological problems of dependence, separation and individuation. As Lasch commented, 'It discourages the moral realism making it possible for human beings to come to terms with existential constraints on their power and freedom' (1979, p. 248). Described within the psychological sphere of individuals, narcissism is shaped and influenced by the backdrop and context of our times. 'The psyche is a kind of field in which experiences as bodily lived and as culturally expressed come together' (Jones, 2003, p. 624).

The conundrum

Many seem interested in narcissism, and the phenomenon occurs in a variety of relationships from parental to business to intimates to friendship. The topic represents a seductive conundrum and has gained attention as many people have or are subject to this personality type. Numerous interpretations abound to explain this personality constellation, and each writing on narcissism emphasises different aspects. The topic can seem overwhelming with its myriad descriptors be they psychoanalytical, psychological, behaviouristic, philosophical, sociological. These indicate how relevant the topic, how difficult it is to grasp and how it can be interpreted from many perspectives.

Narcissism is a powerful force in our world, affecting many with both frustration and sorrow, curiosity and the search for understanding. It is this search that intrigues. It reaches back to the lack of sufficient love and affection from childhood, which fosters narcissistic reactions to loss with disappointments and melancholia turned inwards. The narcissist keeps the narrative originating from the set of reactions and emotions laid down early and rigidly followed. In a sense the early self-images become intrinsic and influence current psychic configurations. This channel, unconsciously experienced, becomes accessible to consciousness via the symbolic expressions in dreams, synchronicities, cultural events, relationships. Not getting enough, these people always need more. As Jung said and this applies to the narcissist, 'We rush impetuously into novelty, driven by a mounting sense of insufficiency, dissatisfaction, and restlessness' (1963, p. 159). Sadly, the narcissist is self-destructive and destructive to anyone in relationship with them as they are unable to access their soul because the inner connections are disjointed.

The approach here presents a unique combination of perspectives with a focus on the intrigue of the narcissist along with their carefully masked sorrow and isolation. They often feel like the living dead, unreal, almost depersonalised, enclosed in their own capsule. The forms of emotional neglect in childhood have led to deprivation within the personality. The predictable characteristics tend to highlight the difficulties in relationships whereas the real issue is the extent of disconnection from the unconscious and from the well spring of the Self. Inner reserves are ignored, and the depth of the narcissist's personhood is damaged – but not ruined. An incomplete or divided self contains myriad different voices that over time become the transgressions against knowing oneself.

Superficial quick fixes appeal to those wanting directives and simple answers to distress. Therefore, a cross-disciplinary approach expands and challenges the very things the narcissist fears about difference, intimacy and knowledge of others. In describing narcissism in a person, relationship and culture, throughout the book I include thoughts from other psychoanalytic perspectives, illustrating yet again the singularity of narcissism and its disastrous attitudes eliminating otherness. Basically, narcissism is both a part of and an obstruction to the development of the Self.

Narcissism has been interpreted and reinterpreted numerous times and in myriad ways since the beginning of psychoanalysis with Sigmund Freud in the early 1900s. From the many psychoanalytical perspectives there have come the ideas of Lacanian psychoanalyst Julia Kristeva; British psychoanalysts Herbert Rosenfeld, Ronald Britton, John Steiner and Donald Winnicott on the false self; and André

Green, the French psychoanalyst. The activity of combining and contrasting their concepts enriches the fabric of understanding. Weaving together these multiple threads gives the discussion a generative quality.

The language here is both somewhat technical and theoretical, mixed with case examples and dreams from Jungian analytical treatment. It is not narcissism light as there is no such thing, no simplicity in this part of the personality and resolution is not immediate. People desire to understand the intricacies of relationships and their entanglements, their hurt, the lack of intimacy and the walls of isolation. The subjectivity and sensitivity gained in dealing with narcissism provide a deeper understanding of this aspect of the psyche. This approach emphasises symbolism for exploring the multifocal and mysterious nature of narcissism.

We live in times fraught with much outer upheaval from the climate crisis to the proliferation of wars around the world, starvation and so many people barely existing in refugee camps. All these crises reflect the imbalances in the collective and the personal psyche struggling to find ballast. In the midst many escape through their narcissistic responses, closing out others, avoiding differences or dishonouring those in need. There is no inclusion. Understanding narcissism can inaugurate personal and collective openings to new directions with creative and innovative possibilities.

The human need is for connection, relationship, difference and collaboration, although the narcissist is uncomfortable with these. The challenge is to develop our individual nature without shutting out or isolating in the narcissistic-imagined safety of sameness. The narcissist tries to maintain a euphoric façade through dynamic ideas and constant activity to avoid getting close. Seeking constant attention, this rather manic approach has become the ideal of the modern ego, pressed to manage ever more information, faster and with a conscious emphasis on the computer screen, with shorter and shorter reels and screenshots. Cultures worshipping competitiveness, euphoria, exhibitionism, youth and speed sweep under the carpet reflective, thoughtful and methodical attitudes. Feelings like sadness or being mindful, contemplative and slower become unbearable, daunting when all must be light, quick and relatively easy. In this scenario the depths with their richness as well as the heights remain unexplored and unexperienced.

Social media presents the narcissist on stage, in their limelight, but altered in an exploitative glitz in the attempt at covering any internal distress. The ignored emotional states plead to be gathered and recognised. The narcissistic attitude makes all seem unreal, time seems turned upside down and life a threat rather than a pleasure. Narcissists cannot bear to be considered ordinary or average. If apprehending defeat, they withdraw. In compensation, they crave the world's applause and love, using externals to avoid the deeper levels of the psyche. The unending search for place, recognition and freedom parallels the loss of direction and the inhibiting tendencies dissolve desire into feelings of impotence.

This writing can shed light both on how the narcissist engages in therapeutic and clinical work and reveal the complex issues of this personality type. Modes of relating and the separating of the real from the virtual and hidden contribute to narcissistic and addictive behaviours. In extreme form, distancing and singularity exacerbate internal issues. Jung described these as complexes. 'Certain complexes arise after painful or unpleasant experiences in the life of the individual. They are personal experiences of an emotional nature, which leave lasting psychic wounds behind them ... capable of suffocating, for example, a person's precious qualities' (Jung, 2002, CW 8, para. 594).

The formation of a complex has its origin in emotional experiences and leaves an imprint, a psychic wound, when these are difficult. Discontinuities in the psyche, the fractured places and failed bonds are manifest through loss and despair, inner disintegration and frozen emotions, and linked with a de-somatised relationship to one's own presence (Goss, 2006, p. 681). The narcissist experiences disenchantment, emptiness and loneliness from the various forms of psychic suffering and coverups. This can be influenced by the impress of the narcissistic parent and early life events casting a devastating shadow, until the narcissist figures their way through the mire. They are left searching for the opportunities to expand the consciousness so necessary to create inner and outer resources and resilience. The need to garner approval leads to the desperate search for ever more achievements and attention.

Significant here is the inclusion of Echo from the myth. Echo represents the feminine ignored yet present our lives. She expresses her voice but does not initiate, and her body is lost from the lack of response or love from Narcissus. She represents symbolically and attitudinally rejection towards the feminine and the body. The search for love includes finding a part of us in the other as Echo continually strives to do but she is ultimately thwarted.

Lying deep beneath our histories, vast regions of the psyche beckon the ego to awaken into the fields of the imaginal and symbolic. Jungian analytical treatment is an in-depth exploration emphasising both the despair and hope within narcissism. Tapping into the unconscious facilitates transformation. The emphasis is on the growth potential within the narcissist, regardless of how polished, confident and successful they appear from the outside.

As narcissism is a major symptom of our current era, we will want to understand this approach to life in its possibilities and hindrances. The need for understanding this personality psychologically and culturally is evidenced in the narratives depicting conflicts and divisions, life and death, Self and world. The point is to comprehend the complex dilemmas and cope with them personally and relationally. Essentially, the task in Jungian analysis is to open the psychological, personal, relational and collective doors. The process of plumbing the psyche is lengthy, arduous, and the rewards are unending.

Here are some of the questions and ideas addressed in this book:

- What narcissism is and why it is misunderstood
- The paradoxes in a narcissistic relationship
- Unpacking whether narcissists are capable of love
- Insight into what it's like to be a narcissist

- The perfectionistic burden of the narcissist, including physical
- Forging health, knowledge and emotional transformation with a narcissist in clinical treatment.

References

Arendt, H. (1998). *Love and Saint Augustine.* University of Chicago Press. (No page number available.)

DeArmitt, P. (2014). *On the right to narcissism.* Fordham University Press.

Goss, P. (2006). Discontinuities in the male psyche: Waiting, deadness and disembodiment. Archetypal and clinical approaches. *Journal of Analytical Psychology, 51*(5), 681–699.

Hillman, J. (1998) The practice of beauty. In Bill Beckley (Ed.), *Uncontrollable beauty: Toward a new aesthetics* (pp. 261–274). Allworth Press.

Jones, R. (2003). Jung's view on myth and post-modern psychology. *Journal of Analytical Psychology, 48*(5), 619–628.

Jung, C. G. (1963). *Memories, dreams, reflections.* Vintage Press.

Jung, C. G. (1967). *The collected works of C. G. Jung: Vol. 5. Symbols of transformation.* Princeton University Press.

Jung, C. G. (1968). The psychology of the child archetype. In *The archetypes and the collective unconscious* (Vol. 9i). Princeton University Press.

Jung, C. G. (2002). On psychic energy. In *The structure and dynamics of the psyche* (Vol. 8). Princeton University Press.

Kristeva, J. (1983). *Tales of love.* Columbia University Press.

Lasch, C. (1979). *The culture of narcissism: American life in an age of diminishing expectations.* W. W. Norton & Co.

Munro, M. (Trans.). (2024). *A new region of the world: Aesthetics 1* by Édouard Glissant. Liverpool University Press.

Ovid. (1922). *Metamorphoses* (B. More, Trans.). The Cornhill Publishing Company. http://data.perseus.org/citations/urn:cts:latinLit:phi0959.phi006.perseus-eng1:3.337-3.434

Phillips, A. (2013). *Missing out.* Picador.

Winnicott, D. W. (1960). *The maturational processes and the facilitating environment: Studies in the theory of emotional development.* Karnac Books.

Chapter 2

The vagaries of narcissism

What kind of attention is narcissistic? What is it seeking? How are we involved, or not? These questions can propel the Jungian process of individuation. Equally true, narcissism can be regarded as lethal – a killer of relationship to self and others. Exploring both the concept and reality of narcissism can reveal its purpose and psychological manifestation, even in its most extreme form. After all, the psyche naturally attempts to heal through psychological illnesses and aberrations. The regulatory function of the psyche is compensatory and seeks balance. This hopeful and expansive perspective is at the heart of Jungian analytical psychology.

Here I am approaching narcissism as an aspect or trait of the personality to be understood and integrated consciously, rather than ignored or shunned as being impossible. Writing and reading about narcissism helps clarify it. But this is neither easy to do, nor is there a system for quickly understanding narcissism as its complexities are many. Contemporary psychology too often presents simplistic ideas of human life along with easy solutions, yet only by delving into the deeper meanings, do we gain the impetus to persist in unravelling narcissism and expanding the psyche.

This exploration does not focus on the more extreme or character-disordered aspects of narcissism. Like any personality aspect, it appears along a spectrum. There is general agreement that narcissism ranges from the normal to the pathological. We are all fall somewhere on this narcissistic spectrum. It appears in addictions, isolating behaviours, and in salving oneself in grandiosity and separation from others. Narcissism is a complex web of love, desire, loathing, envy, imperfection and pain, all needing compassion. Without understanding, these aspects have the effect of refusing to be seen, affecting relationships to self and others. Vilifying a narcissist is not helpful; instead, an alternative is to be curious about one's own narcissistic tendencies.

The more severe narcissists are those rather small number of people who are unreachable, hyper-grandiose and self-glorifying, totally unemphatic, aggressive, ruled by exploitation. As difficult as they are and while some do not change, the narcissistic responses are mechanisms developed to deal with pain, suffering and early losses. The narcissistic struggle is to let the pain go, by examining it and finding a way through. Some cannot imagine this possibility and thus will not open themselves, slamming the relationship door as well as on their own emotions. Although self-love is necessary and deepens relationships, too much of it kills and destroys by excluding others. This narcissist remains lost.

This chapter explores the vicissitudes of narcissism and how its disturbances lead to emotional dysregulation and destructive behaviours. Growth brings awareness of the defences of grandiosity, greed, destructive envy, singularity, false superiority and the secret suffering of aloneness and despair – and how to use rather than be abused by them. What is the unconscious conveying? What does it want us to understand?

The narcissist can be described as a person without a Self, unable to access the real and authentic, uncomfortable in the world and in their own skin. There is a wretched feeling within, a despair, and the Self turned against oneself. Also, there are extraordinary leaps, innovative and original flights of ideas and projects. The narcissist needs to be somebody, a real person, not a nobody as they often feel they are. They are shut in unconsciously, taking up a small space inside even when seeming to take up much more space and be louder. The cases in this chapter map the stories of narcissism leading to self-awareness rather than narcissism as a dead end, drowning in the pool of unconsciousness.

The definition of narcissism has altered, morphed and developed over time. How interesting that what is called superficial impels us into the psychologically murky and slippery realms. Expounding the symbolism within narcissism brings us to a sensitive reflection on the nature of our wounds and the analytical repair needed. Rather than being regarded as solely pathological, narcissism can promote a search for meaning and increase in consciousness. Connection to the unconscious brings relationality out of the narcissistic defences of singularity, grandiosity and its unemphatic envy directed towards the self. Hope emerges from the conundrum of those caught in the throes of narcissism, whether about themselves, a partner or the effects from a narcissistic parent. This includes the culture of narcissism with its psychological harm from insistence on sameness and lack of plurality.

As has been said, narcissism is composed of sorrow, loss and lack and all these are obscured by the façade of a glamorous persona. The origins of narcissism can be traced in childhood to being neglected or overly lauded, humiliated or leaned on to satisfy and fulfil caregivers. Looking back allows forwards movement as the narcissist retraces early lack and absence to eventually begin to replenish and grow. Jungian analyst Erich Neumann stated,

> A negative primal relationship characterized by withdrawal of love and the accompanying anxiety gives rise to aggressions and is the worst possible foundation for social behavior. ... an affirmative attitude toward oneself and one's personalities is not innate but develops in the course of the primal relationship.
> (1990, p. 42)

He then went on to say, 'If a negative primal relationship has produced a negativized ego, the resulting aggressions can no longer be integrated, and then we have the phenomenon onto which the term narcissism properly applies' (p. 76).

Narcissists are plagued by the anticipation of repeating the abandonment by significant caretakers deficient in providing correct care. Unfortunately, without really understanding why, narcissists begin to doubt themselves. As children they encounter the disconnect between parents' unrealistic view of their capacities, either as being too outstanding or too neglected. They are rendered unable to face the emotional vicissitudes of life and cannot bridge the disparate gap between the projections from caregivers and the world. Rejection, lack of acceptance, neglectful and emotional abandonment and unrealistic parental demands all contribute to the development of narcissism.

The narcissist begins a lifelong search for the validation they didn't receive originally, seeking adulation, attempting to obscure the inner loneliness. Grandiose enactments are compensations to counteract the feelings of alienation, helplessness and vulnerability. Self-disillusionment and the need to be right combine with the inability to be sceptical of themselves because it feels too threatening. They cannot reconsider their position as they feel attacked and therefore cannot learn from past experiences.

Imbued with a seemingly enchanting bravado inflates the narcissist's fragile self-image. The inability to tolerate negative feelings and the tendency to destructive behaviours combine with insecure engagement, compromised intimacy and a lack of involvement in relationships. The narcissist can be boring and pedantic, not knowing how to cherish relationships as they do not know how to cherish themselves.

Through this journey key archetypal patterns are revealed in the Greek myth of Echo and Narcissus. The archetypal layers of this myth quite powerfully inform today's collective phenomenon of narcissism. Many think they understand this myth, but few have read it as a profoundly singular refusal of life, differences and the unrecognised self while simultaneously being absorbed in oneself. Union within and with others does not occur. In this complex kaleidoscope, narcissism reveals experiences of blockages to the emergence of transformational spaces for living.

Although the word *narcissist* is blithely used, as mentioned previously it is often misunderstood. The psychological unbalance is different than popularly assumed. Narcissism is one of the numerous manifestations of the 'psychic texture of the self' (Bollas, 1992, p. 5). It involves a combination of psychological, social, historical and relational factors influenced by the culture and historical epoch we inhabit. As Marcel Proust, 19th-century French writer, said, 'The Future sometimes dwells in us without our knowing it, and the words thought to be untruthful describe an immanent reality' (2002, p. 45).

Our reality is currently being shaped by social media and computerised responses from artificial intelligence. The virtual world, like the narcissistic show, can circumvent reality and obscure the sense of being lost from oneself. Jung commented, 'But the self comprises infinitely more than a mere Ego. It is as much one's self, and all other selves, as the Ego. Individuation does not shut one out from the world, but gathers the world to oneself' (1960/1968, CW 8, para. 432). The magnitude of uncertainties and transitions we are now undergoing indicates we are in a particularly challenging time. Narcissism is experienced worldwide, with many cultures lacking regard for others' needs, exhibiting isolationism and bringing about the decline of the planet.

My attempt to portray the complexities and archetypal roots of narcissism is part of an effort to understand how to recognise and cope with our shadows and talents. This releases the narcissist from their chamber of self-deception, singularity and internal isolation. *For example, a therapist dreamt about working with a person on Zoom and in the dream the sound suddenly cut out.* What happened? This dream occurred after only the second session. Each person was now left alone on the screen able to see but not be heard by the other. What did the dream say about this person, the therapist and the quality of their communication? Can it verbally continue? Is there a nonverbal component needing attention?

This man described himself as unable to accept or receive love and any relationships were short term. Now in his mid-fifties, he recalled people trying to get into relationships with him, but like Narcissus, he deflected their attention and left. With each one, he reached a point when he became bored and checked out. He had spent a lifetime escaping intimacy or being known, and at times the avoidance became intensely self-destructive. The dream scene portrays him as unable to communicate, unable to be heard and disjointed from himself. It also asks the following questions: What is behind the disconnect and what does it imply about the reluctance to unite with any other? Does the dream reveal a similar hesitancy by the therapist? Or is it a forewarning of the work stopping prematurely and repeating the old familiar pattern of isolation?

The description

Although the narcissistic persona can be highly attractive, such a façade is a coat of many colours. The flash and shine mask alienation from oneself and others. The paradox is the seductive charm of the narcissist seems to offer closeness, but to no avail. Reality is fraught with anguish, panic, absence and void. The myth of Narcissus and his exclusion of Echo and other suitors poignantly illustrate what prevents this type of person from connecting and loving others. The inner work requires entering a portal into the psychological depths to learn to be in love and to be loved while the other person inevitably imposes their presence in unexpected and dissimilar ways. As James Hillman writes,

> Love not only finds a way, it also leads the way as psychopompos and is, inherently, the 'way' itself. Seeking psychological connections by means of eros is the way of therapy as soul-making. Today this is a way, a via regia, to the unconscious psyche as royal as the way through the dream or through the complex.
> (1972, p. 90)

Narcissism is the love of an image, but one unrecognisable as oneself. The mirror is distorted in many directions, both inwards and outwards. The man in the previous dream commented, 'What do I like? What do I want? I want to be desired, but I don't believe I'm desirable. I want excitement, but I can't excite myself with anything that is not taboo. I want to die, I think. I'm selfish and don't really care about anything more than my own comfort, stability, peace and legacy. And all of this is starting to ring hollow. I am scared and what can I do?'

What pain is expressed within these words. What draws us to the person suffering in this ontological insecurity, living yet half-dead, feeling flawed yet covered in sparkling appeal? How can this paradox exist? The scenario is a perspective on why love is difficult for a narcissist who finds it hard to give but is greedy to take. This person circles around but does not get into the intimacy, feelings and emotions of love. Too busy pursuing their own needs, those of others remain unseen. 'This is the dismissive, denigrating, even exacerbating to murderous, condemnatory rejection, which is the narcissistic obliteration of the other' (West, 2022, p. 350). This attitude assumes getting rid of any other will make one better and alleviate suffering and emotional pain.

Often appearing as a shiny object, adored and idealised, narcissists need glamorous projections onto them to prevent collapsing into what feels like the void of interiority. Narcissism has been described as a grandiose sense of self with exhibitionism; the narcissist needs reassurance of their uniqueness but suffers in disturbed relationships. The capacity to kid oneself is huge and arises from the fraudulence the person fears in being discovered. Living on illusions and then continually having to re-establish these illusions require much effort. The narcissist is 'turning against oneself in shame and annihilation, enacting against others in separation, hatred, and even engaging in envious and raging attacks' (West, 2022, p. 353). This person struggles to establish an integrated sense of 'I'. Yet, the overriding question within this personality is 'If I am not seen as exceptional, who am I?'

Healthy narcissism

There is a part of narcissism that is healthy. From the perspective of Jungian analytical psychology expanding the meanings within narcissism transforms us by moving us further into the depths of the psyche. Jungian analytical treatment aims to 'consider symbolically the psychic narcissistic wounds. These refer to everything that comes to diminish the self-esteem of the self or its feeling of being loved by valued objects' (Rubini, 2020, p. 60) and the effects on people's lives as well as the healing potential. Narcissism is delineated in a sensitive and deep reflection on the nature of one's wounds and their unremittingly inconsolable nature. These are the complexes forming the shape of the personality. This means exploring and unpeeling the origins of the wounds, composed of the painful places and tangled emotional knots. The analytical process of piecing together disparate parts brings about a belief in oneself as having value. It can be the creative impetus to bring the unusual into the world combined with the hope for repair.

The challenge in healthy narcissism is to confidently express the different without annihilating others by staying related. Narcissism contains the passion arising from a sense of one's own importance and uniqueness. We experience this on social media with its proliferation of ideas, platforms and innovations. This medium can be a connector. Equally it can create distance as we sit behind a computer within a virtual reality of made-up selves, avatars floating in cyberspace.

Given so much popular hype around the impossibility of dealing with narcissism, the process of Jungian analytical psychology opens a gateway into the agony and loss, despair and compensatory façades to find aliveness and love of self and others. We are made of many, not one, and this can be interpreted as listening and responding to the voice of Echo reaching out rather than remaining in the singularity of Narcissus who is shut off. There is energy and strength in the innovative narcissist who must stand out, create, be outstanding and extraordinary, pushing boundaries. This form of narcissism can be a conduit to the depths of the self. An individual can believe in who they are in ways that do not exclude but rather include others. Narcissism is part of healthy development because self-love is part of the ability to love others. It encourages our survival and watches out for us in natural and constructive forms.

The therapeutic and analytical challenge

However, the narcissist is often known to rely on defensive strategies like grandiosity, false superiority and entitlement for self-protection, making it challenging to maintain relationships of all kinds, including the analytical and therapeutic one. It is difficult for a narcissist to realistically perceive their limitations or their need for psychological help. The full development of self has been damaged. In fact, the hurt remains and must be defended against recurring as it was so intense and occurred too early. 'The drama of the narcissistic patient is the enigma of resonance probably connected to early experiences of traumatic lacks preventing authenticity. The narcissistic reward is a serious depression which is often organized around the avoidance of contact with the world ... aimed at suspending any process of resonance' (Leo & Riefolo, 2019, p. 156). What remains is fragility, acute sensitivity and precarious life balance. Sadness and aloneness haunt the narcissist's inner world; the grandiose provides a protective cover.

Typically, a narcissist will enter therapy after a breakdown in relationship or some collapse of their carefully constructed world. Vulnerabilities combine with low self-worth and poor self-esteem leading to strong reactions to the hurt with feelings of fragmentation, shame and criticism and projections onto others, which works against openness. Each infraction from others, whether real or imagined, affects self-doubt and arouses feelings of loss and powerlessness. Spontaneity is impeded as guardedness takes over. Realistic self-evaluation is tinged with negativity, worry, unease. This person, no matter what their accomplishments or status, is never sure they are good enough. Self-coherence is lacking. The grandiosity covering any underlying insufficiency can be quite off-putting.

Characteristics of grandiosity include arrogance, exaggerated self-importance and demands for attention oblivious of the impact on others. Narcissism is a complexity of personal grandeur mixed with fantasies based on confusions and insecurity about relating covered with aggression, sharp edges and envy. Grandiose people devalue others and can be unrealistic and aggressive when challenged, making analytical work and the transferences a complex and treacherous road for both participants.

The narcissist cannot help but lean into self-centredness leaving the personality structured around a singular, isolated and lonely false persona. Narcissus represents the disconcerting process of inverting one's gaze. He neither looks outside himself nor does he recognise how he is. And this is the point of the tragedy. In the myth Narcissus said to Echo, 'Why, credulous youth, dost thou vainly catch at the flying image? What thou art seeking is nowhere; what thou art in love with, turn but away and thou shalt lose it' (Ovid, 1893, 3.432–33). This line draws our attention to the plight of Narcissus and Echo who both died failing to attain the love they each desired and leaving the self unfulfilled.

The psychic wounds of narcissism affect the Jungian analytic process and any relational treatment. In analysis the transferences might become stillborn, caught in the patient's network of mummified objects and thus paralysed. These factors can block transference connections and halt the deeper analytical work. The narcissist wants sameness and is threatened by any opposition or difference. The analyst who represents difference might be excluded with a multiplicity of defence mechanisms against the regression (Green, 1975, p. 4) necessary for traversing inwards. What seems unaddressed by the narcissist is the ability to find meaning-making and developing a symbolic attitude.

'In the same way that the body needs food … the psyche needs to know the meaning of its existence' (Jung, 1968, CW 9ii, para. 476). In the confrontation with what they do not know of the other or of themself, the narcissist is entangled in desire and lack, and this can initiate a skirmish for recognition. However, the 'narcissist has trouble reflecting on their own mind in relation to the mind of others, to recognize intentions and motivations as differentiated from actions and behaviors' (Colman, 2007, p. 566). These defences block communication and halt the intimacy necessary to develop both within and beyond, obtruding upon the analytic encounter, and resulting in a walled-off connection.

Narcissism is a study in self-deception. It is defined by singularity occluding a relationship with the unconscious as it is also considered other. The insistence on sameness becomes a defence against assumed inferiority and shame, and the narcissist resorts to protecting themselves behind a defensive impenetrability. From the deep-seated belief there is nothing within or of value, the narcissist fears plunging into the unconscious (Schwartz-Salant, 1982, p. 65). The American analyst Nathan Schwartz-Salant recognised narcissism is not love but hate of self. More globally, the narcissistic conundrum characterised by non-love signifies a lack of connection with self and others and the ramifications reverberate both personally and culturally. The questions remain: What does healthy self-love look like, and can a narcissistic person develop a receptive and reflective attitude for loving?

The problem of forging a coherent self from the warring fragments of the psyche is a challenge typical of narcissism. It is a crisis in belief, a disappointment in what is and a desire for not just more but the refusal of the unknown although this means sacrificing the reach for meaning. The narcissist becomes stymied by anxiety arising from the immensity of the task to just be. The flight from oneself results in various forms of avoidance. Their *anamnesis*, or life history, illustrates reasons for developing the defences of the self, the psychological masks and façades, and why relationships do not fully take. The complexity behind the masks and illusions and the attempted dissimulation work to mystify and deceive oneself and others.

For the narcissist, love is a difficulty, not a pleasure, as relationships threaten the image needed to sustain the known and to avoid arousing anxiety. The increase in what looks like the self-love of narcissism coincides with the decrease in the ability to engage in love with others. It might seem otherwise, but they cannot handle other universes than their own. This is a type of oneness that does not know how to integrate or expand to include twoness.

The psychological process takes patience as the unmasking of reality connotes threats to an ego and persona so tightly relied on. The total personality is hidden and cleverly disguised by persona adaptations. Behind the well-calculated front lies the tender vulnerability and grave suspicion that their personhood will be invalidated. The need for unconditional love is stymied by anticipation about both expected refusal and acceptance. This is normal for the narcissist who withdraws at the slightest injury. Involved in their own strivings, the narcissist insists on sameness while desperately needing to stand out, to gain the sole focus and be on the stage, but alone and applauded from afar.

This personality has a penchant for illusions and poses, an imposter based on inner distress and psychological confusion. We perceive the narcissist to be confident, assured, self-centred and satisfied. This pose is a cover for the fragile and vulnerable ego of one who cannot mature or feel their entire Self, who remains in stasis and has a false superiority. The person has yet to face the truths they know unconsciously, including revealing suspected flaws, discontent and discontinuity. However, the narcissist cannot stop long enough to reach the depths of the personality and the unconscious because it hurts too much to tarry there. At some point life catches up, and they must address what has been the formerly denied. This entails a journey inwards to evolve outwards.

For the narcissist, the qualities of being harmonious, emergent and engaged are stunted and the personality is adrift. The narcissist often finds themselves in a state of self-dissatisfaction, pining after the beauty they cannot embrace or possess to fill the gaping hole within. The inner protest becomes silenced against the wounds and the voice of despair takes over. Depression, self-loathing and desperation occur at any hint of imperfection leaking through. Often the narcissist gives up and dons the cloak of grandiosity. Donning a sense of entitlement, they attempt to mitigate these hurts, sidestepping the losses associated with the deeply painful original emotional betrayals.

We see this in the narcissist observing the world with distant aloofness and false superiority, regarding others with disdain while flaunting and exaggerating their own achievements. So far removed, they have difficulty seeing how they affect others. Through the analytic work there are moments when a person is faced with their anxieties and hurts. These issues affect intimacy, including the sense of not belonging and encountering the dissociated or split selves. The narcissist has yet to access the empathy, the hope for finding meaning in the symbolic, the use of imagination for healing and finding a semblance of union within the personality.

The myth of Narcissus reveals the paucity of self-connection. Knowingly or otherwise, the risk of being seen intimately is governed by an insistence on being right, creating a significant impact on others to gain their approval. This mindset infiltrates the personal and private moments, turning every choice and action into a strategic move in the frenetic game of advancement and achievement.

Mirror image

Narcissus is alienated from himself and does not recognise his own image, indicating the lack of relatedness to self. The narcissistic tendency towards self-absorption, narrowness and individual subjectivity prevents growth. Because they cannot see themself, for the narcissist time is fungible, non-existent and youth the lauded aim. Preserved, suspended in time, can this person realise what has happened to them?

The narcissist becomes ossified, attempting to avoid the natural processes of life, especially ageing. The marks of age are often disparaged in the continual pursuit of glittering and constant approval. The narcissist stares with surprise and horror into the mirrors of life and ages with maladaptive responses to its arc. Harshly limiting narrowness can prevent growth and the narcissist can turn into a tragedy of changelessness, remaining stuck and intractable. Without recognising the span of being, which is at the essence of the archetypal spectrum, there is no movement from here to there. Isolated within, the narcissist becomes the prisoner of their own idealised and frustrated ego ideals. How can they find any ground of being or foundational self when this is the very thing they assiduously avoid?

In the myth Narcissus was captivated by the face reflected in the water, and he could not see or love anybody else, nor did he recognise himself in the image. The general exclusion of all others and enclosure within himself left no other to match his enchanted gaze. No other body could compare with the beauty and enchantment he looked upon. Narcissus remained gripped by his own look and image, ignoring and refusing all others. This describes the fundamental limit of the narcissistic vision, ignoring the richness of their own or any other personality.

This is a self refusing to depend on others in any significant way with alterity and otherness dismissed. The mirror image is portrayed as an object of fascination while the other person is needed to hold the mirror in which the narcissist can see themself reflected. It is in the eyes of the other that we discover ourselves. In fact, we are made of many mirrors, but the mirrored image of Narcissus is one of numbing transfixion, self-absorption and fantasy. In the myth it became a loss of life, drowning as he did in himself when he failed to grasp the love of his own image while simultaneously letting no other in.

The 'as-if' personality

The narcissistic approach to life encompasses the 'as-if' personality, an imposter type written about in my previous books (Schwartz, 2020, 2023). The 'as-if' person feels unable, unworthy; they hide in a tower surrounded by a façade of grandiosity. The concept of the 'as-if' personality reflects only partial engagement with others and the world while remaining emotionally hidden, mostly to themselves, unable to find their internal roots or fulfilment. These people seem to be in opposition to their more authentic selves. Instead of desiring individuation, they appear more concerned with maintaining a particular false image of themselves – that is, to maintain an illusion (Mollon, 1993, p. 131).

Freudian psychoanalyst Helene Deutsch, in her original conceptualising the 'as-if' personality, referred to

> a completely passive attitude to the environment, with a highly plastic readiness to pick up signals from the outer world and to model oneself and one's behaviour accordingly. The identification with what other people are thinking and feeling is the expression of this passive plasticity and renders the person capable of the greatest fidelity and the basest perfidity.
> (1943, p. 304)

In a later paper (1955), Deutsch described a related personality structure – the imposter. These characters actively assume a false identity and attempt to persuade others of its validity. Whereas the 'as-if' personality may dissolve in numerous identifications with external objects, the imposter seeks to impose on others a belief in their greatness. An omnipotent and manic quality severely compromises contacts with the authentic Self.

The 'as-if' personality (Solomon, 2004; Schwartz, 2020, 2023) is one in which the façade takes over as a distancing technique, keeping anyone from discovering who they really are. They exist in a crisis of sterility and stagnation. This coagulates into emptiness, fostering anxiety and addictions of all sorts, occupying time and energy in avoiding oneself and others. The enlivening qualities are continually countered by deadening ones. The soul feels wrecked from within, forming a swarm of instability, and the pain of existence is inevitably and forcefully imposed on others.

Hiding in a grandiose tower, the narcissist fits the concept of the 'as-if' personality. They often feel alone and lonely although with a creative edge and energy that compensates for the underlying morass of sorrow, inability to mourn and unending disillusionments. The idealised and illusionary are ways to avoid the real, as it is assumed to be disappointing. Not uncommonly, many remark on negative inner thoughts, interfering and highly critical self-evaluations. This is why they must always be on, persona in place, no sign of any disorder. The unanswered questions posed are, Who am I really and am I interested in knowing you when I need so much to be seen myself?

The 'as-if' personality and narcissism signal the superficiality, lack and absence typical of and promoted by social media ego and persona images. There is an avoidance of reflection and an absorption with how many likes one gets online – how much life and death anxiety are ignored in the process? The 'as-if' personality includes psychological impenetrability, avoidance of self and others combined with the failure to be present. Even as they might seem present, much living occurs without their conscious awareness. Unconsciously and pervasively little sense of self inhabits the personality, subtracting energy and creating an internal weakness that needs to be compensated and embellished outwardly. Jung did not directly discuss narcissism but recognised an overemphasis on the ego and persona meant denying the shadow with adverse effects on the process of becoming oneself.

Like the narcissist, the 'as-if' person is enchanted with youth. Living in the virtual world of video games, online pornography and Facebook can perpetuate lack of development and the tendency to hide. The pursuit into fantasy as compensation for perceived lack arouses its own proliferation of defences. Engaging in social media often creates shame, depression and mindless absorption. This person is drawn to the computer and unable to stop. This allows them to avoid the comparisons with externality that can hurt when they are assessed as less than, when needing to be the best or most marvellous.

All this is accentuated during periods of uncertainty, times lacking deeper reflection and accompanied by negation and the absences of inner focus. Narcissism is or has become a defining characteristic of our current era and also represents a need to control others. The illusory world apparent in social media and narcissism opens discussion about what in the psyche prevents and what engages with others internally and externally. Stuck between the mirror and the mask, the 'as-if' personality confuses reality and illusion in a search for affirmation. The question is how to bridge the gap between the fantasy and reality of self and others.

Narcissistic anxiety and apprehension of the 'as-if' person is covered by developing an idealised persona to hide the fissures underneath, lying like a silent but deadly fault in the very ground of the personality. When self-esteem easily plummets, inadequacy and failure take over, and the 'as-if' person is fearful of the imperfect and needs to cover the shamed and vulnerable. This person is so intolerable to themselves and so fragile they can hardly reveal themself in therapy, worried about being seen and falling apart and then perceived as helpless.

This is all perplexing when the person appears verbal and pleasant, enchanting and highly functioning, basking in the limelight. What is unnerving is the yet to be discovered layers behind the veils, mirrors and empty cheer. Like today's diagnosed narcissist, in the myth Narcissus sees an idealised likeness, one without warts and blemishes. Narcissus's self-identity is inflated, unrealistic, incomplete and in denial of the shadow. The modern narcissist in the 'as-if' person wants to keep it this way.

Given so much popular hype around the impossibility of narcissism, we run the risk of obscuring the urge for transformation embedded in this personality type. *Primary narcissism*, as originally described by Sigmund Freud, is constitutive of the human condition and the egoism within it is also an instinct for self-preservation. As subjects we are also objects to other subjects and thereby connected to each other. Self-consciousness is the consciousness of the other's consciousness of oneself. And this tension between self and other, between the moments of union between the self and the other is also the moment of difference when one is conscious of otherness.

However, Narcissus gives in to loving only that which represents himself, and he is lost in his self-absorption. The 'as-if' person narcissistically struggles, suffering a lack of being real. It is as if the soul is lost, compromised, stalked by isolative and defensive thoughts and feelings. Such people have difficulty being alone even though they are wrapped in singularity. 'In the erosion of their identity by themselves, the narcissist is faced with their own emptiness, inflexible defensive system, unable to let go and enjoy' (Hirigoyen, 2000, p. 130). The internal undermining narrative is critical and loaded with envy; they covet what others are assumed to have, whether they do or not. Inferiority lies at the base of it all, orchestrated by a darkened and limited vision of the self.

The 'as-if' person feels anxiety and apprehension about life because of early narcissistic injuries – feeling slighted, ignored or treated without respect or empathy. As adults, this protective closing off and withdrawal response quickly arises in the face of even minor slights. 'It often may take the form of a ruminatory retreat to a mental state of sado-masochistic self-flagellation, or to an equally ruminatory preoccupation with feelings of grudge and fantasies of revenge and triumph' (Mollon, 1993, p. 66). This reflects the complex yet driven task of finding one's truly original voice.

The melancholia of these people reveals a 'marked "narcissistic intolerance", a tendency to react strongly and depressively to relatively minor disappointments and insults, and also an inordinate need for "narcissistic supplies" of love and approval' (Mollon, 1993, p. 66). That is why Freud (1917, p. 254) defined melancholic loss as '"an object-loss which is withdrawn from consciousness" or an "unknown loss". Melancholic, without knowing what he is mourning for, he not only loses the capacity to love but also loses all his interest in the external world' (Tuzun, 2002, p. 89).

Narcissus's self-identity is unrealistic, incomplete and in denial of the shadow. To understand the underbelly of narcissism is not easy. There is a 'complex web of fear and avoidance of hurt mixed with grandeur, the narcissistic issues of esteem, idealization of the other and merger prompted by shame in the self' (Homans, 1981, p. 84). Lacking real autonomy and self-cohesion, narcissism indicates a detoured search for self. The problem is in the singularity of being, the fear of intimacy, the inability to be known or real, the sneaking behaviours that hide the real self from others and mask basic, raw desires and needs.

The image portrayed to the world is meant to impress with daring, risk taking, boldness. This person appears confident while the foundational layers of the self are precarious. No one is to guess this or know the difficulty the 'as-if' person experiences to be present and seen. After all, this narcissistic part of the personality has to be a proficient performer, a star, driven and running on seemingly indomitable energy.

Negative capability

The narcissist insists on being right, no errors, nothing to disturb their world order. They are unable to remain in uncertainties, limiting the element of surprise. This is aligned with the concept of negative capability as described by British romantic poet John Keats in 1817. He said, 'I mean Negative Capability, that is, when a man is capable of being in uncertainties, mysteries, doubts, without any irritable reaching after fact and reason' (2011). These lines by Keats were written in a letter to his younger brothers, George and Thomas Keats, on 21 December 1814. Keats references the ability to remain with mystery and doubts, in a state of openness, suspending judgement and not needing to explain what is not understood. All this is necessary for change and for living and loving. Paradoxically, this is a way of bringing the new to bloom and emerge so it can be more fully met. Negative capability takes courage and can be likened to Jung's concept of holding the tension of the opposites. It means letting in whatever is present rather than shutting out the unexpected or unpredictable, accessing the unconscious, the unknown and surprise beyond the safety and control of the known. It means allowing for loss, vulnerability and the passing of time as they all imply change and are integral for increased self-knowledge. This mirrors the Self guiding and revising the plots of our lives.

Typically, the narcissist tries to control. It is a paradox in that even though they are often creative and imbued with unusual perspectives, able to see around corners into new ways with wild ideas and energy, they must also be in control and appear confident. This is a confusing aspect of the narcissist and contributes to their being so difficult to understand or get close to. They are not what they seem to be.

Negative capability implies all is not comprehended while being receptive to whatever will emerge. Although uncertainty unravels, it also opens us to the imaginable. It is a tolerance for frustration and expands the mind beyond its narrow perspectives. There is a short saying by the Greek philosopher Heraclitus in 500 BCE who propounded contradictory propositions are also true: 'If you have no hope, you will not find the unhoped-for, since it is undiscoverable and no path leads there.'

British psychoanalyst Wilfred Bion described negative capability as the ability to tolerate the pain and confusion within and not knowing. Rather than imposing ready-made or omnipotent certainties upon an ambiguous situation or emotional challenge, we become open, waiting for the unconscious, the unknown, to give us symbols and provide the way into consciousness. This indicates the time for creativity when the unconscious emerges, insights and unusual ideas surface, and the mind is adrift in reverie. It becomes a relaxing of the borders, being fluid to whatever surprise is presented. Negative capability 'overturns convenient certainties. It subverts the game of mental habits and defamiliarizes what appears as known, and which for this reason now goes almost unnoticed, so that it can be effectively known' (Citivarese, 2019, p. 760).

Negative capability is tolerance of mystery, enigma, the unexpected, the unknown. The concept centres on suspending judgement about something in order to learn more rather than quickly explaining away what we do not understand. This avoids the neat and easily formed answers to complex questions and experiences. One cannot cloud comprehension with false arrogance and this attitude opens rather than closes possibilities. However,

> [A]n absence of Negative Capability appears in the relentless need to interpret, leaving no space for doubts the negative which impregnates and enriches us, turning it into tools and contents for thinking ... suggest that the traumatic experiences of a child frustrated in her need for a response from the mother [or father] may lead to a situation in which only what is negative is real.
>
> (Ferro, 2021, p. 356)

Negative capability is a means for containing the emotions and working with them without defending against anxiety or needing to provide immediate answers or solutions. Receptivity comes at the cost of certainty as the latter can be like a noose around the neck, smothering and stifling. Rather than rote answers the unconscious is a reservoir of hope, creativity and unknown emergence. This awakens and releases us from the clutches of repetitive and mindless pathways; we are no longer living passively in acceptance or mindlessly following but opening to thoughtful alternatives.

British psychoanalyst Adam Phillips (2002, p. 23), quoting Wilfred Bion, wrote: 'The capacity of the mind depends on the capacity of the unconscious – negative capacity. Inability to tolerate empty space limits the amount of space available.' Although the narcissist wants to be most unusual, stand out, have a grand effect, their rigid pose and lack of confidence limits them. Some grandiosity is needed for change, but for the narcissist this is falsely built on foundations of sand. The conscious mind has become constrained in a past patterning laced with fear and uncertainty. The issue is how to be present in the moment, unattached to a preconceived goal, unstructured and open.

The narcissist needs a certain and positive outcome, and these notions could restrict the emergent possibilities. Life becomes prepackaged, determined, compromising the creation of themself. Too often for the narcissist new ideas or change from others brings catastrophe, threatens and fragments the psyche. Equally this is part of why they are always slipping away, avoiding being held, needing the ready escape.

This perspective questions reliance on the easy search for solutions and recognises the subtleties and nuances of life. We are contradictory and complex, filled with paradox. The narcissist seeks to avoid the anxieties and quell uncertainties. Certainty is sought as it seems reassuring to access the known, familiar, the understood, managed. The fixed roadmap, the control of relationship to self and others, limits exploration and the making of the mistakes required along the way for learning. In contrast, negative capability is the art of embracing the uncertain with open mindedness.

The concept of negative capability resists quick explanations while sitting with doubts and questioning ready-made assumptions. Not only can it lead to wider creativity, but also negative capability can help us become more curious and thoughtful. All this threatens the narcissist who lives within a small frame. But it is by accepting the unknown and living the questions that knowledge becomes an ever-evolving process, strengthening the creative impulse.

Fantasies

Narcissistic fantasies defend against feared rejection and humiliation. The tender and fragile ego of the narcissist makes sure to refuse any challenge to their position. Jung commented on the fantasies that 'have more the character of wonderful ideals which put beautiful and airy phantasms in place of crude reality' (Jung, 1913/1961, CW 4, para. 404).

However, the narcissistic regressive fantasy may be mobilised as a kind of psychic protection when the narcissist is faced with a present-day situation that feels unbearable or seems insoluble. About this Jung said,

> I no longer seek the cause of a neurosis in the past, but in the present. I ask, what is the necessary task which the patient will not accomplish? The long list of his infantile fantasies does not give me any sufficient aetiological explanation because I know that these fantasies are only puffed up by the regressive libido, which has not found its natural outlet in a new form of adaptation to the demands of life.
>
> (1916/1961, CW 4, para. 570)

Such fantasies are maladaptive to the present life and perpetuate the narcissistic responses.

Perfection is sought to defend against anything seeming out of place, perceived as wrong or lacking based on assumed inner flaws. The inside of the narcissist is so fragile they build high walls to keep themselves protected. The intolerable psychic pain, fear and anxiety feel severe enough to anticipate psychic disintegration if anything is amiss. This is the underlying feeling, often unconscious but firmly held. It is too frightening to be seen for real, and any vague hint sets up the defence of perfectionism. Any missteps are to be avoided as they shake the narcissistic foundation. They must be above it all, untouched and removed, aloof from the average. Underneath, a narcissist is easily harmed, feeling inadequate yet simultaneously omnipotent and helpless.

The inner world is attacked when the narcissist senses outer threats to the stability of self. The defence against others is necessary because it is unbearable to feel unloved and of no value. Internally they demand perfection to maintain love and being valued. These are the experiences learned early in life that the narcissist guards against repeating. 'These defensive fantasies then continue to form an integral part of the core internal working models, which organize the sense of self in relationship with others and with the world' (Knox, 2003, p. 224).

The self-blame and defensive wrapping within the narcissist's cloak of isolation is easier to bear than feeling powerless. They regress to previous responses, inhibiting development. Defensive avoidance of distressing memories is also brain related, and studies increasingly show 'the brain enters into a vicious cycle of emotional and cognitive excitement' (Knox, 2003, p. 227). There occurs a form of repression or defensive exclusion in avoidance of the former experiences aroused by the current situation. The narcissist is then chemically drawn back into childhood reactions where the distorted defences arose.

> Defences serve to fragment painful meaning, rendering it less unbearable by a process of dissociation and compartmentalization. On the other hand, defences are also attempts at repair, constructing new and less distressing symbolic significance which renders trauma less threatening to one's personal sense of worth and identity.
>
> (Knox, 2003, p. 226)

We are left wondering about the fantasies and flights of imagination so valuable for growth and development. Does the narcissist let these evolve or are they reduced to control and limits? This paradox opens the value to the narcissistic daring and also points to whatever will arise from the unconscious, presenting the mystery of life. Jung said,

> When an inner situation is not made conscious, it happens outside as fate. That is to say, when an individual remains undivided and does not become conscious of his inner opposite, the world must perforce act out the conflict and be torn into halves.
>
> (Jung, 1968, CW 9ii, para. 126)

References

Bollas, C. (1992). *Being a character: Psychoanalysis and self-experience*. Routledge.
Citivarese, G. (2019). On Bion's concepts of negative capability and faith. *The Psychoanalytic Quarterly*, *88*(4), 751–783. DOI: 10.1080/00332828.2019.1651176
Coleman, W. (2007). Symbolic conceptions: The idea of the third. *Journal of Analytical Psychology*, *52*(5), 565–583.
Deutsch, H. (1943). *Psychology of Women, volume 1: Girlhood* (p. 304). Allyn & Bacon. Cmd+

Deutsch, H. (1955). The imposter: Contribution to ego psychology of a type of psychopath. *The Psychoanalytic Quarterly*, *24*(4), 483–505.
Ferro, A. (2021). Negative capabilities, play and the negative. *The American Journal of Psychoanalysis*, *81*(3), 351–360.
Freud, S. (1917). *The Standard edition of the complete psychological works of Sigmund Freud: XVII. Mourning and melancholia*. The Hogarth Press.
Green, A. (1975). The analyst, symbolization and absence: On changes in analytic practice and analytic experience. *International Journal of Psychoanalysis*, *56*(1), 1–22.
Hillman, J. (1972). *The myth of analysis: Essays in archetypal psychology*. Northwestern University Press.
Hirigoyen, M. F. (2000). *Stalking: Emotional abuse and the erosion of identity*. Wilsted & Taylor Publishing.
Homans, P. (1981). Narcissism in the Jung–Freud confrontations. *American Imago*, *38*(1), 81–95.
Jung, C. G. (1913/1961). The theory of psychoanalysis. In *Freud and psychoanalysis* (Vol. 4). Routledge.
Jung, C. G. (1916/1961). Psychoanalysis and neurosis. In *Freud and psychoanalysis* (Vol. 4). Routledge.
Jung, C. G. (1960/1968). On the nature of the psyche. In *The structure and dynamics of the psyche*. Routledge.
Jung, C. G. (1968). *The collected works of C. G. Jung: Vol. 9ii. Aion*. Routledge.
Keats, J. (2011). *Letters of John Keats to his family and friends*. Project Gutenberg eBook #35698. https://www.gutenberg.org/files/35698/35698-h/35698-h.htm
Knox, J. (2003). Trauma and defenses: Their roots in relationship. *Journal of Analytical Psychology*, *48*(2), 207–233.
Leo, G. & Riefolo, G., (Eds). (2019). *Enactment in psychoanalysis*. Frenis Zero Press.
Mollon, P. (1993). *The fragile self: The structure of narcissistic disturbances*. Whurr.
Neumann, E. (1990). *The child* (R. Manheim, Trans.). Shambhala.
Ovid. (1893). *The metamorphosis of Ovid, Books I–VII* (Henry T. Riley, Trans.). George Bell & Songs. Project Gutenberg (eBook #21765). https://www.gutenberg.org/cache/epub/21765/pg21765-images.html
Phillips, A. (2002). *Promises, promises: Essays on literature and psychoanalysis*. Faber & Faber.
Proust, M. (2002). *Sodom and Gomorrah* (J. Sturrock, Trans.). Penguin Random House.
Rubini, R. (2020). Psychic wounds, Jung and narcissism. *Junguiana*, *38*(1), 57–72.
Schwartz, S. (2020). *The absent father effect on daughters: Father desire, father wounds*. Routledge.
Schwartz, S. (2023). *Imposter syndrome and the 'as-if' personality: Fragility of the self*. Routledge.
Schwartz-Salant, N. (1982). *Narcissism and character transformation*. Inner City Books.
Solomon, H. (2004). Self-creation and the limitless void of dissociation: The 'as-if' personality. *Journal of Analytical Psychology*, *49*(5), 635–656.
Tuzun, D. (2022). [Safe] in a Narcissistic Closure. Yedi (27), 87–94. https://doi.org/10.17484/yedi.963673
West, M. (2022). Healthy narcissism and individuation – clinical, cultural and political manifestations. *Journal of Analytical Psychology*, *67*(1), 345–362.

Chapter 3

Emotion and desire obstructed by envy

The Grimm's fairytale 'Three Little Men in the Woods' begins with a man and woman who each have a daughter. The two daughters are playing together. The man's daughter complies when the woman initiates the idea of marriage with her father. After the marriage, however, the woman's daughter receives preferential treatment and more wholesome drink than the man's daughter. This daughter becomes the stepmother's enemy who from one day to the next does whatever she can to make the stepdaughter's life miserable. Furthermore, the stepmother is envious because the stepdaughter is beautiful and kind, whereas her own daughter is ugly, disgusting and envious.

And on the story goes …

Fairytales illustrate the journey into the Self and the elements encountered along the way. This journey involves conflicts, challenges, the unexpected, and it often entails a demotion in status for a time. The destructive forces of envy are prominent in this tale. Similarly, from Cinderella to Rapunzel and in numerous other fairytales, envy leads to heartless attempts to destroy others, on one hand, and on the other how the protagonists thrive from the experience. Thriving requires a certain attitude of openness, an ability to manage uncertainty and surprise. Jung commented, 'What is it, at this moment and in this individual, that represents the natural urge of life? That is the question' (Jung, 1966/1969, Vol. 7, para. 488).

Adding to this are additional commentaries. Wilfred Bion said the following about painful experiences:

> They result in experiences of unrepresentable destructiveness owing to their devastating power, both external and internal. Deadly anxiety and limitless destruction fill the entire psyche … destructiveness is unable to face psychic pain, nor put a stop to it … as if it were a cyclone that nothing can stop.
> (Levine, et al., 2023, p. xvii).

Jacques Derrida, the 20th-century French philosopher, said:

> By introducing the theme of illness into this thesis I am introducing, infecting, and contaminating this 'self' with an ill or an evil that affects it with a certain

negativity: a 'self' infected by an 'other' to produce a seemingly 'improper', 'ill-functioning' self. Yet, the impropriety of the self ... not as a *hetero*-infection, but as an *auto*-affection that auto-infects itself.

(2005, p. 123)

Psychologically, this quote refers to the destructive impact of envy eating away at the envier from within. Although it is projected, the envy causes decay in the envier who remains unaware of their destruction to themselves.

Narcissistic envy also entails lies as the unconscious deceptions compensate the lack of self-connection. As Jung has said, 'Memory often suffers from the disturbing influence of unconscious contents' (1939/1968, CW 9i, para. 504). The deadly form of this destructiveness is

... based on being gripped by an unbridgeable will ... too often an empty will, feeding its own existence without giving the individual much in the way of nourishment. It is a state of affairs too ghastly to bring to conscious awareness for the envier and prevents any life-enhancing activity.

(Eigen, 2001, p. 9)

The psychological fruit is quickly deadened rather than becoming nourishing. With no way to quell the destructiveness, there is avoidance of truth telling. The truth thus denied and refused, it hides from the envier their fears and experiences of personal annihilation projected to annihilate the other.

The basic self cannot be elaborated, and its development has been halted. No doubt the experience of severe lack has already occurred, but this pain and distress, panic and confusion cannot be accessed emotionally. As noted for the narcissist, caregivers were unable to promote the transformational aspects of the self. The envier sees this possibility in others and wants to grab what they desire but cannot access it within themselves. The connections and the unconscious are smothered and inactive, rendered null and void.

Libido

This is the envy described as 'libido withdrawn from the object – the other, to protect from the painful affects from the anxiety connected with experience with the other, to protect against being at the mercy of the other' (Jacoby, 1990, p. 82). 'Dictionaries tell us the word libido originates from the Latin for desire or lust and has an etymological connection to the English word love' (Jones, 2018, p. 22). Emotion and desire express who we are, our preferences and what makes us tick, defining how we are seen and how we see ourselves. Jung said, differentiating himself from Freud, 'Subjectively and psychologically, this energy is conceived as desire. I call it *libido*, using the word in its original sense, which is by no means only sexual' (Jung, 1916/1961, CW 4, para. 567). Emotion and desire change us, alter the world, create other visions pointing us in several directions.

Libido as energy is part of human nature and reveals desire, but with envy it goes the way of greed – never satisfied and with a disregard of others. Libido is also the energy needed for the narcissist and for anyone to access the more complete self. The rejected and uncomfortable emotional material contains the pressure needed to counteract the repression and release its libido or energy.

The narcissist often feels anxiety about exploring or acknowledging the emotions leading to the inner world. They feel vulnerable admitting this, as such an admission opens them to the search and recovery of what was lost. Yet this is necessary so the personality can grow. If the information is not integrated consciously, it manifests in increasingly difficult symptoms calling ever more insistently to be known. This brings about various emotional reactions, as 'there is no change from darkness to light or from inertia to movement without emotion' (Jung, 1938/1959, para. 179).

Narcissism accentuates the importance of the search for what is lost, what desires to be found. This means recognising and remembering the lack and absence that led to the unmet desires to find satisfaction. If not accessed, the personality withers over time and the lost objects, the aspects lacking within, remain unused, dormant and the possibilities of life untouched, love and enthusiasm submerged. The narcissist goes to sleep and remains unconscious of the wealth within their personality. Something must be given up to fill the insecurity and lack of trust of the narcissist.

Emotion and desire carry us into the depths of the psyche where we discover its hidden treasures. Unaddressed, these can turn corrosive, damaging, deadly and cruel. The Jungian process of individuation, or finding the self, entails going into the areas where we flounder. These hold the promise of restitution should we persevere in the quest. As Jung said,

> It is nothing less than a revelation when something altogether strange rises up to confront him from the hidden depths of the psyche – something that is not his ego and is therefore beyond the reach of his personal will. He has regained access to the sources of psychic life, and this marks the beginning of the cure.
> (1928/1969, CW 11, para. 534)

Disenchantment

The common dictionary definition of *disenchantment* is the act or state of being free from enchantment, fascination or delusion. It refers to a love gone sour, leaving disillusionment, disappointment, dissatisfaction, discontent and cynicism in its wake. The dissolution includes ending, disbanding and discontinuing. Psychologically, this represents breaking down the artifice of the psyche to immerse in the unconscious and bring the rejected parts into consciousness. In other words, it provides an opening.

In the process the ego structures previously in place dissolve. As a physical as well as psychological process, dissolving accesses the energy channels in the body, recharging the cells, and can be experienced as a flow of creativity. With the idealisation of self and others dissipated, disenchantment instigates psychological change as the older and more familiar patterns dissipate. This includes the enlightening, painful yet growing awareness of the dilemmas that led to the disenchantment – a dissolution and reordering of the psychological elements. The masks covering our true selves disappear and we are revealed to be who we are, exposed and vulnerable. However, this is a where the narcissist, who prefers sameness and to be idealised, creates many mechanisms and obfuscations to avoid.

Nevertheless, desire opens the world. Passion is part of love, and although wanted can seem overwhelming due to the diversity of love and the inherent complexity in all relational situations. Jung contended,

> The unrelated human being lacks wholeness, for he can achieve wholeness only through the soul, and the soul cannot exist without its other side, which is always found in a 'You'. Wholeness is a combination of I and You, and these show themselves to be parts of a transcendent unity whose nature can only be grasped symbolically.
>
> (Jung, 1966, CW 16, para. 454, n. 16)

The personality grows from both inner and outer relationships. The questions narcissism raise are what get in the way and what provide the strength to push through. As Jung said, 'She started out in the world with averted face ... and all the while the world and life pass by her like a dream—an annoying source of illusions, disappointments, and irritations' (Jung, 1954/1968, CW 9i, para. 185). This quote describes what it is to walk around with apprehensions and aversions to living. Similar feelings appear in our dreams as the fearsome situations, monsters and people we encounter there and in daily life. These become apparent so we can address them and learn to cope with the emotions aroused because they are change agents for expansion of the personality. Little do we realise how hounded we are by unfulfilled emotions and desires.

For example, a woman appeared in therapy because she had trouble keeping her interest alive in any relationship. She began relationships with energy but then it would slowly begin to wane. She was upset and wondered what happened. Each relationship began to fizzle after the same amount of time and at about the same stage of getting close – or not. She traced them back and found, to her surprise, they each lasted only a few months. She assumed there was more substance, and she was more committed, but she was not.

She began to question her role in the demise of each relationship. It seemed after a short time she began to complain, was disenchanted and would comment about how the person did not get her, was too distant, or did not give her enough attention. There were regulated times for seeing each other, and it was not very spontaneous. Sometimes they had fun. Sometimes they discussed how to get deeper. Yet, the nagging sense that she needed more remained. And she was bored. What did she need? How to ask for it? Was she apprehensive? If so, about what? All these are the questions people ask as they enter therapy and search for relational fulfilment.

So, she tried yet again to express her distress, but again it was insufficiently met. The issue behind it all was not so much the other person as her own reticence and fears surrounding intimacy. She was left questioning how she could discover what was at the core. She could keep a journal of feelings, record her dreams, set up a quiet reflective time. Her task was to get into the conundrum of intimacy and discover what was unconscious yet running her life. By doing so, she might be more able to embark on a journey of love. As Jung commented, 'Desiring always wants what is closest, and feels through the multiplicity, going from one to another, without a goal, just seeking and never fulfilled. Love wants what is furthest, the best and the fulfilling' (Jung, 2009, p. 255, n. 240).

Love brings with it vulnerability. It causes upheavals in life, upsets us and brings us to ourselves in unknown ways. The emotions are disruptive, arising from unmet needs. These are all too disturbing for this woman as she wants life smooth, relationships romantic and without struggle. However, love is shadowed by past events and composed of paradoxical juxtapositions. To really love means embracing and accepting the imperfections of oneself and others.

Powerful emotions are important for living and experiencing as they lead us into the psyche and the discovery of what has been absent, lacking, in need of fulfilment as well as what brings joy and pleasure. The narcissist avoids the interest in what is different whereas love requires nuanced and emotional responses, rather than a dismissal of differences as they sidestep curiosity, dulling enthusiasm and not questioning what is lacking. The longing to find the one with whom to feel complete is followed by catastrophic collapse.

It turned out this woman wanted a replica of herself, an agreement and seamless matching. This was impossible. Dissent reaches into the depths while the superficial and search for the same repeats the status quo endlessly. Denying the different erases the challenges, mirrors the superficial and becomes a way for merely gaining adulation. She wanted the energy turned to her always and sadly her romantic view of what love should be obscured reality, and she remained alone for the time being.

Envy and rage

The evocation of the emotion and desire that accompany envy is a prominent theme of the narcissist. It recalls what the envier lacks, the needs unmet and desires frustrated. The envier lives in the unrealistic fantasy that they can have what they cannot and do not have the talent to manifest. The potential self remains just that, potential and unable to become actualised. In the refusal to see oneself, and to distance from any painful realisations, envy creates intolerable inner cruelty without tenderness to self or others. The envied one becomes a target to fill up the emptiness. The focus on the envied is to obliterate, turning into acts of violence, idealising the annihilation. No one can breathe freely in this surreal encounter.

All frustration is projected while the risk of the descent to self-development is avoided. In fact, there is a moral vacuum, derailing inner attention. Refusing to look at the effects it has beyond its own walls, the shadow side of the self escapes. In fact, this helps the envier deny their own apprehensions about trying and failing to get what they want. The envier is unrealistic, cannot acknowledge their limitations and, as a result, refuses their own development through projections onto the envied other.

Life feels like it has escaped the envier, and the envy embodies what is wished for but felt as unattainable. Life itself feels unfair. The envier refuses to see themself, so taken are they with destruction of the envied who seems to have it all.

> If the envy is turned inward it leads to low self-esteem and a sense of inadequacy; or if the individual is at the 'favourable' end of the interpersonal comparison there may be a fear of being envied and the person can limit themselves to avoid the envy.
>
> (West, 2010, p. 471)

An envier feels nothing special and is deprived, obsessed with their own lack, their pleasure taken away by the envied other. All the energy of the envier becomes an attempt to dominate the envied. 'Envy's vengeful quests reveal the narcissistic needs and rage ensuing when the needs aren't met. And, it resists change' (West, 2010, p. 460).

Envy arouses aversion to separation, a primary and often painful emotion. Narcissistic psychological organisation denies the otherness of the envied object and highlights the envier's limitations. This intricate scheme defends against experiences of separateness and simultaneously promotes the rise of envy.

> The experiences of envy and gratitude depend on an awareness of separateness – an awareness of the otherness of the other. It is hard to formulate a concept of envy which could take place within a relationship of absolute fusion between self and object.
>
> (Roth & Lemma, 2008, p. 6)

Predominantly destructive narcissism is an extreme aspect of envy and arises from the hostile attitude to love objects arising from past painful disappointing experiences.

Envy wears many masks and often is blurred or denied because it requires the envier to admit their needs, wants, limitations and intimidations. It also reaches into the dreaded anticipation of abandonment. Envy is destructive and self-annihilating, originating in people whose early experiences lacked sufficient and correct relationality, leaving them alone in their suffering.

Envy promotes the pull to dissolve in fantasy and magnify a romantic illusion of themself. This reaction also takes the form of a refusal to live in the world or to bear life's difficulties. It becomes an impossible situation when no one can be better or more desirable than the envier.

Often associated with shame, envy constricts, restricts, hardens and turns the heart into an arid patch. Envy is a perception of inferiority, and the envier is diminished over what the other person is imagined as having that the envier does not. Envy is based on lies to self and others. It separates while being attached like Velcro. This indicates a painful abyss defining an insecure self, unable to be found amid all the convoluted made-up narratives believed by the envier. Envy fuels destruction and connects with fury and rage to annihilate anything threatening this fragile self, supported by lies and deceptions.

Under the guise of envy lies emptiness, isolation, alienation and rootlessness, a feeling of void seemingly impossible to negotiate. Originating when the loving and safe parental objects were absent, neglectful or mis-attached, envy enters the consulting room through the transferences. At the same time, envy understood leads into and out from the shadows for psychological transformation, increased consciousness and personality development. 'Envy is a signal of an important need rooted in a legitimate hunger for full selfhood' (Stein, 1990, p. 163). Envy comes essentially from envy of the qualities of the self projected onto the other. It is 'the self that is the ultimate object of envy ... [it] seems to refer to what in analytical psychology we recognize as the self' (Stein, 1990, p.163).

British Jungian analyst William Meredith-Owen (2008, p. 459) called envy 'embittered desire'. Envy hides within the shadows. From the fear of being envied, a person can limit themselves in the attempt to decrease the envy of others. However, this brings in its wake increased frustration and avoidance of themselves. Any way it is framed, the envy loop ties one in knots against being who they are. The tragedy is the inability to receive or fully give, so the envying narcissist winds up feeling cheated and chronically unfulfilled.

British Jungian analyst Barry Proner wrote about those suffering from the envy of themselves as people who are contemptuous of themselves (1986, p. 276). The good inside has become split off, inhibiting enjoyment. The energy for life turns into self-hate, disgust at the body, feeling flawed and internally attacking. These parts are not only projected outwards but are also eaten away from within. Narcissistic envy keeps the bad inside to obscure interior reactions from the view of others, presenting a façade for approval. However, these attitudes arise from the sting of their own envy and the fear of recognising their own good parts (Proner, 1986, p. 148). The good parts are held in secret inside and the external focus is on the approval of others. The whole setup compromises self-acceptance and avoids knowledge of any self with good.

The attacks on the self by inner envying figures can be quite vicious and tenacious. They keep the envier stuck in destruction against themself, ripping all to shreds, leaving them without internal support or confidence. Internal conflict, self-hate, body despair, distance from others and obsessive thoughts clog the system and prevent anything else from evolving within. They impinge on taking in anything else from the world so they can maintain the destructive status quo, which by now has become normalised. It is like being alone in one's room, safe, protected and without being intruded upon except by oneself. It indicates 'parts of the personality that do not interrelate ... a deadly anti-self distorts' (Proner, 1988, p. 161).

This can be seen as a form of narcissism turned inwards coinciding with the prevention of the intimacy of connections with openness and freedom. The envy Proner describes is one of the self, eaten up from within, destroying any connection to one's vibrant centre, creating instability and leaving a person with the ponderous drag of emptiness and lack of fulfilment. The inner feels blank, without substance, an abyss of nothing. The brutal self-attacks begin so early that its lethal quality and distancing from others go unnoticed until much later. By then the envy is in a place with room for nothing else. All this mix-up of emotion has derived from the chronic lack of healthy and restorative mirroring and frustrated rather than met needs.

Meanwhile, the hurt resides inside as powerful energy halting the self in its development. The symbolic images of the uroboros, or snake swallowing its tail, as a symbol of wholeness is altered to an image of a snake eating away at the self, increasing the pain but with no resources for relieving it. This creates a circular system of oneness, a singularity not open to twoness, a need to stand alone, feeling damaged and full of self-hate. Envy of the self destroys so thoroughly the envier is without relationship to the self. No one realises this destruction mangles the personality. It is brutal, like the self-attack of Narcissus who is willing to die rather than move beyond his narrow border of singularity, seeing no others of value. In a sense Echo does this as well because she persists in a futile search for love from only Narcissus although she is continually refused. The self is unfulfilled and succumbs to destruction.

The envious narcissist is consumed with vexation and resentful longing. Their vengeance against what the other has reveals their narcissistic needs and rage, their unmet needs. Envy derives from what the other person has or what is projected they have and want for themself. In the frustrated anger and rage the envied person becomes no longer a person but something to get rid of, to smash and crush. Whether it be about wealth, success, accomplishments or happiness envy takes over as a devouring beast and a raging thing. Narcissistic rage can grow to huge proportions and can be ferocious and grossly destructive with the aim of destroying what is felt to be withheld from the envier ever having (Schwartz-Salant, 1982, p. 41). In this cyclone of emotion all comparisons to oneself come up short and the envy is again refuelled to focus on devouring what the other has. All emotion and desire concentrate outwards, and the envier feels only lack and deprivation without facing realistic limits and avoiding their own work and development.

The frantic need behind envy is to avoid the impact of the emotions of shame and self-hatred instigated by the continual desire for more while feeling less. Self-hatred is enacted through the projections and is motivated by the need to protect the envier from feeling lack and the assumption of being deficient. The result is the person transported outside themselves. The bond, although distorted, is between hatred, destructiveness and projection.

The attitudes of self-hatred, degradation and negation of self derive from early threats to the self and the need to preserve one's being. It is like body and psyche have been snatched by the attraction to the other and one is robbed of who one is. Such strong emotions are not easily eradicated because what is wanted is also considered to be too much to accomplish by the envier, loaded with the early material of loss, longing and deprivation. What takes over is a form of sadistic energy (Schwartz-Salant, 1982, p. 48), an attack, set out to hurt, destroy, take. It is a battle without end as there is no satisfaction even when the other is eradicated. Nothing is ever enough. The poet and writer H. D. wrote about the heart and how it is fed by hate (Doolittle, 1986, p. 379).

The self-hatred associated with envy originates in early feelings being denied and tragically unmet; rage is internalised and deposited in unreachable areas of the personality. Envy is destructive, angry energy that prevents the envier from becoming themself. An 'extreme anxiety accompanies envy with dread, although it is ill-defined' (Steiner, 1993, p. 30). It is impossible to keep the destruction completely split from conscious awareness, and the envier is overwhelmed not only with resentment but also with what feels like unbearable material to contain.

All this shapes the resulting hatred, roiling not just under the surface but also aroused in any interaction. 'Hatred is paradoxical. It emerges from traumatic origins and involves primitive defence mechanisms of the self ... but it manifests itself at a sophisticated level of consciousness where ego fragments have coalesced, albeit in a distorted way, to form a fixed complex' (Weiner, 1998, p. 499). In other words, hatred turned against oneself is driven by the lack of healthy self-attention. This arouses the reaction of envy, causing both envier and envied to become frozen, separated but entangled with each other, loaded with projections in the attempts to expurgate the frustrated desires. Meanwhile, envy makes the envier feel full and denies the emptiness of mind and consciousness and re-creates defeat.

Being envied

Being the object of envy is unbearable; it is killing, sadistic, meant to humiliate, discount, nullify, wipe out. This is how the envier feels as they project their intense feelings outwards. Envy is a mix of pleasure and pain negating the personhood of the other in an intertwining psychological embrace (Ulanov & Ulanov, 1983, p. 18). It can be like a stranglehold. The attachment is an entanglement, disorganised, strong, powerful, sweeping the envier away in its turmoil. It rules with a vengeance and the envier feels persecuted, disavowed, subject to erasure, enacting the magnified vengeance onto the envied.

All the bad is dumped into the envied with no empathy as the other is regarded to be the threat, the enemy and intruder and held helpless in the barrage. Impotent, with connection broken, there seems no way out for either the envied or the envier. It goes on and on, unremitting, all emotion and desire distorted. Greed abounds. The envier cannot fix what feels broken within, and the envied is held hostage to the destruction the envier creates by shooting their poison arrows.

The envier feels without any good as this belongs to the envied who then must be eliminated. Any desired excellence is assumed to be owned by the one who is envied. 'Envy is in the lack of something assumed inaccessible within the envier' (Ulanov, A. 1983, p. 78). The devouring aspect of envy is hungry, starving, glutenous and seeks to eradicate the other or eat the other as it can find no inner nourishment or sense of fulfilment. Hate and attack are the mechanisms for this form of attachment. Envy is never fulfilled; envy steals or does whatever it takes to obtain the good from the other who is considered better. These reactions are insatiable and cannot satisfy the intense and desperate suffering and loss. So, on and on envy continues, halting development. Anything good in the mind of the envier will not occur. The envier steals rather than develops, a predator who eats on carrion bodies. Their core identity remains unformed, unfed or fed on the poisoning of unnourishing attachment. Envy is outwardly a glutenous expression to the envied one who is to be torn apart and eaten alive. The envier attaches to the envied one in this destructive, sadistic and unconsciously driven brutal energy.

The envier misses accessing their own vitality, and their consciousness is clouded with distress while confusion, despair and desperation take over. In the swirl of emotion, the envious narcissist and the object of their envy are both affected, subject to be demolished in a destructive rage and sabotage against life. The entitlement, the early deprivation of love and attention pull the envier out of themselves into a one-sided shadow existence. The world narrows as the only thing that counts is the demise of the envied. This is symbolised by the devouring lion Jung referred to in the alchemical images and narrations, eating and eating with no end.

Behind all this are the vulnerable and suffering areas, the tenderness, hurt and lack. To avoid dealing with this and the inadequate self-esteem confronting the envier, even more envy gets activated. The cycle is never satisfying but it continues. The shadow has overtaken the envious personality and access to the deeper layers of the self are demolished. In the idealisation of others, the envier is felt as never ideal enough and sorely lacking. The powerless response to devalue and kill the other increases. Access to any self-reflection is gone but it never was present. The envier treats others from the pain they experience, the emotional deprivation and insufficient love. They continue in this fruitless stream. The roads giving access to any other path within are blocked. All is ego and persona driven. The death instinct, the desire to kill and destroy, have the upper hand.

The envious narcissist is immersed in the lack they cannot repair. It becomes projected, and the locus of the projection is the problem, not themselves. So strong is envy and hatred it destroys their personality. But they do not feel this as only the envy can be registered. Contempt and rage are the outwards expressions of envy, overlaid by devious methods of destruction to the other to avoid any self-feeling. The fantasy is if the other is killed, the cannibalistic envier will live off the remains. This narcissist is conflicted, enacting both the abused and abuser, and cannot manage their aggression balanced with the need for protection (West, 2013, pp. 88–89).

One woman, who described herself as being from a lower social class, continually felt as if she did not belong, as if she were unaccepted, not as good as others, never able to find her way. This was projected onto anyone, including the analyst, as being more fortunate, richer, with more opportunities while she suffered and never got anything. The suffering turned to envy, disguised but leaking into the analysis in oblique ways. It emerged in feeling criticised, and all commentary was taken as negative. She assessed she could do nothing right, and in the defence against growth and change, despair took over, while the envy remained and grew.

She described a defensive and desperate fight response against her father. She knew it was not safe for her to express and thus emotion was repressed and held in her body as tension in her arms and torso. It changed into envy of others whom she assumed had more while she did not. There was too little recognition, too little safety, and no respect or confidence from the father. She feared him and this transferred into her scathing verbal criticisms of others. It included turning against herself in the form of lack of internal support or care, anxiety mixed with despair about anything ever changing and her body being a constant source of dissatisfaction and discomfort. She felt less than those who were fortunate to be born into a higher social class and more secure economic bracket. All she could recount were the places she wished to live but never could, money she desired but was thwarted from earning, loss of weight. She felt she never learned the basics richer people had as her family came from a lower class. This was a metaphor for what she wished for and knew would never happen. This attitude created inner bitterness, a hidden but strongly felt resentment. Her unbearable experience of being less than almost automatically was ejected into any other. The analyst and the entire analytical process seemed insufficient and unattainable, and she was never good enough.

Many people like her have experienced various forms of early trauma (West, 2013, p. 92). The wound became the central organising factor in her personality dominating her identity. Through the unsatisfied envy she 'continued to prosecute the world for re-traumatizing her. The projection remains with no material difference in her world to prove otherwise' (p. 92).

The hurt and pain from this wound and its associated complex can have a mesmerising effect on both patient and analyst, and both will need to recognise and deal with it. So long as the analyst simply identifies sympathetically, overlooking the talion responses constellated, she is colluding in maintaining the distortion of the patient's identity. This attitude is an aspect of the narcissism and envy keeping the patient in the role of a helpless victim. This response impedes her emerging from the underworld of a less than, underdog position. She does not take her place in life. In fact, there is refusal to do so, and this indicates resistance to change, much as she professes otherwise.

'Working with the bad object and the wounded self reaches into the wounds from the violation of the core self' (West, 2013, p. 81). This woman was so intimated by the father, so beaten down by his verbal attacks and challenges to her competency, that she projected a similar attack would come from others, especially those she envied, as occurred in the analysis. She could not relax, let her guard down or ever be challenged or attach with confidence and safety. The fragility of self was so armoured by envy, she remained impervious to any other form of connection.

When the original primary caregiver does not model a sense of self for the developing child, psychic wounds accumulate, and the loss becomes unbearable. This woman is an example of someone who clings to a precarious pretence of self-sufficiency. Her illusions defend against feeling helpless and powerless. This experience traces the residuals from the father's overpowering presence and emotional absence, disconnecting her from self. This is the most sensitive, precious and vulnerable part of her needing protection and acknowledgement in the analysis.

The core self is the part enlivening the personality, orienting us towards what gives meaning, and its affects are the most true, profound and fulfilling. 'The split in the self occurring early in childhood leaves no inner harmony nor is there life within an understanding of self and other because she does not know it' (Kohon, 1999, p. 101). When this self is violated, the reaction will be extreme and powerful, the outrage and murderousness intense. The sense of betrayal can feel unforgivable. The situation is dire.

Resentment, hate, the rawness of envious emotion rules the life of a narcissist as they feel inadequate and robbed, deprived of both inner and outer resources to succeed. She assumed she could never rise above her social class and spoke about it as if marked and damaged by it. Arrogant, competitive and then ruthless describe this personality with its envy; even though, the outer presentation can appear helpless and obedient. The façade of inferiority is buoyed by the puffed-up emotion of envious rage, whether apparent to others or not. All these lead away from any inner work and the larger self recedes within, hardly to be found. The envy attacks fuel the status quo and continue until they themselves come up against something that might make the envier realise there is no joy or happiness in any of this, but then the narcissist has not experienced much of either. The narcissistic envier only sees their failure to have what the other has.

Part of the analysis is to plumb the internalised depths of these reactions and differentiate the emotions and desires. In analytical treatment this will entail a descent into what resides in the unconscious as revealed in the dreams and active imaginations as well as synchronous events and relationships. These all have the potential of radically altering former positions based on lack that fuels envy. However, the narcissist can be a chronic talker, needing to fill the empty space and busy deflecting from themselves. This is based on the vulnerability and poor self-connection that must be hidden.

It is a difficult process as much of the inner life has remained silent and unknown, sunk in sorrow. She was unable to value self and others. The violation to her nature was so complex that, although addressed in part, it did not facilitate trust or confidence in the analytical container. She remained closed, envious, adamant and the analysis stagnated, stuttering to an end. The analyst was unable to connect or alter the course of the analytical demise. The painful original pattern was replayed and remained in place.

Sadism

The sadism of the envier is meant to humiliate and nullify the envied person who is both idealised and persecuted (Ulanov, 1983, p. 17). The envied one must be reduced to nothing, relieving the envier of any responsibility to look inside. 'Sadism kills the other and masochism kills the subject' (Levine, 2023, p. 26). Narcissistic people sadistically try to humiliate those they envy just as their own humiliation replicates a childhood of insufficiency, inner support or self-esteem. Like in the previous example, the personality is left fragile and unable to find inner stability.

British psychoanalyst Melanie Klein brought to awareness envy as a manifestation of human aggression (2002). She propounded envy developed early in life, dividing the feelings and reactions into what she labelled as the good and the bad breast. She defined it as the angry envier who possesses, takes away, spoils, destroys. It arises from an internal world filled with fragmented self-representations and their cruel feelings of shame and humiliation given by caregivers rather than love. The other is violated as the envious person was violated or negated and their rights demolished. 'Libidinal (or energic) forces are confused with destructive ones and the destructive seem to destroy the libidinal ones' (Hinshelwood, 2023, p. 20). Love and hate stay undifferentiated. One is frozen, lost in the torpor of the near-living or half-dead, suffering the painful absence of connection while denying the capacity for accepting, embodying and manifesting their potency.

The envious person feels tormented by their image in the mirror of the envied, which reminds them of their mundanity, limitations and imperfections. The envious are haunted and suffering from this mirror into which they gaze; they gain no assurance, but only restrictions and imperfections. They cannot tolerate these and are overshadowed with blight.

Left with a mixed sense of impotence and rage, the mental state of the narcissistic envier is one of self-depletion, full of feelings of inadequacy, low self-esteem and self-pity. Unable to escape the obsession taking over the mind, the self is disconnected from the ego and the larger self cannot be accessed. The person is bereft. The pattern of emotional exploitation, targeting and psychological theft is immoral, manipulates and purposely hurts others. Without any ethics towards oneself, entitlement and false superiority are run by an immoral disregard for anyone or anything. There are no codes of conduct, and there is less self-reflection. The envier does not realise how hurt they are because they are so busy projecting envy from the absence of love, security or trust. The murderous effects of envy destroy the narcissist from within and prevent development of self-reflective states.

Eros or relating is demolished in the envy and the hate within the narcissistic response. The person kills what they seek to kill in the envied but have already killed in themselves. No relationship is possible. The self with its healing properties is prevented entry and the envier is submerged. The envious narcissist only feels the mortal injury to themselves and desperately requires excessive praise and success to compensate.

Vengeance and diabolical thoughts and deeds are obsessive as the envious are set to destroy, not develop. Grandiosity and omnipotence fuel a path leading away from finding any spirit of their own and focus on destroying everything in the envied person. There is only the wild, untamed and unconscious hurt and pain. Because so much was taken from them early in life or just not there to be given, the unconscious needs and rage exacerbate.

Envy separates a person from the Self with its dehumanising energy, projecting all outside and leaving the inner empty and powerless. Although the psyche is self-regulating, the narcissist feels only deprivation resulting in their cruel acts of destruction. 'Envy, that great distance maker, that connection destroyer, can, if suffered consciously, close the gap that its own wounding operations have opened' (Ulanov & Ulanov, 1983, p. 10). However, for some there will be no repair as it requires gaining the very consciousness envy negates.

The unclaimed shadow material and hatred keep the ego fragile. Unmitigated and uncontrolled, the envier feels less than. The singularity of the rage of envy wraps them inside, isolated from others. Without the symbolic and unconscious, without delving into deeper meanings the totality of a person is inadequately addressed, leaving one stuck in a quandary of pain and distress. Jung (1968, CW 9i, para. 563) explained this as follows:

> An inflated consciousness is always egocentric and conscious of nothing but its own existence. It is incapable of learning from the past, incapable of contemporary events, and incapable of drawing right conclusions about the future. It is hypnotized by itself and therefore cannot be argued with. It inevitably dooms itself to calamities that must strike it dead.

The disavowed energy destabilises and de-potentiates the personality as the envier joins the culture of the narcissist, envious and descending into a zombie-like existence.

Meanwhile, emotions and desire take the envious to realms of the unknown – intense, uncontrolled, imperfect, upsetting the precarious balancing of one and others. The person's psychological structures include being split from the sense of 'I' and demand engagement. This is manifested through eating disorders, compulsive behaviours or recurrent relational difficulties. It should be noted, however, that the split-off not-I within is not just negative but cannot yet be engaged with consciously. Envy obstructs. Being seen and unseen, the verbal and nonverbal, subjective and intersubjective provide both the tensions and the places of growth.

The transformative

Love's transgressive power when expressed in envy is also double-sided and can be transformative as the shadow aspects come into the light. We become revealed to ourselves and the other as the inner phantoms emerge. Emptiness holds the possible and the yet to be filled. Love opens to this emptiness and is an opportunity to plunge into knowing the makeup of our psychology. Accessing the emotions can lead one into a state of rawness where they encounter the shadow in its undeveloped and unknown aspects. Listening and responding to the nature of these desires consciously keeps us from apathy and psychological stagnation.

The envier desires relationship and this is the perversity. The envied becomes a locus of attention and affectation in the search for feeling. The narcissist often is unfeeling as all is captured by the deadening effects of envy. Caught within a complex, they fear love and these desires are frustrated. The aggression turns inward, and they feel defective and like something is missing. What is missing is the modus operandi for self-love.

The child has become 'the carrier of the parents' unconscious fears, impulses and other repressed or disowned parts of themselves and these negative attributions become an integral part of the child's sense of self' (Knox, 2011, p. 341). This in turn becomes a basis for the apprehension and distrust of love and the envious defence against relationship. The denial of the self thus begins early with negative or neglectful reactions by caregivers. The rejecting response leads to shame and is embodied in the physical. It is 'founded on the embodied resonance of the mirror neuron system ... discovery of mirror neurons has given us, for the first time, an account of the neuroscientific mechanism that underpins this embodied interpersonal knowledge' (Knox, 2010, p. 31). The child becomes absent and unable to find presence. Acknowledging this is necessary for stepping toward consciousness. Coming to the Self, experiencing love and joy, these emotions entice us to a journey towards self-expression.

Emotions are played out in the theatre of the body, but these frustrated passions can bring us to relationship. Passion is part of the dynamism necessary for change elaborated through the psyche and the body. Desire to unite with one's real self, with its wide-ranging emotional life, is a complex and many-layered process. As Jung said,

> Individuation is a heroic and often tragic task, the most difficult of all, it involves suffering, a passion of the ego: the ordinary empirical man we once were is burdened with the fate of losing himself in a greater dimension and being robbed of his fancied freedom of will. He suffers, so to speak, from the violence done to him by the self.
>
> (1948/1969, CW 11, para. 233)

References

Doolittle, H. (1986). *Collected poems 1912–1944* (L. Martz, Ed.). New Directions Publishing.
Derrida, J. (2005). *Rogues: Two essays on reason.* Stanford University Press.
Eigen, M. (2001). *Damaged bonds.* Karnac.
Hinshelwood, R. (2023). *Herbert Rosenfeld: A contemporary introduction.* Routledge.
Jacoby, M. (1990). *Individuation and narcissism: The psychology of self in Jung and Kohut.* Routledge.

Jones, R. (2018). The stream of desire and Jung's concept of psychic energy. In P. Bishop & L. Gardener (Eds.), *The ecstatic and the archaic: An analytical psychological inquiry* (pp. 19–27). Routledge. DOI: 10.4324/9780203733332-2

Jung, C. G. (1938/1959). *The collected works of C. G. Jung: Vol. 9i*. Princeton University Press.

Jung, C. G. (1916/1961). Psychoanalysis and neurosis. In *Freud and analytical psychology* (Vol. 4). Princeton University Press.

Jung, C. G. (1928/1969). Psychoanalysis and the cure of souls. In *Psychology and religion: East and West* (Vol. 11). Princeton University Press.

Jung, C. G. (1939/1968). Conscious, unconscious, and individuation. In *The archetypes and the collective unconscious* (Vol. 9i). Princeton University Press.

Jung, C. G. (1948/1969). A psychological approach to the dogma of the trinity. In *Psychology and religion: East and West* (Vol. 11). Princeton University Press.

Jung, C. G. (1954/1968). Psychological aspects of the mother archetype. In *The archetypes and the collective unconscious* (Vol. 9i). Princeton University Press.

Jung, C. G. (1966/1969). The structure of the unconscious. In *Two essays in analytical psychology* (Vol. 7). Princeton University Press.

Jung, C. G. (2009). *The red book: Liber novus* (S. Shamdasani, Ed.) (S. Shamdasani, M. Kyburz, & J. Peck, Trans.). W. W. Norton & Co.

Klein, M. (2002). *Envy and gratitude*. Free Press.

Knox, J. (2010). Response to 'Emotions on action through the looking glass'. *Journal of Analytical Psychology*, 55(1), 30–34.

Knox, J. (2011). Dissociation and shame: Shadow aspects of multiplicity. *Journal of Analytical Psychology*, 56(3), 341–347.

Kohon, G. (Ed.) (1999). *The dead mother: The work of André Green*. Routledge.

Levine, H. (Ed.). (2023). *The Freudian matrix of André Green*. Routledge.

Levine, H., de Mattos Britto, G., & de Mattos, J. (2023). *The clinical thinking of W. R. Bion in Brazil*. Routledge.

Meredith-Owen, W. (2008). 'Go! Sterilize the fertile with thy rage': Envy as embittered desire. *Journal of Analytical Psychology*, 53(4), 459–480. https://doi.org/10.1111/j.1468-5922.2008.00741.x

Proner, B. (1986). Defenses of the self and envy of oneself. *Journal of Analytical Psychology*, 33(2), 275–279.

Roth, P. & Lemma, A. (Eds). (2008). *Envy and gratitude revisited*. Routledge.

Schwartz-Salant, N. (1982). *Narcissism and character transformation*. Inner City Books.

Stein, M. (1990). Sibling rivalry and the problem of envy. *Journal of Analytical Psychology*, 35(2), 161–174. https://doi.org/10.1111/j.1465-5922.1990.00161.x

Steiner, J. (1993). *Psychic retreats: Pathological organizations in psychotic, neurotic and borderline patients*. London: Routledge.

Ulanov, A. & Ulanov, B. (1983). *Cinderella and her sisters: The envied and the envying*. Westminster Press.

Weiner, J. (1998). Under the volcano: Varieties of anger and their transformation. *Journal of Analytical Psychology*, 43(4), 493–508.

West, M. (2010). Envy and difference. *Journal of Analytical Psychology*, 55(4), 459–484.

West, M. (2013). Trauma and the transference-countertransference: Working with the bad object and the wounded self. *Journal of Analytical Psychology*, 58(1), 73–98.

Chapter 4
Emptiness and boredom

As American psychologist William James put it in the early 1900s, scientific thinking regards our private selves like 'bubbles on the foam which coats a stormy sea ... their destinies weigh nothing and determine nothing' (1902, p. 495). He described the reality of an 'unshareable feeling which each one of us has of the pinch of his individual destiny', a feeling, that 'may be sneered as unscientific, but it is the one thing that fills up the measure of our concrete actuality' (p. 499). These quotes might describe love, what it adds to life and how its lack is gravely felt by the narcissist.

Authenticity

'What compels us to create a substitute from within ourselves is not an external lack, but our own inability to include anything outside ourselves in our love' (Jung, 1967, CW 5, para. 253). What occurs emotionally within a narcissist is not displayed on the outside. The variety and complexity of this person is shrouded in mystery, yet the veil between inside and outside is quite thin. Feeling lost, caught in indecision and a lack of confidence, the narcissist's life becomes an insincere act, a fabrication of their world; they are desperate for others to recognise their value as they cannot find it. Or, if found, it does not last, as value is contingent on the next achievement or shiny thing. There is a constant need to be replenished. At issue is the narcissist's arrogance, which obstructs the value of other people as well as themselves.

In the words of existential philosopher and French feminist writer Simone de Beauvoir, 'The paradox of [the narcissist's] attitude is that she demands to be valued by a world to which she denies all value, since she alone counts in her own eyes' (1949/2010, p. 682). Denying the reality of life results in dissatisfaction, never satisfaction. Hidden from oneself and the world is the feeling within that the narcissist's mind is empty. This realisation must be escaped. It is too painful, fraught. Assuming there no exit, there can be an insistence on movement and activity, as they run from the threat of the empty, bored and boring. The languor of being unable to go within comes from the fear of penetrating the psyche only to discover nothing is there. This apprehension of just nothing is haunting. Hence the need for the illusions that are the mark of the narcissist.

Narcissists try to ignore the nagging feeling that the centre is shaky or the recognition that the original lacks in attachment form part of their maladaptive life response. Psychological dissociation and relational distancing develop as survival skills and, along with the illusionary setup, compensate a weighty, depressive anxiety. Natural body instincts and feelings fall into the unconscious. Frequently uneasy, this person is subsumed with obsessive drives and self-persecutory impulses, the oppressive weight of mindlessness as they binge on the internet, gaming, television, shopping and so on.

This is the boredom the narcissist tries to escape. But it leaves them still apprehending the lonely inner chamber. The light of pleasure and stimulation is needed to counteract what feels like emptiness, what feels hollow, aimless, even deathlike. The boredom so easily felt by the narcissist signals the need to know their own significance and value. To compensate, they seek the highs, the adrenalin rush and the unusual.

Boredom is also part of natural contemplative moments, of solitude and stillness, creativity and daydreaming. Boredom can offer a time away from the hectic to focus on what counts and the inner life. However, the narcissist too often flees from their inner world, unable to stay with their own emotional experiences. They cannot imagine themselves on the other side of change because the current self is the one needing to die for the other one to emerge.

The narcissist's daily habits and patterns and their repetition provide balance but can seem to be a prison if the rhythm becomes monotonous rather than foundational. Herein lie the restive questions necessary for change. The narcissist becomes restless to do, accomplish, quickly fill in the empty spaces. An answer for the narcissist is to surrender, open the portal, expand the perspective. However, the narcissist has yet to experience this.

In the meantime, the narcissist makes themselves the subject and project of life. This is someone who regards themself in a deeply incoherent way, an object for others to glorify. But this proves to be unattainable, and the exalted ideal position is not reached. Meanwhile underlying this pattern is a sense of disinterest and distrust in the environment. Or the narcissist cannot take in what is offered or, when they do, immediately require more as nothing is digested or integrated. It is like empty calories. The narcissist believes they cannot be fulfilled and remain in need. They are unnourished, any emotional food undigested. As Simone de Beauvoir pointed out, 'even the most perfect narcissist realizes the hollow, alienating nature of [their] existence' (2010, p. 681).

Yet, it is often surprising to discover for the narcissist 'the self is felt as fragile and vulnerable, empty, and dead, as if nothing was there' (Modell, 1996, p. 151). They appear full of themselves yet are subsumed with lack, feeling flat, flawed; their beauty is imperfect; they fear vanishing from importance and are desperately holding on. 'Estranged from one's affective core', the loss of contact with an authentic self means closing off from others (Modell, 1996, p. 150).

Jung opined, 'The self would be an idea; an entity which embraces the ego. The self expresses the unity and totality of the personality' (Jung, 1921/1971, CW 6, para. 425). What defines the narcissist is not knowing how to access the contents of the unconscious. This hampers the personality, constraining it in tight bonds and the false security of singularity.

There is consistency between a person's primary experience and their outward behaviour, reflecting values in sync or not with the Self. When authentic, there is flow, a flexible mood, attitudes and openness to new experiences. The inauthentic part is associated with various addictions, self-silencing, low self-esteem, and internalised anxiety and depression. The narcissist has little inner ballast; they are stuck in predictable needs and seemingly unattainable unremitting desires. They are

> ... sensitive to the slightest disapprobation, always wearing the stricken air of one who is misunderstood and deprived of his rightful due. He nurses a morbid pride and an insolent discontent – which is the very last thing he wants and for which his environment has to pay all the more dearly.
>
> (Jung, 1928, CW 7, para. 226)

Grandiosity

Grandiosity enters at the border between ego and self where they are sufficiently undifferentiated and unrealistic goals of perfection indicate a disturbed self-evaluation (Jacoby, 1990, p. 89). The basic feeling that they are not taken seriously dominates, and this propels much of their narcissistic behaviour. The narcissist's internal worldview reveals an unstable sense of self-worth, shame and the need for constant validation. Of course, nothing will be enough. 'The suffering is from emptiness combined with a search for meaning, burdened with negative self-image and blockage in self-realization' (Jacoby, 1990, p. 188).

Narcissistic grandiosity is a merger of the ego with the Self, an identification with the Self, rather than development of a relationship with the Self. Swiss Jungian analyst Mario Jacoby noted, 'The rejection of one's inner vitality and isolation from the environment draws on the proneness to interpret as offensive the reactions from others' (1990, p. 179). Maintaining a grandiose sense of oneself requires a withdrawal from or denial of any situations putting that grandiosity in doubt. Occupied by alternating grandiose and vulnerable aspects, the narcissist brings hypersensitivity to any negative evaluations. This heightens their aspirations for perfection as well as their need for masks to cover any social awkwardness and feelings of inadequacy.

The central problem is that the narcissist accesses self-esteem through the continual approval by others. This is a difficult task often misperceived by others and impossible to be maintained as an internalised self-imposed demand. The narcissist might feel like a fraud, knowing they desperately need adulation. Paradoxically they feel rightfully deserving although each achievement becomes insignificant once accomplished. They quickly seek new challenges, but these are never sufficient for establishing solid positive self-esteem.

Francesco Bisagni described the fascist state of mind as a place where complexity ceases and the symbolic is eliminated. The heart is emptied with no opposition, and there is no real contact with others. American psychoanalyst Christopher Bollas originally coined this term and described the aggressive aspect of the narcissistic self-state achieved by 'killing their loving dependent self and identifying themselves almost entirely with the destructive narcissistic parts of the self provides a sense of superiority and self-admiration' (Bollas, 1992, p. 198).

Bisagni also depicted this as a narrowed capacity for experiencing emotions (Bisagni, 2022, p. 441). This state of mind is based on internal emptiness and a narrow range where little is accepted and tolerance for difference is non-existent. The personality is run as if by a dictator, submerging spontaneity, fascist in attitudes and rigid in conformity, preventing change or exploration. Distance from others becomes the order, and nothing is to disturb the personality from maintaining this status quo.

Narcissists struggle and feel they have few choices. They chafe against and try to rebel, to find a way out, to escape the bonds of life, assessing they are limited by them when they are limited by their own narrow fascist focus. Life goes on hold; fed by a repressive and miserly dictator within, their existence lacks nourishment. Hard to satisfy, the narcissist is ever searching for more. The dictator is a voracious being; the narcissist feels like they are in an abyss lobbing epithets of insufficiency to themself and others. As one person said, 'I could eat the world in one bite and still be hungry.' Worried about being average, this person carries within a sense of being ruptured but is terrified of showing any of these feelings. 'Consciousness needs a good working unconscious to support it or undergoes warp and semi-collapse' (Eigen, 2001, p. 48).

Melancholia

What makes a person feel dead and feelingless? Deeply felt experiences are compromised, blocked by the need to be viewed as exceptional but not intimately known. Life must fit an ideal image rather than encounter any overt struggle. As the need for illusions become stronger, they serve as a defence against anxiety and maintain the narcissism of singularity. The narcissist is in a rage of self-masochism and devoid of self-love. Their negative reactions strike outward through emotional distancing but are most painfully inward hitting. Loss of love ignites depression and the closed state of narcissism along with the self-destructive intensity of unconscious self-hate (Green, 2023, p. 71). Any contradiction to the narcissist's viewpoint and perception is met with refusal, denial and insistence on being correct.

Because inner and outer relations are twisted, the narcissist feels lifeless, filled with negative self-judgements, alone and unloved. Within melancholy, the narcissist carries sorrows, early experiences of loss, an unshored ego, the self unattended and an overwhelming despondency. There is loneliness and hunger from the dormant and unused aptitudes and melancholic passivity in avoidance of spirit and soul. This person eventually must go through some sacrifice to access their knowledge, find relationship and regain feeling. Here lies the richness of the personality plunging them into the sea of what seems unbearable.

The old traumas put a person on the brink where 'a sad voluptuousness ... depression is the hidden face of Narcissus ... where we see the shadow cast on the fragile self' (Kristeva, 1992, p. 5). There is meaning in this despair as it leads deeper along the labyrinthian path to the Self. However, the self-devouring of the narcissist erases existence. The narcissist bypasses the depths and suffers from the absence of self-connection while simultaneously assuming unacceptability from others. These feelings operate unconsciously and powerfully, whereas experiencing the depression consciously could bring the person into themselves.

The predictable analysis

The narcissist is difficult to approach as they are usually not just hiding but also busy filling any empty spaces with grand plans, rapid speech and frenetic activity. They rarely are still; they are internally churning, energy moving, ideas flying. All of this is an attempt to stave off being known, to remain in control, but this highjacks the richness of the personality. The flatness underneath, although carefully hidden, becomes ever more apparent as it seeps into all relationships, including the therapeutic by subverting connection.

An example is an accomplished woman in her fifties. Outwardly she is put together, conscious of the right labels on her clothes and jewellery. The persona is managed, in place, staged to be alluring and unapproachable. She is carefully orchestrated and manipulated. Everything is for effect and to appear intact. She expresses little thought about having any adverse effect on others. On the contrary, she recounts her successes and how well she does in their eyes as they all approve of her. People are pawns in her world and used to her advantage. There is a cold, hollow and removed quality and one cannot imagine getting close to her.

She relayed a childhood filled with aloneness, secrets in the family, marriages based on money and status in society. The outer image counted; emotions did not and were to be managed, held within, out of sight. Although her early life sounded grim, she had no emotional expression but relayed the events as stories she was removed from. 'One needs presence combined with early experiences of appropriate absence to form thoughts and make creative use of the symbolic and the imaginal' (Colman, 2007). She was not imaginal except in a self-aggrandising way and seemed to be operating only to gain adoration.

At a young age, she developed an elaborate system of deception. Originally it came about when no one seemed to notice the difference between the truth or falsity of her tales. Her truth was neither wanted nor questioned. Now it was operating to deceive the partner she complained did not pay attention to her. She sounded vengeful, engaging in affair after affair. It was a vengeance against everyone involved. She seemed not to mind and was rather cold about the whole thing. It was about her, not the others. What this meant for her own psychology, much less for those engaging with her, seemed to mean little if anything as relationships were manipulated like bargaining chips. She revelled in the fact that she got away with it all and was only concerned she appear enchanting to anyone she encountered. Meanwhile, she counted on her spouse remaining ignorant of it all and rationalised the affairs by projecting he was neither emotional nor caring.

It was she who could not or would not be emotional. Her secrecy and the need for perfection plus her deftness in hiding truths kept people away. She compartmentalised friends and told each some aspect of her life but not the whole story. Each friend felt special as she had a charming quality but any pathway into the real person was blocked. It became apparent over some time she operated with similar guile in the analytical situation. Her persona of having no needs or dependency and no ripples on the smooth plane of life was all she knew about relating and relationships.

Scattered remnants of her past slowly and almost carelessly emerged as the stories she told portrayed her as removed, an observer in her unemotional retelling. She described parents as deceptive and having affairs themselves, but she did not tie this to her own behaviour. She expressed feeling for those at a distance, a dead father, an emotionally unavailable mother. She said mother was busy when she was a child – an only child left for long hours to play alone. Her parents divorced when she was young, and father never contacted her. She had no memory of tender moments with her mother or stepfather nor any recollection of feeling close and loved. She learned early not to expect what was unavailable and not to want intimacy or affection and loving expressions, at least this was what she told herself. How and what she might otherwise expect remained unknown, and an empty space inhabited her psyche. Emotions such as shame, fear and grief had no place.

But what was the truth? Even when questioned, she had a glib answer. When this was pointed out, she shrugged it off and went on telling yet another story. She could hardly be interrupted from the rapidity of her responses, allowing for little pause or reflective space.

What was she seeking or running from? Why? Would anything be admitted or hint at what was sorely amiss and not discarded into the gutter? On neither end of the emotional spectrum was she touched. Analytical treatment and self-exploration bring forth chaos as part of the development of personality. But with her, it seemed any chaos outside of her purview was quickly denied. And she lied.

She had a dream, told in a flippant manner, that she robbed someone. Because she did not know the dream people or have more details, she felt it did not really apply but told it as she knew dreams were considered significant in Jungian analytical work. Few dreams populated her verbiage, and because she needed approval also in the analytical treatment, she provided the dream. A dream contains layers of meaning and symbolic significance. Obviously, the dream was indicating something inside was stolen. Intellectual, she conceptually gathered the implications, but they did not seem to sink in or have a deep effect. Where were the self-feelings and the concern?

I considered the dream and its apparent lack of impact on her, sharing my observations and questions. She did realise she had little emotional reaction and took the dream as a commentary about her but did not know what to do with it. How could she take in and manage the information when it could not penetrate? She is an example of the difficulty of the narcissist in any psychological work when the depths to the personality barely open. What lies beyond the same stories, repeated by rote with little emotion, lack of attachment and the sorrow unexpressed?

Here is the lure of the narcissist. One can sense there is more but cannot grasp it. The promise and possibility in the dream portrayed a need to find something serious eluding her, taken from her. Yet, she became bored, stationed herself at the edge of the unconscious and carefully thwarted any penetration. Here could be the crime referred to in the dream. Maybe it was also a message to me, the analyst. She could be the robber as well as the one who was robbed and was robbing us – me and the analysis. The dream was a signal, a signpost for the analytical work. The question was whether she would take it up and whether together we could unpeel its meaning to enhance her life.

She did not realize she had lived solely out of her persona in order to survive, like many narcissists. It was all she knew. She experienced

> ... an abyss of sorrow, a noncommunicable grief that at times ... lays claims upon us to the extent of having us lose all interest in action and even life itself ... Within depression, if my existence is on the verge of collapsing, its lack of meaning is not tragic – it appears obvious to me, glaring and inescapable.
>
> (Kristeva, 1992, p. 3)

She had rejected her deeper self without knowing there were consequences. She did not realise the maladaptive patterns formed from early in life. Being intelligent she coped as best she could, even though she received little guidance or expressions of love as a child. She covered the heartache with an impenetrable shield as there was nowhere else to put it all. But this left her alone, shutdown, frozen.

The analytical or therapeutic process creates new patterns and an ability to shore up the personality with the richness from the unconscious. She was dimly aware of all this, having read books, attended online lectures and seemingly acquired knowledge. But all was held at a distance from her heart. The actual work of self-discovery meant opening to others, but she was stymied by the need for performance, skimming the surface and cheating herself. Perhaps here was the robber taking from her as the dream referenced.

In effect she refused to acknowledge the shadow parts. As Jung notes,

> The shadow is a moral problem that challenges the whole ego-personality, for no one can become conscious of the shadow without considerable moral effort. To become conscious of it involves recognizing the dark aspects of the personality as present and real. This act is the essential condition for any kind of self-knowledge.
>
> (1968, CW 9ii, para. 14)

She could not open to her inner secrets and emotional longings and instead covered them with an enchanting façade. Under it all was a dry place, emptied of life and energy, into which she was loath to proceed. She feared the roiling unconscious contradictions, impulses, instincts awry because she had never learned to handle the plurality and paradoxes within. Admitting and feeling what she had experienced was obviously overwhelming or she would not deny it so ardently. The pursuit of psyche for a narcissist can be propelled by the nag of emptiness, leading to boredom yet also needing to hide and deny any problems.

As Jung said,

> It seems as if it were only through an experience of symbolic reality that man, seeking his own 'existence' and making a philosophy out of it, can find his way back to a world in which he is no longer a stranger.
> (1954/1968, CW 9i, para. 198)

The point is we individuate or become ourselves in relationship to self and others, and although this can feel terrifying, it is a natural process.

The emptiness within the narcissist is often unacknowledged or even unknown, and this causes the lag of boredom. To face difference is to enter rather than transpose reality. The hole of the emptiness is an opening to other experiences, allowing us to transcend what seems impossible. As we revisit events, like in analysis, memory changes and perspectives alter with reflection. Things are re-seen, re-membered, re-ordered. Emptiness so opened leads to self-discovery and erases the need to forget. It takes courage to be vulnerable, and this is hard for the narcissist to admit.

She recounted an early memory, before kindergarten. She wanted a hot pink dress. Mother said she bought it but when they got home the dress was not there. Mother said it was not available in her size, but she knew her mother had lied. Her mother's lie had a profound impact and, even then, she knew the deception could not be countered. Nothing could erase the emotional wounds, the unfilled promises, the betrayals from the parents. Although this was unconscious and she consciously turned from them, she found herself adopting similar false fronts and rigid defences.

The persona of a narcissist works to obscure the disturbed self-feeling in order to convince others of their beauty, power, wealth, attraction. The false enchantment leads to self-deception, supported by delusions and illusions and the boredom of unconsciousness. This helps deny the heavy load made more intense by negating what is natural. To become conscious of our truths and unmask the falsity means penetrating wishes and desires and encountering the assumed risk of intimacy the narcissist tries to avoid.

Dealing with emotion from a solely thinking or intellectual perspective cheats the pursuit of depth. Thinking the rational protects one from suffering avoids duality, multiplicity and surprise. It flattens curiosity. The narcissist, although filled with themself, feels the absence, and this creates the need for stimulation and false comforts, wrapping them away from openness. Avoiding or covering the wounded, tender areas only steals from ourselves. Dulling the emotions is mixed with the search for the highs of excitement but not transformation.

Emotion is reduced to the singular, and the flash and show are to keep the narcissist's world safe and untouched. Dreams arise from the psyche unexplored, the personality considered too risky to enter, yet it calls her to venture within. Drawn to other versions of herself can feel destabilising, incomprehensible and reprehensible. It requires learning a new way of listening, without self-judgement. Yet, she was loathe to take the time to reflect or think about what she could not. She entered analysis with no particular or spectacular crisis but unconsciously was drawn, unaware of what was previously unacceptable and still unconscious.

Here is a short vignette illustrating she and her partner in a narcissistic deception to self, other and to the world. The image is often lauded as one desired, yet it describes the narcissistic vacancy, the fear of discovery, the lack of inward focus from abject fear. Vacillating between the longing to connect to an object world, between the pull towards life and death, this is an example of narcissistic destruction and death to the movement of the psyche needed for life.

This couple developed a firmly entrenched narcissistic defence in which there was a profound commitment to the repetition of psychical deadness of their early lives. Each was unconsciously resistant and operated to avoid the awareness of despair and defeat. These aspects were disallowed into their lives of lies. They were image driven to remain away from themselves, busy creating one image after another to present to each other and the world. They contributed to the right organisations, seemed active in community, attended the showy spectacles and events, all these activities colluding against change or growth, freezing any psychological movement. The therapeutic task raised the possibility of experiencing absence and what had been missed. However, they had a pact, unsaid it seemed, to remain in the land of the psychologically dead where 'the some-thing of absence must take the space of the no-thing' (Sekoff, 1999, in Kohon 1999, pp. 122–123).

Their image was maintained by both appearing to the world as the epitome of success in looks, status, money. Everything the culture of narcissism says is wanted and desirable, they had. Yet, she entered analysis. What unfolded was a series of narratives of aloneness, serious events of loss in the family, but she excluded the process of mourning or acknowledgement of anything wrong. Parents were self-involved, and she had to proceed with no emotion demonstrated, no solace offered. Her comment was the partner did the same.

There were affairs, always with those who were unavailable. Complaints abounded about being bored and nothing changing. It seemed nothing wanted to change. The surface remained placid, held in place by the right facelift, the right car, the right label. Nothing challenged them. She complained but could not leave. Pain receded momentarily with the acquisition of the next shiny something. And this portrayed the narcissistic collusion for remaining unconscious, singular, untouchable, impenetrable, yet with the adulation preserved. She did not grapple with 'experiences that feel unrepresentable, empty, void, and laden with threat to the status quo' (Scuderi, 2015, p. 65). Analysis was threatening as it brought forth the absences, the internal space with its psychic productions yearning to be filled. When these were revisited, they reanimated with their potential, but when nothing happened, they soon died.

When a person makes the decision to undergo psychological and analytical treatment, it is propelled by some displeasure, a creeping discomfort. Rather than deadness, an opening occurs in analysis for exploring potential presence. Narcissism, whether it seems so or not, carries the desire and opportunities for change and the hope facilitated by the psychological treatment. Some of these people can move beyond the deadly repetitions of singularity and the boredom of sameness. Underneath the powerful, destructive deadness there is a spring of life waiting to be released. But unable to tackle the unconscious as it would surely disturb the status quo, neither person could afford to go there. Further development or opening did not occur nor was the analytical work ever deepened beyond the superficial and repetitive narratives.

Finding the meaning in repressed material helps a person discover their value – aspects unavailable from self-absorbed parents who lack intimacy nor show affection to each other or the children. Jung said,

> We doctors are forced, for the sake of our patients ... to tackle the darkest and most desperate problems of the soul, conscious all the time of the possible consequences of a false step ... concerned with the total manifestation of the psyche as a natural phenomenon.
>
> (1946/1955, CW 17, para. 170)

Narcissists are usually not prepared for the realities of life as they have been given an unrealistic view of themselves from either overindulgent parents or ones who neglected them. The child becomes the object of unfulfilled parental dreams, and they did not attach in a clearly loving way to the child. This child was unseen and in this unmet need the gap within remained. As result there must be constant reinforcement to the system of sameness. She felt empty without it. The emptiness may represent the potential of fullness and fulfilment, but it can also remain a void state, an abyss without beginning or end.

Puer and puella

Fear and an inability to grow up à la the famous story of Peter Pan is an actuality for many and an obvious reference to Narcissus. Both characters refused union with any other and retreated to sameness without realising the harm to their own lives. In Jungian analytical psychology they represent the archetypes or typical ways of being, an outline filled in a certain pattern called *puer* for male and *puella* for female. These are not gender specific but apply to anyone as inner figures.

These figures represent the continuation of adolescence in attitudes to the whole span of life. This means living what has been called the *provisional type*, contributing to the lack of reality, and resisting development with its back-and-forth movement and awkwardness (Hillman, 1979, p. 24). They become paralysed in eternality, refusing adulthood, and nothing develops with no discipline to hold the personality, but just desire to escape the day with its drag of the average. Yet, out of the pathos of the problem comes the search for soul, the very aspect the narcissist seeks, often in vain (p. 147).

The narcissist, characterised in part by the archetypal concepts of puella and puer, signifies immaturity, lack of intimacy or genuineness. Wanting to be most special keeps this person out of touch with *mater/materia* as psyche and soma are dissociated. They feel empty and emotionally deprived at the core, without connection to their natural instincts. So why do we love them so much? Or try to love them? Or get caught in their desire for more as nothing is ever enough? How are we narcissistic personally and culturally, and where is this healthy or not? These and other questions are part of the complexity of narcissism enacted by the puella and puer figures in the psyche.

Puella and puer cannot adequately make the leap to the threshold of adulthood and its responsibilities for development of the self. The split and subsequent integration from the parental world does not occur. To refuse development means remaining unconscious and a child, unreflecting and self-centred without consideration or knowledge of the other, without intimacy or knowing love.

The puella and puer are taken with body perfectionism. They are caught in a narrow myth reducing all to a sameness of rigidified beauty and body image. The illusion of identity leaves no solidity of self. This is the fragile self, based on shaky foundations and unable to face the vicissitudes of life. Youth is sought through body alterations and facial adjustments, over and over and often to extremes. The mirror they gaze into is always critically demanding and unrealistic.

Seeking pleasure is singular, not in union, or is only temporary as there is resistance to the limits and grounding of time and commitment. If all is for the short term, what can grow? The narcissist recoils to escape the anticipated boredom involved in any development. All must be fast paced and shiny, or there is depression and a refusal of the transformational parts of life. Adulthood creates new patterns and links, the ability to dissolve the adjustments of childhood and re-create anew as an adult. Differentiated relationships to self and other are part of the process of individuation. Love catapults one out of solitude, eradicates narcissistic defences and expands psychological realms. In love we come alive, engage in intense attachment to others and reveal vulnerability to intimacy.

However, the flattening of this personality type makes them noncommittal, a fleeting love interest. There is an inner emptiness and living in the fantasy when real life will begin, but always it is later than today. The magical belief is somehow it will be better, they will be more prepared, but it never happens. Puella can be confused with childlike unsteadiness and an incapacity for perseverance, lacking tenacity, giving up too soon. Restless, inundated with ennui, bored but also comfortable in the waiting, entitled while languishing in wasting time, she feels disconnected from her body and especially fears being reduced in any way and earthbound to the average while the future remains elusive.

Puella has been referred to as ethereal, hazy, undeveloped.

> Unfortunately, many puella types relate to the world through hiding, mimicry, and adaptation at the expense of authenticity. The deep longing for connection has been an area hurt, cut off, afraid, damaged. The remnant and the tragedy are changelessness, stuck, unmovable, and presenting with rigid persona. They feel lost, stagnant. Reality is fraught with anguish, panic, absence and void.
>
> (Schwartz, 2023)

This is hidden behind an appealing but elusive façade. Puella takes flight from reality as she does not know it. Eventually life is no longer sustainable in an illusionary world solely reliant on the ego and persona.

Puella are described as doll like, a girl, objectified, shaped according to the dominant collective traditional male desires. Likewise, puer remains the boy, and in both instances – puer and puella – they are in the grip of the pull of powerful energy, compromising individuality, subsumed by parents rather than assuming adulthood. They can be rebellious but are caught in the very patterns they try to escape. Their internal distress signals they are trapped in unconscious personal, cultural and historical wounds; unfinished mourning processes; intergenerational issues and archetypal anxieties indicating emptiness and disillusionments. Seeking impossible ideals interweaves with the failure to live as the destructive elements hound them internally, each day creating sterility and inertia. They could remain stuck, bored and empty.

Fear of being inadequate

Gabriel seemed a puer type male, younger looking than his late middle age, attractive, appearing confident and above it all. The instinct for intimacy was obscured behind his overt sexual desire while he remained unmoved emotionally. Life had little meaning as he glided smoothly from one accomplishment to another and one relationship to another. He described himself as blown by the wind and settling for whatever presented itself. No emotion was involved in any of his serial affairs. He called these temporary partners friends and did not see how he controlled and used them. He thought he was loyal to each. Of course, his wife did not know. He pretended and played the role. With her or anyone, he did not argue, show passion or emote as he considered it weak. He never let himself go into the area of feelings or anything intense. Affairs were common for him, and while the women fell in love, he did not. He could easily walk away and did. He kept himself intact this way, always a step removed from living, seemingly cool and collected; nothing ruffled the placid surface of rationale and distance.

Gabriel was taken by surprise when he found himself in tears in my office. He did not cry, always kept his composure and did not just hide; there was no emotional response. Yet, he was internally caught in negative thought cycles, self-denigrating to the point of being paralysed. In these cycles he could not find where he fit or what to develop. No one knew what he felt but he also did not know. His feelings were searching for connection, but it was a cold, intellectual and sexual physical connection. He remained uninvolved.

It did not cross his mind to rely on anyone or even that he lacked the ability to love. Self-reflection was simply not part of his life. It was not rational. Until now there had been no urgency or commitment, nor did he take himself seriously. Even at his work, although conscientious, he knew he could do more, go further, but just did not. Given the rigidity of these patterns, no growth was internally or emotionally available. Transformation of the personality was blocked. Nothing and no one from the outside penetrated, and he did not notice. Emotions were damaged, flattened with the façade of rationality and he was seemingly uncaring. As Julia Kristeva commented, 'The pain that nevertheless remains bears witness to this experience of having been able to exist for, through or with another in mind ... A fragile crest where death and regeneration vie for dominance' (1987, pp. 4–5).

Only when a divorce occurred again did he begin to feel something, but he knew not what. He began analysis to figure out what had happened. He chose the Jungian approach having recalled a book he read many years prior speaking of Jungian analytical treatment. The vague memory was not coloured by emotion but by intellectual curiosity.

Gabriel was split off from his more complete self, living a half-life. He knew he was fraudulent as he admitted in the first analytical session. His inner psychological composition had been split off and was now demanding engagement. He had not been lonely and miserable before but busy with rather compulsive behaviours – the affairs, rigid exercise and eating patterns. The relational difficulties and feelings were missed, submerged, buried. In fact, he was taken aback his wife wanted a divorce. He would have gone on the way it was as he felt no discomfort. The world was coloured by the sameness of routine and bland without emotion or desire. He was removed from himself and had been unaware of the cost. Now he began to feel something and did not know what to make of it.

As a child he recalled being lonely and sensitive but without goals or ideas of what he wanted. There was little opportunity to express feelings or have his subjective reality recognised. However, the split-off others, those dissociated parts within, were not exclusively negative or painful material as he assumed prior to beginning his psychological quest. It was only that he did not know how to feel or engage with them. Other options did not enter his mind. For him desire coalesced into sexual expression rather than expanding into life pleasures, professional achievements, or development beyond the safety of the small envelop in which he was ensconced. The breakthrough needed to arouse emotion and desire was this third divorce.

His aliveness had been suppressed in living below his potential, preoccupied in the routines of exercise, food, affairs. Underneath this pooled the psychic energy seeking expression and now bursting forth. He was surprised. It was to bring his entire personality forward out of the mediocrity he had accepted, hiding his depth and lying unconsciously at the core of his being. Engaging with otherness in general is engaging with the 'not-I' elements to bring possibilities for personality expansion out of the narrow sameness of narcissism. And it can be unsettling. Gabriel is an example illustrating the difficult process of accepting oneself, dropping the illusions and grandiosity and facing the hungry, empty, lonely ego searching for the self.

'As-if' personality

Gabriel said his façade was fraudulent. It was not apparent, but he sought attention, was in secret competition with others, and experienced harsh self-judgement and criticism. For years his sexual affairs seemed defiant and greedy. He grabbed all he was told he could not have by breaking boundaries and getting away with it. He enacted a similar relationship to food and did not know when he was hungry or full. His inner world was populated with myriad accusations, and this enacted a defensive and aggressive dynamic that kept him from other feelings.

Gabriel never had a good or acceptable self-image, and he punished himself with excess, seemed restless and did not know when he lost himself in food, drink and sex. He learned low self-worth, and it remained. Each morning, he had to masturbate; it just was a fact, but he did not know why. Similarly, he needed the stimulation of pornography. Again, he did not know what drove this or what satisfied him; he just kept the sameness of routine. He did not contemplate he might be searching for himself.

In the absence of any containing or comforting spaces, his emotional world must be protected from the anxiety and threat of annihilation by the overwhelming affects he could not manage. In the absence of adequate internal and external containers it became necessary to resort to increasingly forceful projective attribution – perhaps in the hope of finding containment and relief from what in the moment was felt to be the unbearable hollowness inside.

The subjective relation to and relationship with our interior informs our capacity to create meaning, connect to people and engage life in fulfilling ways. The relation to interiority evolves over time and demands we analyse ourselves and reflect on authenticity and self-honesty. However, Gabriel had been split inside, numb and cut off from feeling, as if he were a robot.

The fantasy is to protect but Gabriel was unwittingly caught in the split between his private and public self. Feelings of being fake, unseen and worthless were tangled up with a sense of entitlement and fury. When a person feels so deeply flawed, they cannot imagine ever fitting into human society; so narcissistically wounded, they must imagine being above it all. This makes the sense of isolation more acute, the need to be both seen and not seen ever sharper, and the façade finely honed.

The narcissist like Gabriel grows up suffering in extreme loneliness and a confusing sense of despair. The singularity of addictions of all kinds and their predictable patterns – sneaking, theft of being, isolation, hiding of self – seem to be the solution to avoid the lack inside. 'The [psychic] retreat then serves as an area of the mind where reality does not have to be faced, where phantasy and omnipotence can exist unchecked and where anything is permitted' (Steiner, 1993, p. 3). Although this person is very alone, they cannot easily be alone, and they are busy being drawn to their addictive patterns. For Gabriel this was sexual, physical and orchestrated to defend against self and other relationships, although he did not realise this.

Being run by disillusionment and always needing to be filled deflect from the deeper issues and are based on the need to control. Sometimes this means lulling others into the make-believe world of the narcissist, setting up a false image of confidence and aloofness. The mask of façade comes into place to avert anxiety and avoid critique; the persona is a masquerade and defence to survive. Underneath is the personality fearing retribution from the outside world and anticipating not being enough of anything. These fears plague the narcissist who does not know how to cope if not perfect or not completely adored. Stability is never flawless, and this is what the mask covers – the felt inadequacy and insecurity lying just below the surface. The person worries about anything being wrong or mistaken, obsessed with the need for reassurance that proves to be never enough.

The history of this personality has long roots and goes by different names in psychoanalysis. Freudian psychoanalyst Joan Riviere, in 1928, wrote a paper called 'Womanliness as Masquerade'; Helene Deutsch, in the 1940s, named the 'as-if' personality; and in the 1990s Ronald Britton also referenced the 'as-if' personality. Jungian analyst Hester Solomon resurrected this concept, bringing it forward in 2004. Her perspective provided hope with the twist that these people were analysable and did not inhabit just a vacant and superficial shell. My book on this (2023) aligns the concept with the currently popular jargon of the imposter, a person who knows they are fraudulent and needs to cover what they consider basic flaws. Others would be amazed at this, but the person feels it and knows it deeply inside. The centre does not feel strong enough, and they must keep on the move, stir up and create stimulation to deflect from anyone getting close enough to perceive the severe lacks.

As noted, this has been an aspect or personality type weaving in and out of the psychological lexicon. The person is a shell of attraction and charisma. The outer shell seems well developed and the person confident. However, even though they are in many ways reflecting the real person, once the outer layer is peeled off, they are felt to be bored and empty because they are separated from the energy and stimulation of the unconscious. In the silence of their being, these people are without vitality. To explore this will require inner work, but this process can become their stumbling block.

The phrase 'as-if' can be characterised by the narcissism of façade, fragility, fraudulent and vulnerable, bounded by a wall of impenetrability (Schwartz, 2023).

The person is veiled in an appealing but elusive persona based on a precarious sense of self. Distress occurs when the outer accomplishments formerly shoring the personality are used up and the inner reserves collapse, as they are no longer sustainable due to the lack of attachment at the core, creating part of the maladaptive life response.

The personality is trapped in an image, attempting the ideal and needing to be idealised, lauded and applauded at each endeavour. They must be the best. The consistency of self is porous, and the sense of self-value lost to one's purview. It is like a hole at the centre that nothing fills permanently. It is difficult to bear any absence, discomfort or lack.

The cost is the inability to find the real self. The inner disconnect is diverted to the outer show and attention is turned to the surface. The inner misery and bewilderment are put away, isolated. Sometimes the dreams are so circuitous the person cannot be located. The self is shame filled for this person whose life is based on self-deception. If sufficiently protected by what has become a tightly defensive organisation, they do not have to feel. They can avoid distress because they do not know how to enter or cope with the inner conundrum.

Rooted in the need for the image of self-reliance, the imposter shapeshifts the perceptions of themselves to fit each event. What remains elusive is a definitive identity combined with the need to jump to the next project or event. The 'as-if' person exists in a crisis of sterility, an emptiness fostering anxiety, and addictions of all sorts occupy time and energy away from the self. It feels empty and boring to just be. As in the novel *The Picture of Dorian Gray* by Oscar Wilde, the protagonist commits crimes and gets away with it, remaining unsuspected. No one can see the truth due to his impeccable public persona. Meanwhile, the portrait of himself secreted in his room and only for his eyes becomes transformed into an image more and more twisted, a wretched picture of the wretched side of humanity, stained with each infraction until ultimately the portrait explodes, killing Dorian Gray.

To the world these high-achieving individuals function well. They are simultaneously lively and lifeless, yet ideas proliferate and accomplishments accumulate. With lightning speed and seeming ease this person dances to a frantic beat, as if continual movement will fill the emptiness, jettisoned by the anxiety and worry they are a sham. Life itself must be filled with as much as possible, and this preoccupation diverts from the deeper rivers running within. The 'as-if' person has difficulty with the absent spaces, the pauses between events, life transitions and the up and down flow of life. Few realise it is not easy to be this person.

There is an underlying sense of distrust and lack of confidence in one's place in the world. Filling the emptiness with people, places and things is an attempt to compensate the feeling of being unreal. The emptiness arises from early emotional wounding and lack of correct or close enough attachment with consistent caregivers. As adults these people are performers, needing attention and seeming superficial. The question is how to bridge the gap to access who one really is.

The way of relating to the world is through mimicry and imposter façades; however, the adaptation 'as-if' comes at the expense of authenticity. One feels as flat as the social media screen, yet they often hide this from themselves and others. The unconscious calls to be more deeply known, relationships with self and others open rather than closed, life no longer avoided with emotional distancing, compulsions or perfectionism (Schwartz, 2023).

Saddened and struggling to be otherwise, without sufficient or basic attention Gabriel learned to put off his real desires. There was no comfort, instead only nervous watching and hypervigilance. He did not know love. Peace and contentment were also unknown in the need to exert control and eliminate suffering. The gnawing emptiness signalled the lack of a secure identity. He must be stellar and without any issues or there was the crush of despair and defeat. The sense of solid identity was easily jeopardised in the anticipated abandonment for any infraction. Self-negating thoughts and actions were set up against imagined standards of perfection. In the progressive deadening of the self, one enters a sort of wandering, repeating the original losses while escaping introspection.

With the narcissist, relationships are based on disguise and learned inauthenticity. Although social and seemingly capable of warmth, emotional depth is stunted when the person feels unable to emerge or be safely seen. The creative can occur when authenticity acts in accord with one's entire self. As Jung said,

> Our consciousness is aware of resistances, because the other person seems strange and uncanny, and because we cannot get accustomed to the idea that we are not absolute master in our own house. We should prefer to be always 'I' and nothing else. But we are confronted with that inner friend or foe, and whether he is our friend or our foe depends on ourselves.
> (Jung, 1950/1968, CW 9i, para. 235)

References

Bisagni, F. (2022). Digressions on the fascist state of mind: Psychoanalytic perspectives on narcissism and 'social-ism'. *Journal of Analytical Psychology*, *67*(2), 434–444.

Bollas, C. (1992). *Being a character: Psychoanalysis and self-experience*. Routledge.

Colman, W. (2007). Symbolic conceptions: The idea of the third. *Journal of Analytical Psychology*, *52*(5), 565–583.

De Beauvoir, S. (1949/2010). *The second sex* (C. Borde & S. Malovany-Chevallier, Trans.). Alfred A. Knopf.

Eigen, M. (2001). *Damaged bonds*. Karnac.

Green, André (2023). *On the destruction and death drives* (Howard Levine, Ed.). Karnac Books.

Hillman, J. (1979). *Puer papers*. Spring Publications.

Jacoby, M. (1990). *Individuation and narcissism: The psychology of self in Jung and Kohut*. Routledge.

James W. (1902). *The varieties of religious experience*. Longmans, Green and Co.

Jung C. G. (1921/1971). *The collected works of C. G. Jung: Vol. 6. Psychological types.* Princeton University Press.

Jung C. G. (1928/1969). The relations between the ego and unconscious. In *Two essays on analytical psychology* (Vol. 7). Princeton University Press.

Jung C. G. (1946/1955). Analytical psychology and education. In *The development of personality* (Vol. 17). Routledge and Kegan Paul.

Jung, C. G. (1950/1968). Concerning rebirth. In *The archetypes and the collective unconscious* (Vol. 9i). Princeton University Press.

Jung, C. G. (1954/1968). Psychological aspects of the mother archetype. In *The archetypes and the collective unconscious* (Vol. 9i). Princeton University Press.

Jung, C. G. (1967). *The collected works of C. G. Jung: Vol. 5. Symbols of transformation.* Princeton University Press.

Jung, C. G. (1968). *The collected works of C. G. Jung: Vol. 9ii. Aion.* Princeton University Press.

Kristeva, J. (1987). *Tales of love.* Columbia University Press.

Kristeva, J. (1992). *Black sun.* Columbia University Press.

Levine, H. (Ed.). (2023). *On the destruction and death drives,* by André Green. Phoenix Publishing House.

Modell, A. (1996). *The private self.* Harvard University Press.

Schwartz, S. (2023). *Imposter syndrome and the 'as-if' personality in analytical psychology: The fragility of self.* London: Routledge.

Scuderi, L. (2015). *The work of André Green: An introduction* [Master's thesis]. Smith College, https://scholarworks.smith.edu/theses/661

Sekoff, J. (1999). The undead: Necromancy and the inner world. In G. Kohon (Ed.), *The dead mother: The work of André Greene* (pp. 109–127). Routledge.

Steiner, J. (1993). *Psychic retreats: Pathological organizations in psychotic, neurotic and borderline patients.* Routledge.

Chapter 5

The body talks – does a narcissist listen?

Are you talking to yourself about your body as if it is something separate? As Virginia Woolf wrote,

> There is some check in the flow of my being; a deep stream presses on some obstacle; it jerks; it tugs; some knot in the centre resists. Oh, this is pain, this is anguish!... To whom shall I give all, that flows through me, from my warm porous body? I will gather my flowers and present them – Oh! To whom?
> (2000, p. 57)

The habit of self-talk is typical of narcissists who ignore, negate and exist in the disconnection between mind and body. The instinctual connection to our body begins from birth when we freely express enthusiasm, curiosity and desire. As we grow, many scenarios and patterns step in to disrupt or foster the psychological and emotional relationship between body and psyche. Without body appreciation we miss out on intimacy, love, feeling, emotional reactions. These arise from relational and physical issues, both overt and subtle, social and private, to which we are exposed. All reflect the extent of our present and future sense of agency, self-regard, encouragement or discouragement and authentic expressiveness. The early environment gives us numerous messages about how to act that we continue to listen to throughout our life. This is where we learn to be narcissistic and whether to reveal the truth or cover-up, physically and psychologically.

Body narcissism is about the narcissist's attitude to the body and its display. For a narcissist it reveals a person needing positive and adoring reactions. The narcissist is embroiled in conflict around the body although they often receive projections that they look fantastic. It is not evident this person has an internal distorted body image. Body narcissism is exemplified in a poem written by Sylvia Plath called 'Mirror', which I discuss later in this chapter.

The body is also where psychological transformation occurs as the body affects our feelings, and these feelings circulate within in a continual loop. The body is where we live, experience and heal from trauma, loss of love, and where we express or suppress our feelings. Without the body there can be no total life experience.

And yet the narcissist turns away from their body by instituting various distractions. One of these is being wrapped in singularity, like a computer, living in a virtual reality, shielded from the effect of others upon themselves.

Embedded in the body are experiences extending from the past to present time, connecting us to ourselves and our history. However, usually the narcissist feels disembodied and not present. Our personal and collective story is sequestered in bodily memory – losses, victories and events often unable to be recalled solely through language and narration. The body discloses openings to these silent, but loudly resonating memories. This includes repressed situations, depression and anxiety, longing and suffering, the loss of meaning, joy and ecstasy, and the connectedness or not to love and be loved on conscious and unconscious planes. Therapeutic analysis traces how the learned experiences of bodily negation and appreciation is constructed and how this is shaped throughout life.

The narcissist focuses their attention on presenting a distinctive persona with a striking appearance, avoiding others' judgements in their preoccupation with the surface self. The body shame, sadness and overemphasis on approval masks discomfort, unease and an abyss of self-contempt. Shame arises when a narcissist fails to live up to their ideal standards. Narcissists are upset and angry when the outer world does not match their idealisations of it, or others don't respond the way they want them to. Superficial physical attention is sought, not for closeness or real intimacy, but rather as a barrier from others. Relationships where one is seen and sees the other are unfortunately not part of the narcissist's experience. They are cut off from perceiving this as pleasurable and find it uncomfortable to be real with others. There are always nagging doubts and self-conscious judgements.

Although there is much internal and social pressure to present the perfect body image, for the narcissist it is never sufficient. Their inner shame and self-contempt must not be revealed to others; they support this with rigid defences and a tightly held persona. The focus on physical appearance, preoccupation with looks and a desire to be the centre of attention are attempts to deflect from how deficient they feel inside. The narcissist's bodily experience involves a sense of disconnectedness and fragmentariness, getting in the way with others, building a wall for distraction but not togetherness.

The myth of Narcissus and Echo addresses the lack of relationship between the 'I' and other, body and psyche, inside and outside. The figure of Echo is typically interpreted as the subject who loses her voice and body agency and is doomed to repeat the historical patriarchal attitudes towards the feminine and her physical self. In part she enacts the role of the obedient one, waiting and ultimately disappearing. It is the past and present tale of the female as they experience body exclusion, perpetuation of unconscious body violence, biases and demeaning narratives. As Hélène Cixous, French writer and feminist, advised, it is through the 'emancipation of the marvelous text of herself she must urgently learn to speak. We must kill the false woman who is preventing the live one from breathing' (Cixous, 1976, p. 880).

The lure of the perfect image

The desired image combines messages from culture, family and self. Media, especially social media, bombards us with how to look, improve, get thinner or more buff, be more seductive and thereby more beautiful. The way we perceive and deal with these internal and external images throughout life gives rise to narcissistic reactions. Even though narcissism points to some fundamental aspects of human nature, the social and public mirror for the perfect body is the narcissistic focus. The narcissist reflects an image for adulation. Is this image the real one? The narcissist learns early this is a way to be loved. But it also promotes inner lack, a never-fillable hole. There can be no satisfaction when the narcissist remains separated from the authenticity of their body expression.

Yet, narcissism is a body story. It is physical in its manifestation and expression of desire, although this is ultimately unrequited in the myth. Mesmerised by gazing into his reflection Narcissus expressed, 'Let it be allowed me to behold that which I may not touch, and to give nourishment to my wretched frenzy' (Ovid, 1893, book III, ll. pp. 509–510). This seems vain, self-absorbed, and it is. It is also a commentary on what it is to be separated from one's body and its physical feelings, unable to take in or accept its reality.

The narcissist wears the body, not for expressing themselves, being intimate, loving or authentic, but to attract attention. They might become sexually absorbed, but it is without emotion. They may be attracted to internet chat rooms, pornography and any variety of addictions as the constant need to prove creates insecurity and the pressure to have more. The body itself, although admired by others, is often reviled by the narcissist, a self-hatred necessitating disguise with a grandiose cover. The physical self is not connected to the psychological self but remains absorbed, alone, distant, aloof, admired. Yet there is a violence enacted against the body to shape it, disguise it, make it into an object of wonder, display, the best.

The voice of the body tells a psychological and cultural story and reveals one of the defences of narcissism. The glitzy body hides any internal confusion and disguises any hint of the negative. Moreover, in our youth-oriented societies, the ageing body is automatically seen as lacking physical beauty, strength, mind or wisdom. Rather, ageing becomes loaded with despair, weakness, invisibility. One is assumed to be ugly and worn out, no longer appreciated, sexual or energetic. These ideas of physical appeal are narrow and can produce anguish, self-alienation, eating problems, body distortion, hatred, defeat, illness and distress. After all, in the myth Narcissus was a teenager.

In the early 1900s, Jung recognised the body as a communicator of the unconscious. He used what was called a *galvanometer* from which he derived readings of body reactions as proof of the physicality of the psychological complexes he called 'the living units of the unconscious' (Jung, 1934/1975, CW 8, para. 210). In his *Zarathustra Seminars* on the philosopher Nietzsche, Jung (1988) stated there can be 'no meaning without the body' as the body is an interpreter and communicator of the psyche and interrelatedness. 'Body and mind are the two aspects of the living being, and that is all I know. Therefore, I prefer to say that the two happen together in a miraculous way' (1935/1976, CW 18, para. 70). Similar statements may be found elsewhere in Jung's *Collected Works*. 'The mysterious truth is that the spirit is the life of the body seen from within, and the body the outward manifestation of spirit – the two being really one' (1934/1968, CW 10, para. 195).

Feeling alive and open, shaped by interactions and dialogues with others, brings with it the capacity for physical and psychological presence. In the myth, Narcissus and Echo both lose their bodies, and they physically enact loss, sorrow, longing and desire unfulfilled. Narcissism sadly represents the denial of the body-mind union because the experience of being fully present depends on the body and our mindful consciousness of it.

Mirrored body

Phillipe described a disappeared self, almost dying several times. He lived wild, untethered, no guidance from home, with an absent father and both parents preoccupied with themselves, narcissists in his description. No one watched out for him, and early on he became involved with the wrong crowd – drugs, gangs, petty crime, juvenile detentions, experiences of helplessness, nameless dread, loss, guilt, lack of containment. This was accompanied by his building up powerful defences against the destructive feelings enacted against himself and others. Phillipe prided himself on his sexual prowess, yet he wondered why nothing stuck in relationships. He always seemed to leave as the thrill of yet another conquest lured him away to something more appealing. At the same time, he longed to be loved but really did not know how to garner attention other than for his looks and sexual performance. He seemed to need this reinforcement a lot. His emotions were safely placed behind an unconsciously constructed wall through which he did not reach. He felt nothing.

'It is possible in this way to understand violence as a type of action which fulfils a particular psychological function, namely the ridding of unwanted mental content …' (Mizen, 2003, p. 294). Violence can be a way to mediate and contain psychic pain and is a response to an 'unbearable psychic experience' (p. 298). Narcissistic and self-preservative reactions like Phillipe's serve to compensate for the lack in the inner and outer container where there should be a variety of emotional responses and affects. Phillipe had narrowed his world to defence and hardening and now was just numb. The British Jungian analyst Richard Mizen noted,

> In the unstable category the violence has a reactive character in which its projective quality is intended to expel, perhaps explosively. In this circumstance the violence is intended to actively void mental elements, which are experienced as violating the existing psychic system.
>
> (Mizen, 2003, p. 298)

These destructive elements are stronger than the narcissist realises and keep them from self-confirmation, as they are occupied with compulsive internal games and avoidances. They are continually leaving the present moment; it is considered too painful and fraught. Any underlying unease and vulnerability must be submerged. This is related to the emotional hurt and disappointment often repressed for years yet remembered and enacted in the body. Bodily neglect lurks in the various manifestations of the split-off body complex.

Body and psyche are supposed to oscillate in an energic and dynamic paradigm. The body dissociation for Phillipe was a psychological defence, a way to avoid the feelings he did not understand and that felt too dangerous for conscious psychic integration. It was just not possible to get close to what felt like destructive elements for most of his life. He feared the inner world, unsure what it contained and was not comfortable revealing his inmost self. He reported little experience of being held, loved or cared for. He felt impinged upon, angry, unfulfilled, frustrated and that nothing was of value, least of all him. Lost and confused, he was worried all the time that things would fall apart, no matter what success he incurred.

Phillipe's parents, immersed in poverty, poor education and lack of opportunity, were unable to tolerate or understand the activity and intellectual curiosity of this child. Phillipe did not care if mother died as she constantly demeaned him. Father was preferred, and although softer; he was distant, a solitary figure while mother was more overtly anxious, empty of love and disapproving. Phillipe's body enacted the confusion of feelings and reactions, propelling him to exhaustive gym workouts and emotionally ensuring no one could come close. This was a person who seemed to be buffering himself against the traumatic effects from the other, experienced both personally and socially through economic and emotional lack of confirmation.

The role played by others in the recognition of body image creates synthesis and a comfort of coexistence. The experience of inhabiting one's body is also an expression of interrelatedness and arises from the influences of culture, politics and society on our physical lives, attitudes to body and psyche, conscious and unconscious. But what happens when a person feels discarded socially, living on a lower level, shamed at not having? Or, culturally a minority, of mixed race and ethnicity or religion? Where and how do they fit?

Dreams in various scenarios expose the demons inside that do not allow a child to succeed, speaking in murderous self-defeating voices unable to be faced or stilled. Phillipe said

> *I dreamt yet again and have periodically through my life about the man who always had a strange energy – part erotic, part fear, part draw, part destruction. I know he has killed people. I am not to tell as then he will kill me. I am at a seminar and the man is there but is a shape-shifter, a trickster and has put on a disguise. He is now a woman, but I see in his eyes he knows I know who he is, and he knows I am going to tell. I wake up fearful and then think I must call 911 and get away from this guy or else it will never end.*

The dream reveals an internal figure turning against Phillipe, with threats of possible annihilation. It reveals the pressure and themes of instability mixed with fear and vulnerability. The images illustrate a self that is fragmented and insecure, dangerous and seriously destructive. And Phillipe is reaching out for help.

Upon awakening Phillipe knew there was no way he could assume he had dealt with this inner force. He associated this dream scene with the daily hatred of his body, trying to reshape it, constantly upset at his looks, bombarded with destructive thoughts, anxiety and bewilderment. He lacked security. The dream figure was an instigator, a complex figure ruling his life, sapping originality, diminishing confidence and cutting his potency and confidence. And the figure was like a trickster who changed bodies constantly, shifting, uneasy, devious. Was this the defeat rearing itself before each possibility presented to him? The answer was always no; he cannot do it and will not succeed. He often backed off but just as often pushed onwards but felt defeat no matter what. For years he tried to cope, but the dream made it clear he could no longer deny the destructive inner setup. He had lived at a distance emotionally, his mind and body split, and he had hardened with no tenderness towards himself. He knew he just would not make it if he did not turn this around.

Emptiness

Jung wrote: 'It seems highly probable that the psychic and the physical are not two independent parallel processes but are essentially connected through reciprocal action' (1928/1969, CW 8, para. 33). Dissociation from the body prevails. Although the narcissist seems concerned with body perfection, more often this person remains disconnected from the physical. The body can be an enemy, not to care for, but to get in shape, and it is never or rarely pleasing. Instead, the body is held at a distance, shadowy, distorted, denied, separated from psyche with a thick wall keeping others from entering in any meaningful way. The incessant demand is to present an illusory ideal as the walled-off and walled-in psyche resists being seen except in carefully controlled and superficial ways. Unable to sustain a sense of personal aliveness, body image and illusions obfuscate the internal fragmentation draining into psychic impoverishment.

Becoming othered, separated, facing the unfamiliar compositions of identity, self-belonging and self-estrangement define narcissism. Disconnection from the body arises also from the unconscious and creates division from one's authentic nature. The 'deeper regions of psyche remain elusive, feeling without center, void, empty, nothing fills, the structure not felt as body not felt, objectified' (Connolly, 2013, p. 640). The sensations of lost vitality and emptiness can also lead to profound alterations of the body, attempting to deny yet emphasising the psychic deadness.

The narcissist cannot come face to face with themselves. The disidentification with the body is apparent when Narcissus was captivated by his reflection in the water. He could neither see nor love anybody other than himself, but he also did not know who it was he saw. Narcissus could not find himself in his reflection. And Echo lost her body caring little for herself when her expressions of desire were continually refused.

The self-belonging of a narcissist is threatened by becoming othered, disconnected and estranged, facing unfamiliar compositions of identity. These sensations can lead to seeking the perfect body image but not the real. 'In more severe instances there are pervasive and overpowering feelings of psychic deadness accompanied by the conviction all is without meaning' (Connolly, 2013, p. 640). In states of psychic deadness, there are disturbances in the sense of body ownership. A loss of temporality is characteristic of such states. The self is experienced as detached or dissociated from corporeal reality. Even when exhibiting the desired look, satisfaction is fleeting. Many people compensate and disconnect through various obsessions with mind-altering substances, food, activity or sex. All these can be connectors in moderation but for narcissists they are often used as separators. 'The lifeless dissociation between the subjective self and the body is experienced as something cold, frozen or even dead' (Connolly, 2013, p. 646).

The decorations

Spurred by the fear of being inadequate the fantasy of youth is retained through cosmetic surgery, Botox and augmentation or depletion of the body in many forms. Increasing use of surgical operations for bodily enhancement link a cultural preoccupation to a more basic drive to renew the self. These become an unconscious attempt to manage the unbearable anxiety of self-rejection and loss. To erase the inner experience of ugliness, the narcissist makes the body 'a kind of stage upon which the unfelt psychic pain is dramatized and relieved' (Marles, 2013, p. 150).

Such people operate like zombies who portray the living dead, those without comfort in their own skin, accentuated by a lack of vitality or hyperactivity revealing they do not really exist. Their lives are assumed to be senseless with an invisible barrier between them and others, and their outer and inner selves are disjointed. The world in which they live becomes increasingly empty and meaningless, and they express apathy and have difficulties making decisions or taking initiative. They treat themselves, not as a living body in relation with the mind, but rather as an inanimate object, something distant to be manipulated and attacked, mostly by themself. The body becomes a space of misery and dissatisfaction. They do not know how to self soothe and put energy into seeking attention from others.

Many narcissists assault themselves through self-denial as the disappointments pile up and aggression turns inwards, and these become the means for control and defence. Dissociation becomes the mechanism whereby ideas, fantasies and emotions operate unconsciously and independently. Jung called these clusters *subpersonalities* or *complexes*. His view of the psyche was characterised by an emphasis on establishing relations between the various parts of the psyche and comprehending the ways these parts can come together.

A woman dreamt of an unknown and undefined woman emerging out of a stone wall. This short dream reminded her of other dreams with women also emerging from various enclosures like an old-fashioned bathtub, walking out of the ocean or just standing in a field. She commented about the dream saying she had been sleeping and now is more awake. She had been unconsciously consumed with inner dead feelings, the real self hidden from others, devoting her passion to things but not herself and being with people who did not challenge or seek to know her. Their more shallow and superficial existences fit as she did not want to be seen and did not know how to be known with kindness and love. Now she realised she had backed off from this form of knowledge for years.

Her early experiences fit the following description. 'The non mother, dead, nothing to give, no heritage, no being no related anything there. The patient seemed to be awakening or coming out of the womb during the period of her psychotherapy' (Sebek, 2002, p. 230). Both maternal and paternal figures were distant, unaffectionate, giving her little positive response, and they dominated her psyche and her body as she went in and out of anorexia and sexual affairs, not caring or thinking about it at all. When visiting family, she literally could not eat and lost weight. There was nothing digestible there, and her body disappeared.

Through the analytic process she was beginning to come alive, and it was a slow process. One does not easily emerge from being dead. Over time the sense of aliveness was more apparent, and it arose from the inside. She could be seen, and it was becoming safe.

Sylvia Plath and the mirror image

A poem by Sylvia Plath entitled 'Mirror' describes a woman in the mirror and the disparagement she feels towards the image she sees there. She looks in the mirror and sees herself but distorted, denigrated, separated, like the narcissist who does not know how to access the entire personality. This poem describes the experiences of the woman in the previous section who had become separated from her complete mind and body self.

The woman protagonist in the poem listens to the mirror, described as male in its harsh assessment of her. The poem illustrates a paradoxical situation. A mirror holds the image of oneself but is also not oneself. Looking in a mirror one is the observer and the observed, the watcher and the watched. The power of the mirror image is portrayed as mirrors provide more than mere reflections, and, in the poem, this one is endowed with the power to reflect negativity and lack.

American poet Sylvia Plath killed herself at age 30 after years of psychological struggles and suicide attempts. She was married to British poet laureate Ted Hughes, but the poem does not portray relationship or love. Hughes had many affairs. For years Plath struggled to fulfil the expected and correct female image, to meet social standards, and yet her real self was yearning to express herself. Her writings show intense periods of self-exploration, and their dramas and conflicts were made more poignant as she aligned her intimate struggles with the collective human experience during the post–World War II years.

Jung stated about poetry: 'The unsatisfied yearning of the artist reaches back to the primordial image in the unconscious which is best fitted to compensate the inadequacy and one-sidedness of the present' (1922/1971, vol. 15). Sylvia Plath, like the narcissist, experienced early emotional mis-attunements, which continued throughout her life, creating disappointment in herself due to the insufficient fulfilment with others. From the lack and loss of parental attachment, she learned to develop masks set to please others but also to cover her real self. To this end, 'Plath explored the oscillation between longing for extinction fantasies of transformation, of escape from constriction and engulfment, and of flight, where casting off outgrown selves and overused masks lead to a naked renewal' (Bronfen, 1998, p. 64).

Several of Sylvia Plath's poems describe this in the distance set up between who she is and who she wants to be, although the protagonists continually seek renewal and rebirth. Looking into a mirror, Sylvia Plath wrote in her journal, she 'noticed a big, smudgy-eyed ... woman staring idiotically into my face. It was only me, of course. I was appalled to see how wrinkled and used-up I looked' (Kukil, 2000, p. 17).

Image is 'an expression of the unconscious as well as the conscious situation of the moment' (Jung, 1921/1971, CW 6, para. 745). 'It is only possible to live the fullest life when we are in harmony with these symbols; wisdom is a return to them' (1930–31/1969, CW 8, para. 794). Interpretation of the symbolic starts neither from the conscious nor from the unconscious but rather is enriched by their reciprocal relationship. The symbol is the 'best possible formulation of a relatively unknown thing, which for that reason cannot be more clearly or characteristically represented' (Ostrowski-Sachs, 1971, para. 743). The symbolic world emerges for us to find meaning through analogy and metaphor to restore the psyche and body connection.

The creative function of images and the meaning of symbols derives from the fact that they are embedded in and cross reference a network of other symbols (Connolly, 2013). Analytical psychology includes the imaginal with its inexhaustible resources into the creative. In other words,

> The Jungian symbol tends towards the dimension of the not-yet. It anticipates that which the culture will explicate only in the course of time and in times and in ways that are impossible to determine a priori. Thus, the Jungian symbol has a dimension that is not only individual and subjective but collective and cultural.
> (Connolly, 2003, p. 365)

In the poem the mirror is a symbol. Its silver backing is also associated with the moon and the feminine. While the mirror claims it is without preconceptions, it manages to communicate the woman protagonist is not viewed as she desires. Because the woman cannot handle this, she turns from the mirror to 'those liars, the candles or the moon'. Candlelight and moonlight symbolise the feminine and are shadow makers, concealing as they reveal, distorting images, creating illusions and providing another light onto consciousness. But these also sound disappointing.

Yet, throughout the poem, the mirror supposedly shows the unadulterated truth as the poem comments about being a faithful reflection no matter what it says about the woman. The woman is drawn to the mirror and believes it reveals the truth even though its words repulse and frighten her. She returns to it, morning after morning. The mirror reflects a sense of negation and self-annihilation and the daily search for self effaces her very being. The mirror acts like a rejecter, and the woman sees herself reduced and enclosed within the margins of a squared and linear reflection.

A biographical reading of the poem illustrates Sylvia Plath's self-flagellation as a personal record and commentary on society's limiting and restrictive roles and treatment of women and the feminine (Conway, 2010, p. 41). Although a sense of self includes an appreciative awareness of one's physical body and mental state, this mirror image does not show either. Rather, there is a nagging depersonalisation reflected in the mirror (Ekmekçioğlu, 2008, p. 94). Plath provided a vivid portrayal of the psychic state that speaks of life without feeling alive and of the self divorced from the body. Moreover, Plath and the culture she fought against associated the feminine with weakness and saw the female body as vulnerable, subject to attack. The poem repeats the plight of women, like Sylvia Plath, who feel their 'worth is viable only if they remain young which in turn becomes a limited definition of beauty' (Conway, 2010, p. 45). Plath's mirror is a metaphor of the struggle between the true self and what is internalised from her mother, other women, and the collective images men have of women and the feminine. The woman in this mirror is objectified even as she simultaneously but seemingly unconsciously objectifies herself. Many people still look into and believe these types of mirrors, reflecting disharmony between themself and the image with its negative and critical judgement.

Sylvia Plath portrays an internalised consciousness narrating a lifetime of interactions with a nameless, faceless woman who imagines the natural process of ageing as disfigurement and despair. Although the speaker of the poem is a mirror, the true protagonist is the woman seeing herself both in and as the mirror in a duality and an opposition to the self. It is unclear in the poem whether the woman is visible in her entirety or whether she can take in the whole context of her body. We have no idea what she shows the mirror as it makes up its own evaluation from what the mirror sees.

The poem emanates ambivalence about the mirror, showing it is not easy or pleasant to be confronted by the mirror, described as square, metallic, hard, cold. The flat wall behind the woman in the poem makes her corporeality indistinct, unimportant, rigid and icy. Moreover, this situation has gone on so long the woman is now a non-entity. She has become merely part of the darkness in the background and hardly separate from the wall itself. The mirror also reflects the lack of response towards women by society in the mid-20th century, Sylvia Plath's marriage marred by her husband's betrayals, and the publishing strictures women of her time struggled against.

However, as true with many seeking reassurance and approval, the woman is drawn to the mirror even though it repulses and upsets her. The question is, what is it she sees in this mirror that keeps her coming back, obsessed day after day, even though she is upset by it? The mirror reveals the woman's narcissistic needs while illustrating the impact and inevitability of time, ageing and obsessions with superficial vanity inevitably and inescapably taking her over.

A person who adopts this type of mirror as their belief system can become cruel, primarily and often in secret, to themself. The mirror also represents Sylvia Plath's image as a disciplined achiever, typical of the driven narcissist, striving to surpass all expectations with a glitteringly perfect image, meeting the parental and social standards of elegance, beauty and achievement with a persona encompassing it all. This represents the social cast of her personality aesthetic, a perfect cover girl smile, an image set to hide any hint of vulnerability.

In the second section of the poem the mirror changes to a lake with a woman bending over and searching for who she is. A lake reflects like a mirror and has depth. Both mirror and lake reflect the surface but also the shadows as the woman searches for herself. The lake contains the depths for the inner processes of rebirth and transformation and the woman searches in it for the truth of who she is. The lake is a more natural place of reflection yet contains the possibility of drowning in the unconscious it symbolises. The end of the poem recognises the girl becoming old and seeming like 'a terrible fish' (Plath, 1981, p. 173).

Sylvia Plath was interested in Jung's use of the symbolic and archetypal perceiving images with a wide perspective. For example, the fish can be noted as content of the unconscious, living under water, and has many other symbolic interpretations. The fish is cold-blooded, undifferentiated, primordial and is 'a symbol of the self. It is the highest and lowest simultaneously and is a threat until dealt with and then can become a curative remedy' (Edinger, 1996, p. 93). In the symbolism of the science of alchemy, the preparations for change 'correspond to the magnet that the alchemist holds in his hand to draw forth the fish from the deep' (Edinger, 1996, p. 125). The woman in the poem is both fascinated and abhorred by this image of the self, described as a 'terrible fish'.

This lake contains a monster in its depths that represent the personal demons Sylvia Plath strove to conceal and the unrest she felt lurking just beneath the surface. The monster in the depths, in other words, is also the monster on the surface – perhaps more accurately, the monstrosity of being mere surface and lacking depth. The horror is to be trapped within such one-sidedness without any escape. Or perhaps it is Plath herself as a woman who has accepted the depersonalisation and passivity but longs for authenticity. Symbolically, the fish inhabits the depths as well as the spirit and perhaps Plath was also drawn to this.

The fish or old woman figure represents a depth of transformation upsetting to the ego or persona with its superficial vanity. 'Fish are removed from the human making the thoughts and emotions of a fish alien, unknown, and unknowable, imbued with detachment like the unconscious itself' (Hunter, 2009, 106). The end of the poem leaves the audience slightly shaken, waiting for the moment that the 'terrible fish' will break the surface. 'The fish mirrors the disfigurement and death as one's destiny claiming a doomed, ageing subject who cannot look away from what both appalls and swallows her' (Hunter, 2009, p. 120).

To the layers of the fish symbol is added Sylvia Plath's husband, Ted Hughes, who was an avid fisherman. The fish might reference the broken bond with him, the disappointing inner and outer masculine images that swallowed her youth and then her life. Moreover, the fish and old woman also symbolise aspects of the mother archetype associated with secrets, darkness, the world of the dead, seduction and poison, anything that devours and is terrifying and inescapable. These can coalesce into what is called the negative mother archetype, appearing like the witch, or any devouring and entwining animal, such as a large fish or a serpent, deep water, nightmares, Lilith, and so on. Is this associated with her feelings of her mother, her own mothering to herself and her young children? Yet, the fish can also represent connection to the natural and nurturing aspects in the dark. When dominated by its devouring and destructive side, we lose the value of its introspective and reflective nature encountered in exploring the psyche.

Reflective surfaces demonstrate both the search for self in its multiple disguises and the disintegration of the self into pieces as well as the rebirth of her true self. 'The mirror shows that a life lived by the false self is not life, but an intolerable death-in-life overcome only by dying to that life' (Kroll, 1976, p. 12). Sylvia Plath's traumas were concealed by a tight and superficial composure set up to portray an ideal persona. Her work is a chronicle of the face she put on for others. Through many of Plath's images we feel an 'insistence that clandestine traumatic knowledge not only haunts its host but will strike back and shatter the protective fictions of infallibility with force equal to the effort put into repressing this truth' (Hunter, 2009, p. 123).

The poetic within the psyche is expressed by Plath's life of sorrow, struggle for understanding and expression mixed with many accomplishments, quite like the narcissist. The psychological process includes desire mixed with the destructive powers of the psyche, as she so poignantly expressed in her writings, including her detailed journals. She wrote of the psyche layered with psychological oppression, a desire for release, and layered with intense emotional reactions. Her words put a visage on the inner chaos exposed through her work, tracing the process of self-examination and the issues for establishing a sense of self.

Poetic images arouse feeling. Sylvia Plath revealed her passion and energy, not from the rational but the emotional. She created a style of recording social and cultural history through conveying her personal experience. Her fierceness, originality and descriptive embodiment of psychological conundrums remain powerfully resonant and applicable to this day. The psychological and physical struggle resounds through her narratives, creativity, contemplation and thoughtful reflection. Like Echo, she lost her body perhaps also over an unrequited love combined with the self-destructive aspects of the narcissist. 'The Self experience leads to issues of embodiment' (Schwartz-Salant, 1982, p. 93). Yet, like the narcissist no one knew the complex struggles warring inside her, and she took her own life.

Despite all her psychological issues, until her death, Sylvia Plath continued to write out the process of finding herself. The discontent, disequilibrium and inner tension was also her source for artistic energy in breaking with tradition and defiantly striving to be herself, continually searching for transformation. Artists like Sylvia Plath exhibit the courage to be shaken to truths not easily quelled and model a pathway in search of transformation and authentic body and psyche connection. 'Her appearance would necessarily bring if not revolution ... at least harrowing explosions ... that radical mutation of things brought on by material upheaval' (Cixous, 1976, p. 879).

References

Bronfen, E. (1998). *The knotted subject.* Princeton University Press.
Cixous, H. (1976). The laugh of Medusa. *Signs, 1*(4), 875–893.
Connolly, A. (2003). To speak in tongues: Language, diversity and psychoanalysis. *Journal of Analytical Psychology, 47*(3), 359–382.
Connolly, A. (2013). Out of the body: Embodiment and its vicissitudes. *Journal of Analytical Psychology, 58*(5), 636–656.
Conway, C. (2010). Through the looking glass: A discussion of doubling in Sylvia Plath's mirror. *Plath Profiles, 3*, 39–45.
Edinger, E. (1996). *The Aion lectures.* Inner City Books.
Ekmekçioğlu, N. (2008). Sylvia Plath's mirrors reflecting various guises of self. *Plath Profiles, 1*, 92–102.
Hunter, D. (2009). Family phantoms: Fish, watery realms and death in Virginia Woolf, Sylvia Plath, and Ted Hughes. *Plath Profiles, 2*, 103–134.
Jung, C. G. (1921/1971). *The collected works of C. G. Jung: Vol. 6. Psychological types.* Princeton University Press.
Jung, C. G. (1922/1977). The relation of analytical psychology to poetry. In *The spirit in man, art and literature* (Vol. 15). Princeton University Press.
Jung, C. G. (1928/1969). On psychic energy. In *The structure and dynamics of the psyche* (Vol. 8). Princeton University Press.
Jung, C. G. (1930–31/1969). The stages of life. In *The structure and dynamics of the psyche* (Vol. 8). Princeton University Press.
Jung, C. G. (1934/1968). The meaning of psychology for modern man. In *Civilization in transition* (Vol. 10). Princeton University Press.
Jung, C. G. (1934/1975). A review of the complex theory. In *The structure and dynamics of the psyche* (Vol. 8). Princeton University Press.
Jung, C. G. (1935/1976). The Tavistock lectures. In *The symbolic life* (Vol. 18). Princeton University Press.
Jung, C. G. (1988). *Jung's seminar on Nietzsche's Zarathustra.* Princeton University Press.
Kroll, J. (1976). *Chapters in a mythology: The poetry of Sylvia Plath* (revised edition 2007). Harper & Row.
Kukil, K. (Ed.). (2000). *The unabridged journals of Sylvia Plath.* Anchor.
Marles, K. (2013). Book Review of *Under the skin: A psychoanalytic study of body modification* by A. Lemma. *Journal of Analytical Psychology, 58*(1), 148–150.

Mizen, R. (2003). A contribution towards an analytic theory of violence. *Journal of Analytical Psychology, 48*(3), 285–305.
Ostrowski-Sachs, M. (1971). *From conversations with C. G. Jung.* Juris.
Ovid. (1893). *The metamorphosis of Ovid, Books I–VII* (Henry T. Riley, Trans.). George Bell & Songs. Project Gutenberg (eBook #21765). https://www.gutenberg.org/cache/epub/21765/pg21765-images.html.
Plath, S. (1981). *Collected poems.* HarperCollins.
Schwartz-Salant, N. (1982). *Narcissism and character transformation.* Inner City Books.
Sebek, M. (2002). Rebirth fantasy and the psychoanalytic process. *Journal of Analytical Psychology, 47*(2), 225–234.
Woolf, V. (2000). *The waves.* Wordsworth Editions.

Chapter 6

Echo's tragedy – narcissistic isolation from intimacy

How do we see the other if we do not see ourselves? Narcissus and Echo are the primary characters in the classic Greek tragedy enacting this question. This question has current relevance to the psychological issue of narcissism with its singularity and the inability to love. The themes of the story are complex and interwoven, illustrating one-sided love turning to paralysis, depression, psychological and physiological deterioration and death. A caveat here is to perceive these mythological figures as parts of the personality seeking union while avoiding the strictures of gender. Because they represent suffering, loss and lack of connection to self, at issue is how these aspects are made conscious and what obstructs the process of their union and love. To set the scene for the chapter, here is Echo trying in vain to get Narcissus to see her:

> One day, when she observed
> Narcissus wandering in the pathless woods,
> she loved him and she followed him, with soft
> and stealthy tread. – The more she followed him
> the hotter did she burn, as when the flame
> flares upward from the sulphur on the torch.
> Oh, how she longed to make her passion known!
> To plead in soft entreaty! to implore his love!
> But now, till others have begun, a mute
> of Nature she must be. She cannot choose
> but wait the moment when his voice may give
> to her an answer.
> Presently the youth,
> by chance divided from his trusted friends,
> cries loudly, 'Who is here?' and Echo, 'Here!'
> Replies. Amazed, he casts his eyes around,
> and calls with louder voice, 'Come here!' 'Come here!'
> She calls the youth who calls. – He turns to see
> who calls him and, beholding naught exclaims,

'Avoid me not!' 'Avoid me not!' returns.
He tries again, again, and is deceived
by this alternate voice, and calls aloud;
'Oh let us come together!' Echo cries,
'Oh let us come together!'

Ovid, Metamorphoses (1922, ll. 528–551)

Echo's words

The words of Hélène Cixous, French writer and feminist, can be applied to Echo.

> Through the same opening that is her danger, she comes out of herself to go to the other: she does not refuse, she approaches, not to do away with the space between, but to see it, to experience what she is not, what she is, what she can be.
> (Sellers, 1994, p. 43)

The figure of Echo challenges and calls for accessing the passions, the shadow, the feminine. She mouths the possibility and the hunger for hope and love, reverberating with echoes of what sadly proves impossible. Yet, her language declares an aliveness. In this myth she is a connecting piece to the larger scope of the personality, called in Jungian analytical psychology, the Self. As Hilda Doolittle, an analysand of Freud, wrote, 'Words were her plague and words were her redemption' (1981, p. 67). Echo expresses longing for life, love and the value of relationship. She reaches out to expand the singular existence Narcissus insists upon as she attempts to elicit a response and union with him.

Echo's language illustrates a relationship between the choiceful formation of her words and their meaning. In her words desire reaches out as her narrative expresses thoughts, feelings, wishes, movement and hope. Echo is singularly focused on Narcissus and profoundly affected by her love as undeterred she verbalises her desires over and over.

In fact, her words are reminiscent of the ways many people feel who are shunned and slighted by the self-involvement of narcissists. Martha Nussbaum, American philosopher, eloquently stated,

> Finding and sharing the words is a matter of finding the appropriate and the honorable fit between conception and expression ... certain truths about human life can only be fittingly and accurately stated in the language and forms characteristic of the narrative style of the artist ... [they] are winged creatures, blunt terms of ordinary speech or of abstract theoretical discourse are blind, acute where they are obtuse, winged where they are dull and heavy.
> (1992, p. 5)

Narcissus is preoccupied with himself while Echo is preoccupied with him. Echo desires to be loved, to feel lovable, to have love received and reciprocated; she wants to be special. We can conjecture there is a void in Echo's life, as she continues echoing this although it only became a more deeply painful place. She remains unseen while the myth recounts the hunger to be seen and to see oneself for who one truly is.

From the beginning Narcissus's mother was told by the blind seer Tiresias, 'If he but fail to recognize himself, a long life he may have, beneath the sun.' One might argue that having never known adequate mirroring with a river for a father and a nymph for a mother, Narcissus could only stay with the comfort of his own image rather than seek a relationship with an external other. This piece substantiates the limiting draw to a mirror when it only contains oneself. As Jung said, 'The world is empty to him who does not know how to direct his libido towards things and people, and to render them alive and beautiful' (1967, CW 5, para. 253).

From the moment she sees him, Echo is preoccupied with getting what could be assumed to be the void within herself filled by Narcissus. What she wants ends up bringing harm to herself and her love remains unrequited. Yet Echo reveals the urge for spanning the spectrum from self to another. She finds creative ways to express this through the words she hears, and her echo repeats these words as she attempts connection. The words are those originating with Narcissus. In so doing she talks about herself and her desires (Quinlin, 2021, p. 161), replicating his words but with meaning for union. Sadly, her passion and feeling expressions are ignored by Narcissus whose passion and feelings are singular and only for himself.

The figure of Echo is connected to creation and related to the pre-Hellenic past when she was named the goddess Acco, known as the 'voice of creation' (Cavalcanti, 2003, p. 139). As for Echo's identity, she is a character who desires to be seen, demands space and cleverly uses repetition to seek recognition. Repetition can be a search for recognition or an expression of her essence (Berry, 2014, p. 143–144). It forces us, in one way or another, to listen to ourselves and is pointed out by another, similar to what occurs in the analytic process. This encounter with the other is crucial for overcoming entrenched narcissistic defences and singular character structure.

'Repetition is an acknowledged form of consciousness both here and elsewhere. Relentlessly resuming something you have already said. Consenting to an infinitesimal momentum, an addition perhaps unnoticed that stubbornly persists in your knowledge' (Munro, 2024, p. 45). The repetition can lead to elaboration and gives a sense of continuity fostering the development of identity. 'Echo's creative repetition gives new meanings to the words she echoes ... and their repetition also allows for elaboration and resolution in the need to repeat' (Berry, 2014, p. 116). This highlights Echo's ability to reorganise the meaning of Narcissus's words, shaping them into her interpretive echoing and the literal meanings transformed by her echoing. Speaking the words becomes a form of responding, making it possible for Echo to express herself. In contrast, Narcissus, looking at his image, notices it responds soundlessly: 'and, as much as I can guess by the movements of your beautiful mouth, you tell me words that do not reach my ears' (Ovid, 1922).

Listening to oneself can lead to reflection and the ability to attend inwardly. The actions and speech we cannot stop and keep on repeating indicate the complexes. Repetition itself became the verification of information from Jung's word association test developed early in his career. Jung found the formation of the repetitions revealed the complex and through this the constellation of the self. About this process Jung commented, 'But the self comprises infinitely more than a mere Ego. It is as much one's self, and all other selves, as the Ego. Individuation does not shut one out from the world, but gathers the world to oneself' (1934/1969, CW 8, para. 432).

Narcissus

Narcissus represents the inability to hold paradox. In the language of Jungian psychology, the tension of the opposites is not sustainable for the narcissist. This ability for holding presents a fragile balance for the narcissist as they cannot tolerate the separate or the opposition separation implies.

Connections to others arise through feelings and self-recognition, affirming each other's existence. The contradiction between asserting oneself and recognising another involves the 'lost tension between self and other ... and explains how from our deepest desires the bonds of love are forged' (Benjamin, 1988, p. 94). This balance is a key to establishing personality differentiation and represents the vulnerable place of dependency inherent in connection. This living and unfolding process is enacted somewhat differently within each person and relationship.

Narcissism reveals the distance between who one is and who one imagines oneself to be. The narcissist can become limited by the other, their desires frustrated. They feel badly about themselves, and then self-expression is compromised (West, 2020, p. 174). The resultant sorrow might constitute a substitute object to which the narcissist clings for lack of any other. Desire becomes dissipated as the narcissistic world is barricaded against the intensity of the desire. As Echo communicates, in contrast to Narcissus, her perception of and value towards relationship, they each provide obverse lens for thinking, feeling and perceiving the world.

Narcissus is trapped by singularity and insistence on image and the idea of himself without any other input. From a different form of insistence 'Echo's desire is single focused, particular and direct, articulate, based on one desire' (Berry, 2014, p. 120–121). Her reaching out to Narcissus is an endeavour towards this while he represents the adversarial position against it. As Cixous noted, 'Action consists of the essential: living, loving' (Sellers, 1994, p. 115). These are the very elements ignored by Narcissus.

Christopher Bollas noted, 'The psychic route encompasses a form of dialogue and brings up how to structure our lived experience combined with the messages appearing from the unconscious' (1992, p. 47). These reveal the ways we develop and understand our personality structures and composition. Our subjectivity is composed of dreams lying within, of awakening to new areas and vistas with fragments and visualisations conveying both unknown and current needs while expressing the Self. Hélène Cixous described this as 'the work of un-forgetting, of un-silencing, of unearthing, of un-blinding oneself, and of un-deafening oneself' (Sellers, 1994, p. 83). This is voice as resonance, gesture and embodied reality, expressing the potential of self-agency with intentionality.

> Knowledge of love is not a state or function of the solitary person at all, but a complex way of feeling, and interacting with another person. To know one's own love is to trust it, to allow oneself to be exposed.
> (Nussbaum, 1992, p. 274)

The way we perceive and deal with these internal or external others throughout life brings attention to the concept of narcissism. It is from this place that the persistence of Echo is an expression of love and the union desired of subject and object. The unconscious incorporates the dissociated personality parts into the self, reflecting the multiplicity of the psyche, but Narcissus closes off these aspects and as result does not develop.

The voice in the myth

The myth of Narcissus and Echo reveals the frustration, unconsciousness and psychological distress of narcissists. The complex beyond the ego and persona reveals a lack of self-love and appears in dreams and mis-attunements in relationships. Narcissus has no relationship between his subjectivity and others, like the modern-day narcissists who are trapped in their subjective singular world. For the narcissist there can be no difference whereas Echo represents difference, not only sexually but also in expressing desire for what is not her. Narcissus desires an image he does not realise is himself. But it is also an image that is neither different nor an actual other while he remains autonomous and can see nothing else. In fact, he does not ever see Echo; even though he hears her. She draws his attention, but he resists as Echo is a model of alterity.

Echo disturbs the order and the self-sameness of Narcissus. She attracts his attention whether he wants it or not through her voice with its tone, rhythm and his words accentuated through their repetition. Her voice transgresses his boundaries and psychological walls, challenging and persisting. She represents the desire for difference, not the self-same, while her presence calls into question Narcissus's isolation.

As Cixous noted, 'She went beyond borders ... She paid: she had the possibility of paying the price of love' (Sellers, 1994, p. 90). Echo represents cyclical repetitiveness, listening and operating from her deepest self throughout the myth. Echo '"exemplifies the female trajectory that acquires voice and presence by marking her space and building her story" and expresses herself using linguistic resources in their totality' (Quinlin, 2021, p. 159).

In Cixous's description, 'I discovered that the face was mortal, and that I would have to snatch it back at every moment from Nothingness ... Because of my fear I reinforced love, I armed love, with soul and words' (Sellers, 1994, p. 83). The story of Echo is related to frustrated passions, masochism and restriction to repetition, supposedly without creative possibilities, pointing to what seems to be a one-sided comprehension of her as a mere follower, obsequious, docile (Berry, 2014). But she is none of these.

Many people are caught like Echo. Their echo doesn't end as they contain an ever-gnawing void displayed in a body looking as hungry as their heart is. Bodies shrink to ever-smaller sizes as these sad females lose their appetites, distracted by emotions, longing and grief. They are distraught and cut off from the love of self and other. Lonely, their survival is spare rather than filled with the luxuries of life. These affect attitudes towards the ageing process, the influence of social media as a photoshopped image and the striving after a too thin body. Did Echo die from being rejected or longing for a person unable to receive or give, one who was caught in a solely subjective existence?

Narcissus, according to British psychoanalyst Adam Philips, is 'committed to the absence of otherness' (2001, p. 218). His closed-off being is connected to obliterating difference. These are like psychic retreats, as labelled by another British psychoanalyst John Steiner (1993), functioning to contain and protect him from the destructive impulses arising when feeling out of control and that one has no impact. Any anxiety or difficulty is quelled by closing off to protect against the expected psychic pain. The retreat allows the narcissist to avoid reality, getting close; they shut out the world and growth stagnates. This state is maintained by being alone. However, development is paralysed, immobilised, yet anxiety and fear are dissipated in the fantasy of omnipotence. The narcissist denies dependency needs and eliminates recognition of anything outside themself. The shock of the different is avoided and the doors locked to the outside world.

Hélène Cixous said, 'And as artist of love, her knowing-pleasure overflows her individual activities (psychical cultural, historical) in the direction of the other: she has an unconquerable propensity to unite, join, connect together desires, language, unconsciouses' (Sellers, 1994, p. 60). Echo is open and invites the other's response. Narcissus is enclosed, not seeking self-knowledge, refusing what Echo has to offer and what other parts within himself have to offer as well. 'Love requires a pattern of exchange and mutuality, of mutual attraction evolving over time' (Nussbaum, 1992, p. 344). Yet, the narcissist stands aloof, displaying an omnipotent position, deflecting against anything or anyone including themself. This creates obstacles described as 'destructive forces interfering with the capacity for love and creativity ... while the complexity of the internal organization is cruel and tyrannical' (Steiner, 1993, pp. 40, 43).

The resultant internal division becomes exclusion severing thought from emotion. The separation and genderising of these human capacities can be another exclusion, creating artificial boundaries, compromising the personality with superficial constructions and limitations.

The background story

Echo was cursed and doomed to repeat the words of others. This occurred after the Greek god Zeus enlisted her to distract his wife, Hera, while he engaged in numerous sexual dalliances. Upon this discovery, Hera cursed Echo and, in this action, represents an angry and vindictive feminine element turned against another feminine figure. She does not challenge or approach the masculine, her spouse who transgresses and ravages whomever he wants. There are no boundaries for him, and Hera does not confront his assaults. Rather, Hera's fury was unleashed on Echo, not Zeus. Misdirecting her power, Hera's curse to Echo was only to repeat words and sound but not initiate from within herself. Because Echo did not speak as Hera wanted and Zeus forbade her talking, Echo bore the brunt of their deception to each other. Neither Zeus nor Hera took responsibility to voice the issues directly to each other. Echo coped as well as she could by using her voice to express her presence, desire and love. She was not silenced. Interestingly the word *echo* means sound.

The predominant interpretations of the myth have lacked attention to or held only a narrow focus on Echo, reflecting cultural and psychological positions towards the feminine elements within the personality. The myth sadly tells a story reflecting the current cultures of patriarchy consciously and unconsciously still silencing women, the feminine, and the male narcissist left alone. Echo is an opening to what can be rectified if we listen to the inner voices longing to be heard. Otherwise, there is dissociation from our various selves, and we are left in the narrow singularity of Narcissus.

Silencing any part of the self can bring depression, loss, grief, despair and detachment. This is marked with various indicators of psychological and physical distress. Narcissism with its arms folded in on itself works against life connection. After all, Narcissus lost his life refusing to pay attention to anyone but himself. Echo with her arms reaching out through her voice presents the opposite and supports the process of self and other relating. Yet Echo also remained alone, and her body disappeared.

Analytical treatment involves the other, both as inner and outer figures. This is the basis of the transferences and becoming aware of differences to grow beyond where one is stuck. Analysis deals with what has been repressed and lies in retreat and embraces others rather than stagnating in aloneness. Both analyst and client provide echoes to each other and this interaction promotes growth.

Body loss

The loss of Echo's body paradoxically brings up the body as part of how we define, view and express ourselves. When Narcissus shuns Echo's desire and entreaty to be seen and loved, for she loved him on sight, he says, 'Take off your hands! You shall not fold your arms around me. Better death than such a one should caress me'.

The author of the story, Ovid, continued:

> Thus rejected she lies hid
> in the deep woods, hiding her blushing face
> with the green leaves; and ever after lives
> concealed in lonely caverns in the hills.
> But her great love increases with neglect;
> her miserable body wastes away,
> wakeful with sorrows; leanness shrivels up
> her skin, and all her lovely features melt,
> as if dissolved upon the wafting winds –
> nothing remains except her bones and voice –
>
> (1922)

Rather than this being a simple story of the abjected feminine, it is a complex one depicting the ramifications of the rejection of other, difference and ultimately the Self. Narcissus cannot realise his own personality, although he supposedly only sees himself and ignores all others. This represents maltreatment to the feminine and anything or anyone other as well as the denial of his natural physical and psychological self. The story makes the point that without love, one cannot live.

Although her voice lives on, the scars of rejection and repression are expressed as her body wastes away. Echo's testimony of love is also a discourse of resistance. The silencing of woman and the feminine reveal the one-sided male dominance prevalent in the past as well as current traditions. 'The suffering is the content of this story that tells a human truth' (Nussbaum, 1992, p. 253).

Critics have focused on Narcissus as the chosen subject. Echo has passion as reflected in the tones and moods she expresses, but the narcissistic way has dominated. This 'ends up making the idea and coexistence with difference and otherness unfeasible' (Quinlin, 2021, p. 164). It is a defensive denial of the object's autonomy combined with the isolative autonomy in narcissistic individuals. There is a perception of the other's independence, but narcissists deny this due to feelings of insecurity and have difficulty dealing with complex perceptions of the other. The fear of being abandoned or rejected indicates their fragility, inferiority and vulnerability. Thus, 'the relationship with the other is hampered by persecutory feelings regarding the invalidation and autonomy of the self' (p. 164). Echo defies the narcissistic rejection while simultaneously portraying the suffering of the soul. Her various responses for connection convey psychological truths for union and personality enhancement.

Echo records desire and her reality. 'Echo desiring Narcissus represents the Other in the development of relationships, in the process of identity formation and in the development of sense of self' (Cavalcanti, 2003). Love is a giver and a taker in the way it alters the self and points out incompleteness. It can be both an ecstatic and disorienting admission that personhood is unfinished and requires development beyond the status quo. By entering the world of the other, we enlarge our own world. In this dynamic exchange of energy, we become more ourselves.

'[Narcissus's] rejection of this transformation is associated with the narcissistic refusal to perceive the autonomy of the Other' (Quinlin, 2021, p. 164). For the narcissistic personality, the existence of their individuality is managed through denying the other. Their strength and value are asserted through invalidating the other's strength and value. This silencing of the other is a means of control and falsely verifies that one's needs can be met by oneself. The narcissistic dynamic holds the other in servitude, submissive, passive, responsive primarily to the narcissistic one who demands mirroring. 'Echo represents a reminder of Narcissus' vulnerability and fragile identity, which demonstrates the impossibility of his independence from Echo, since he needs to feel loved in order to feel worthy, and this leads to an intolerance to be criticized' (p. 165). The other's autonomy threatens the narcissistic fragility, vulnerability and abhorrence of separation.

Narcissus deceives himself. How can he know love when he does not allow in other voices, halting plurality? The heart becomes known by opening to the many responses inherent in the emotions and desires of longing, pain and joy. Instead, 'it is the demand that we not rest content … we create our lives with one another with as much responsiveness, delicacy and imagination … dismantling our anger, fostering our gentleness' (Nussbaum, 1992, p. 216). This means an ongoing exchange of reflections and emotions, making room for challenging insights while in the process of the exchange we become more accurate readers of our own selves and reciprocally responsive to the needs of others.

Case example: Jaycee

The child learns through the process of echoing the identification with caregivers who provide the scenario for love. Repetition is at the heart of the psyche for its growth and development. Similarly, a child learns their identification comes from uniting with the other and making themself identical with the other. This occurs in a mystical metamorphosis, encouraging alteration and the transformation of the individual personality. Likewise, in the myth Echo nourishes herself on the words of the other (Kristeva, 1987, p. 36). The verbal and nonverbal mingle together as they are given expression.

However, Jaycee experienced early life without the safety of identification but with the unconscious demand to please, following whatever would make her parents happy. She was to be a salve for them and be the best performer. Jaycee's mother paraded her in front of people to show what a good mother she was. In analysis Jaycee described this mother as a narcissist, and all attention was directed at her. The narcissistic parent's demands inhibit a child's independence and sense of agency and security. The child learns the parent's needs take priority, and so the child must constantly mirror that parent. Jaycee was told she was loved, but the recognition allowing her to experience herself as separate did not occur. It became obvious she was there for her mother's edification and recognition as a good mother, to be verified and praised by others.

Looking back in analysis, Jaycee realised she felt used, like a trophy and not real. She experienced negative body attention even when young from a mother who critiqued her, and this was repeated by other children as she developed physically early. Comments were always made about her figure. She began to retreat into her mind to escape because the attention felt aversive. An excellent and quick student, Jaycee realised early, 'The subjective experience of self becomes disembodied and identified only with the mind' (Connolly, 2013, p. 637). Gradually, especially after the birth of her own children when she could not lose weight, she went numb physically and psychologically. Again, the body was ignored.

Jaycee held a responsible position at work while her partner hardly worked, did little to contribute and spent money without care. Rather than see her and notice her emotional needs for love, he plied her with food while she provided money, status and security for him. Now she remembered she sought to escape any attention and was numb to her partner's passive aggressive actions. Jaycee quietly said nothing and negated taking care of herself, accepted however she was treated and just went along, like she learned to do early on with her mother.

One day in analysis she said she was like Echo and felt almost completely disappeared, devolved into dust from the lack of loving attention from anyone. She became so non-existent and felt like such a non-entity that she was almost completely not present. In fact, she had to become conscious of how destructive she was to her body. Her neglect of herself was dangerous, especially the older she got. In the process, the deadness of her marriage and in herself increased. Her partner hardly saw her, participated little; they shared less and less as she took over more and more financially, seeking to please while her body and psyche were lost. Feeling numb she did not realise she was like a zombie to herself.

At the time, she did not know how disastrous this was to her soul. She learned to perform but not count for much, in part due to a narcissistic mother who never saw or acknowledged her separateness. The process of retreat from her body began young but now was so pronounced she had to work to remain even slightly present each day. Her professional voice was strong; her personal value and the mind-body connection was almost extant. The effect of shutting off from herself had so solidified, she did not comprehend the extent of the damage. All this became apparent not only as she entered analysis but also as she entertained the thought of another kind of relationship than the dead marriage. Now she began to realise how she backed off from intimacy and expected little from others. She was comfortable not being noticed except for what she could do and how she used her intellect. This split of mind from body had detrimental effects on her health. The body and mind discrepancy were striking yet seemed insurmountable. Jaycee's body was ignored, turned away from. The discomfort around being seen made her feel used, on display, not real. Outwardly, the achievements mounted. Inwardly she hardly existed.

Since beginning analytical work, she became increasingly aware, and her tendency to blank out, become numb and negate her body became more evident, while any change was met with resistance as that was the old pattern. The issue was not just body image but the habit of numbness to avoid feeling or being seen. As she became more cognisant of herself, the old patterns became harder to maintain, although they were quite entrenched. Jaycee was divorced by now and considering relationships with others, but she began to realise her apprehension about intimacy was at the basis of her complex.

This modern-day Echo has lost her body, perhaps in a different way than in the myth, but it is lost and needs to be reclaimed. To reconnect is a process of remembering her physical sensations, being aware of herself and including her body. Jaycee began to recognise the narcissism had been repeated in her partner, differently manifested than in her mother but equally numbing to herself. Through analysis she began to gain some healthy self-reflection, and this meant not being lost in the needs of others, trying to save them while they did not look at or see her. She began to note and sever herself from places where there was no good attention to herself.

The self when not ignited early in life brings with it a silent depression. One becomes isolated and metaphorically learns to remain hidden. Self-denial and self-denigration become the modes of being. The self hesitates, disappears and often does not know how to return. Dreamwork and analytical exploration bring a person like Jaycee out of the tangles of narcissism to conscious awareness of body, self and other.

Offence to Eros

Both Narcissus and Echo offended the god Eros, as did Jaycee. Psychologically, both the relationship with herself and the other suffered disastrous consequences. To be a person is to possess otherness, divisions and differences, promoting links in the polarities and opportunities for unity. The psyche seeks balance through internal union and can be likened to a dance between opposites be they feminine and masculine, hot and cold, dark and light, igniting passion and life energy. Dynamically this means bringing new twists to former limiting thoughts and ideas.

The concept of the anima and animus, feminine and masculine, as internalised elements bring up leaving in 'suspension' the 'question of "masculine" and "feminine" ... even, and the word is used advisedly, in some confusion' (Samuels, 1989, p. 94). Especially in our current era of flux and change, it cheapens and is simplifying to prescribe a fixed set of properties to the masculine or feminine. Every archetype implies another, commented James Hillman as he recounted the tandems and coupling of these elements as inner and outer intertwining and interfusing as one archetype implies another in its many dimensions and pairings (1985, p. 169).

The animus and anima include use of intellect, mind, thought, feelings, emotions and various creative connections. Images are not of women and men per se but are 'a metaphor for the richness, potential and mystery of the other' (Samuels, 1993,

p. 143). Without contact between them energy can turn destructive. If this happens, they display a cruel face, cutting at participation in life. There is loneliness and hunger from the dormant and unused aptitudes and melancholic passivity in avoidance of spirit and soul. This person eventually must go through some sacrifice to access the range of masculine and feminine figures, their interconnections and variations and replenish their absence of contact and connection.

In classical Jungian psychology the *anima* and *animus* are terms associated with feminine and masculine, forming a syzygy of dualistic Jungian archetypes. Jung described 'the masculine principle as logos or the tendency to logic and verbal formulations and the feminine principle as eros or the tendency to emotional connections and relatedness' (Jung, 1959, para. 14). These terms, as defined or delineated and understood in Jung's time of the early to the late 20th century, have altered and now take on new meanings, images, ideas and identities with the gender reconfigurations of our current era. The danger is if we fall into concretism (Jung, 1990, p. 151) rather than integration and imagination, constantly morphing and creating new images to be lived.

More complete inclusion of these figures takes us into the unconscious and its energy becomes released into conscious life. They can be fluid, permeable, flexible and their differences not just opposing but also subject to cultural changes loaded with varying and not incompatible aspects (Jung, 1990, p. 197). Recovery of their lost aspects is healing, bringing enthusiasm, vitality and new visions.

Originating in the concepts of the anima and animus archetypes are the counterparts of gender identity. These images have been traditionally considered to be feminine for men and masculine for women. If we can bring these qualities into flexible form and interweave them to fit the individual, we find the unconscious psyche is a combination of both in a vibrant conscious identity. The healthy balance of these functions in the psyche stimulates growth and enhances consciousness. Each person is comprised not only of outward physical form but also of intangible, inward awareness. Repression rather than union causes negativity, depression, anxiety, emotional numbness, an inability to act and general disconnection to the Self. Neither term is hierarchical but equates to subjective forms of integration. The general point is how these aspects are loosened and raised out of unconsciousness to conscious awareness.

Anima and animus, when seen as open concepts, can challenge and open us to new ways of internal and external communication. Addressed with flexibility they put the mind in tune with inner values and open the way into profound depths, taking seriously our various feelings, moods, goals and fantasies. Bringing these unconscious contents into consciousness expresses what is lacking, stultified, restrictive. When regarded with the attitude of plurality and creativity, they can encourage a person to get into direct touch with life and authenticity. When not, they inhibit. Both anima and animus can be vampiric and destructive as well as nourishing and encouraging. They are complementary and compensating forms with interactions between them that enhance the creative process and promote the individuation urge to become who one is.

There is an innate restlessness to the psyche seeking and desiring to emerge into the fullness of the real. Consciousness is a road towards the definitive appearing in an individual often other than in a general or predictable way. This is the process of individuation, as Jung commented:

> What is it, in the end, that induces a man to go his own way and to rise out of unconscious identity with the mass as out of a swathing mist? ... It is what is commonly called vocation: an irrational factor that destines a man to emancipate himself from the herd and from its well-worn paths. ... Anyone with a vocation hears the voice of the inner man: he is called.
> (1934/1966, CW 16, paras. 299–300)

These following lines are from a letter Jung wrote to Olga Fröbe-Kapteyn, the founder of the Eranos Conference, in 1945.

> You yourself are a conflict that rages in itself and against itself, in order to melt its incompatible substances, the male and the female, in the fire of suffering, and thus create that fixed and unalterable form which is the goal of life. Everyone goes through this mill, consciously or unconsciously, voluntarily or forcibly. We are crucified between the opposites and delivered up to the torture until the 'reconciling third' takes shape. Do not doubt the rightness of the two sides within you, and let whatever may happen, happen.
> (Adler, 1973, p. 375)

There are various definitions of masculine and feminine, animus and anima, and ways they can be interpreted and evolve. They partially derive yet expand from the former and outdated assumptions about gender, binary positions and rigid heteronormative frameworks. Integrating the range of masculine and feminine aspects of oneself is central to the pursuit of individuation, while tackling what this means is not an easy task. The symbolic properties of feminine and masculine are a combination of the personal, social, collective and spiritual. Society shapes gender with a determining influence upon its meaning and enactment. Yet, our current era calls for re-balancing and re-examining individual and collective psychic health. It is a transformational journey to manifest the heart within relationships but in one's own way. New paradigms are needed and emerge from continually examining and integrating these personality parts.

Emma Jung stated the following:

> To discriminate between oneself and the animus, and sharply to limit its sphere of power, is extraordinarily important; only by doing so is it possible to free oneself from the fateful consequences of identifying with the animus and being possessed by it. Hand in hand with the discrimination goes the growth of consciousness and the realization of the true Self... when women succeed in maintaining themselves against the animus, instead of allowing themselves to be

devoured by it, then it ceases to be only a danger and becomes a creative power. We women need this power, for, strange as it seems, only when this masculine entity becomes an integrated part of the soul and carries on its proper function there is it possible for a woman to be truly a woman in the higher sense, and, at the same time, also being herself, to fulfill her individual human destiny.

(1998, p. 13)

Jung opined, 'Without the anima and animus there would be no object, no other human being, because you perceive differences through the likeness to the differences in yourself' (Jung, 1990, p. 1357). The unconscious psyche is a counterpart of conscious identity. The healthy balance of different functions in the psyche helps the individual to stimulate growth for the development of consciousness and life fulfilment and satisfaction. The definitions of anima and animus are not literally describing certain characteristics, but their images serve as symbols and abstractions of active and reflective principals. In dreams, the anima and animus archetype manifests also in figures of strangers inviting us to the unknown. Each image is an expression of the psyche by way of a 'shift of noticing – from what is seen and heard to the way in which it inheres' (Hillman, 1979, p. 134).

James Hillman said 'the anima can operate in the personal and archetypal unconscious of both sexes. Perhaps the animus is something completely different and co-existent with the anima' (Hillman, 1985, pp. 89–91). Eros is joined to the anima. The anima is not limited to the male psyche but is a structure of consciousness in relationship to the unconscious within all the sexes. The anima then inhabits her role as relatedness, as the bond to the unknown psyche, not only to other people. Women do not solely carry the anima or soul image for men. They have their own animas to cherish. Similarly, both sexes have equal access to animus or spirit. Anima and animus ideally enact an inner marriage, marking a fertile aspect of psychic development. They are the psychic lens by which the other is known. The opportunity presented to each person is to move beyond the classical traditions to modern interpretations more malleable and flexible with much room to grow beyond the old borders and definitions.

Being real includes both the light and dark with their shadows reflecting the multiple subjectivities of the world. Without these elements in flow, life narrows to establish safety but eliminate otherness when anything outside oneself feels threatening. 'Relationship to the self is at once relationship to our fellow man, and no one can be related to the latter until he is related to himself' (Jung, 1946/1966, CW 16, para. 445).

References

Adler, G. (Ed.). (1973). *C. G. Jung letters: 1906–1950* (Vol. 1). Routledge.
Benjamin, J. (1988). *The bonds of love*. Pantheon Books.
Berry, P. (2014). *Echo's subtle body*. Spring Publications.
Bollas, C. (1992). *Being a character: Psychoanalysis and self-experience*. Routledge.

Cavalcanti, R. (2003). *The myth of Narcissus: The hero of consciousness*. Rosari.
Connolly, A. (2013). Out of the body: Embodiment and its vicissitudes. *Journal of Analytical Psychology, 58*(5), 636–656.
Doolittle, H. (1981). *HERmione*. New Directions Publishing.
Glissant, E. (2023). *A new region of the world: Aesthetics I* (Martin Munro, Trans.). Liverpool University Press.
Hillman, J. (1979). Image-sense. In *Spring* (pp. 130–143). Spring Publications.
Hillman, J. (1985). *Anima: An anatomy of a personified notion*. Spring Publications.
Jung, C. G. (1934/1954). *The collected works of C. G. Jung: Vol. 17. The development of personality*. Princeton University Press.
Jung, C. G. (1934/1969). On the nature of the psyche. In *The structure and dynamics of the psyche* (Vol. 8). Princeton University Press.
Jung, C. G. (1946/1966). The psychology of the transference. In *The practice of psychotherapy* (Vol. 16). Princeton University Press.
Jung, C. G. (1959). *The collected works of C.G. Jung: Vol. 9i*. Princeton University Press.
Jung, C. G. (1967). *The collected works of C. G. Jung: Vol. 5. Symbols of transformation*. Princeton University Press.
Jung, C. G. (1990). *Visions: Notes of the seminar given in 1930–1934* (C. Douglas, Ed.). Princeton University Press.
Jung, E. (1998). *Animus and anima*. Spring Publications.
Kristeva, J. (1987). *Tales of love*. Columbia University Press.
Munro, M. (2024). *A new region of the world: Aesthetics 1 by Edouard Glissant*. Liverpool University Press.
Nussbaum, M. (1992). *Love's knowledge: Essays on philosophy and literature*. Oxford University Press.
Ovid. (1922). *Metamorphoses* (B. More, Trans.). The Cornhill Publishing Company. http://data.perseus.org/citations/urn:cts:latinLit:phi0959.phi006.perseus-eng1:3.337-3.434
Phillips, A. (2001). *Promises, promises: Essays on literature and psychoanalysis*. Faber & Faber.
Quinlin, C. (2021). Echo's calling: Listening to silenced voices. *Junguiana, 39*(2), 157–170.
Samuels, A. (1989). *The plural psyche: Personality, morality, and the father*. Routledge.
Samuels, A. (1993). *The political psyche*. Routledge.
Sellers, S. (Ed.). (1994). *The Hélène Cixous reader*. Routledge.
Steiner, J. (1993). *Psychic retreats: Pathological organizations in psychotic, neurotic and borderline patients*. Routledge.
West, M. (2020). Self, other and individuation: Resolving narcissism through the lunar and solar paths of the Rosarium. *Journal of Analytical Psychology, 65*(1), 171–197.

Chapter 7

Psychoanalysis and André Green's life and death narcissism

What exactly is the attraction to narcissism? And what are the issues? Throughout the ages and for as many years as psychoanalysis and psychological exploration has been prevalent, this aspect of the personality has engaged us in trying to pin it down. It is seductive, as is the narcissist. Narcissism is like a 'black [hole] into which turbulence had seeped, and the empty concepts flooded with riotous meaning' (Bion, 1977, p. 229). No doubt being drawn in reflects our needs to comprehend similar qualities that appear in ourselves.

Narcissism is rooted in the history of psychoanalysis and Sigmund Freud and coincides with the beginning of the 20th century. Like any exploration of the psyche, its beginnings are important as well as the developments that have sprouted from those initial seeds. We are made from our history. When it is fraught, disappointing and diminishing, these replicate the very issues the narcissist must deal with yet attempts to deny.

Our world has radically changed since the beginning of the 20th century and, as a result, disorders of the psyche and disturbances in the soul take different forms. We are in another millennium with particular influences. Yet, the historical norms of the analytic culture remain with us even as other values and prejudices are embedded in our current era. The approach here aims to broaden awareness about the assumptions we make about narcissism. These assumptions are so subtle they are often hidden from ourselves. They impact the clinical and relational processes as we move towards more consciousness, leading to expanded self-reflection. These are natural evolutions, not aberrations. They are reflections found in the mirrors particular to each era. In addition, Freudian and Jungian thought (discussed in Chapter 8), although taking divergent paths, do overlap in their pursuit of trying to understand narcissism, both past and present, personally and collectively.

This rendition of how to understand narcissism is slanted toward the Jungian perspective and the mythology and symbolism revealed in the story of Narcissus and Echo by the ancient Greek writer Ovid in 30 BCE. The Freudian lineage emphasises the pathological whereas the Jungian emphasises the symbolic meanings. The selection of a few Freudian psychoanalysts has been based on my own proclivity and experiences of narcissism in my work as a Jungian analyst. I am drawn to Herbert Rosenfeld and his concept of the destructive inner gang as well as to

Helene Deutsch on the 'as-if' personality. Tangentially mentioned are the famous explorers in this field – Otto Kernberg, Heinz Kohut, and Donald Winnicott on the false self. I hope this brief history will connect some dots for readers in the understanding of this complex personality type, honouring the psychological suffering of narcissism and the narcissist rather than dismissing them as incorrigible.

The caveat at the beginning of this chapter focused on Freudian and psychoanalytic thought is to recognise it is a cursory rendition. Unlike the dense topic of narcissism this is only an overview. This is also because the literature on narcissism, like narcissism itself, can be both enlightening and extremely overwhelming. The psychological complexity of narcissism has brought numerous viewpoints to the forefront, and it is impossible to summarise them all. However, the mere fact of the convoluted and ever murkier waters draws us to the mirror of the narcissistic psychological composition to comprehend it from many angles.

Following my overview, I will explore in more depth the death aspect of narcissism as André Green described. It reveals the inner world often not acknowledged in the narcissist. Few imagine the internal distress so cleverly covered, the dynamic of death silently condemning one to not fully exist. Green describes the disregard of life and the narcissism leading to death-in-life as follows: 'The early emotional lacks form psychic holes, not the loss of something once had, but the absence of love objects that never existed … setting up internal world attacks, time frozen, investment in self dismantled and void occupying the mind' (1986, p. 153).

Basic psychoanalytic concept of narcissism

The psychoanalytic approach to narcissism and its suffering presents it as a solipsistic response that erases relationships to any others. This core reaction rides on experiences of not being heard, seen, felt or responded to correctly from early in life. Such experiences leave psychological lack with empty emotional spaces. The resonance between self and other is gone and a void of confusion remains. The residual effects make the narcissist feel powerless, vulnerable, alone and misunderstood. All this is blanketed with a grandiose exterior, denying any problems and garnering attention but refusing intimate connection.

The concept of narcissism was initially defined in the late 1800s, prior to Freud, by theorists Paul Nacke, Albert Ellis and Karl Abraham. This brief outline charts the early influences on the present day. We are made of and carry within us this history, yet, as said previously, our world has changed over the last century. The process of change will continue to escalate as we live at ever faster speeds and psychological complexity tightens. The symptoms and behavioural manifestations of the narcissistic personality reveal the cultural influences of the era in which we live and those generations from which we derive.

The narcissistic response and way of living traces to early childhood where patterns are laid and ways of coping develop. The unmet needs, frustrations and ways the growing child is seen, or not, leave nuanced and blatant effects. The various analytical approaches are trying to establish what went wrong, affecting the person and their relationships while simultaneously influencing and being influenced by the cultural overlay.

Freud's view

Freud presented two kinds of narcissism. What he called the *primary narcissism* experienced in the parent/child dyad is crucial to the developing infant. It provides a basis to distinguish between self and other, the symbolic and the real. I have selected a few sentences from Freud's original paper 'On Narcissism' to explain some of the ideas originally presented there. As Freud himself said in delineating the history of this concept,

> The term narcissism is derived from clinical description and was chosen by Paul Näcke in 1899 to denote the attitude of a person who treats his own body in the same way in which the body of a sexual object is ordinarily treated – who looks at it, that is to say, strokes it and fondles it till he obtains complete satisfaction through these activities.
>
> (Freud, 1914, p. 73)

Freud described narcissism as a type of attachment to the self rather than the other. He theorised primary narcissism was a stage in infantile development prior to the capacity to relate to others. This creates a particular kind of internal object relationship in which 'the separate existence and particular qualities of the internal object are denied, and an internal narcissistic relationship is created through projective identification' (Britton, 2004, p. 481). This means the child feels unseen and develops an attitude of looking out to verify their impact on others. Freud (1905, SE 9, 218) described the ego-libido as 'narcissistic libido and a necessary stage leading from autoeroticism to object-love. Infatuation with one's own person is a necessary phase of evolution' (Engels, 2013, p. 86). But this is not sufficient for relational development.

The alignment of self-esteem and narcissism originated as a defence against being at the mercy of early caregivers who misjudged the child's needs for their own and as like theirs. What Freud called 'secondary narcissism is a pathological stuckness in fantasies that ought to be re-framed if the Oedipus complex was negotiated successfully' (Samuels, Shorter & Plaut, 1986, p. 98). In his essay on narcissism Freud wrote, 'We must recognize that self-regard has a specially intimate dependence on narcissistic libido' (Freud, 1914, p. 98). This becomes the defensive self-esteem later known as *secondary narcissism* and manifesting as a developmental stage. It is marked with narcissistic vulnerability extending from inferiority feelings on one side to grandiosity at the other end of the spectrum.

The meandering description of narcissism encompasses many qualities. From psychoanalytic beginnings, the myth of Narcissus, its symbolism and the analytical characteristics it exposed have taken a subordinate role in its theoretical explorations. However, many interpretations, critiques and expansions of Freud's original ideas have proliferated. This fact illustrates the viability of the concept and its widespread occurrence as well as its mysterious hold on us. Freud's emphasis in his famous paper written in 1914 addressed states of being in love and the idealisations necessary to foster love between children and parents and then between adults. Freud significantly went on to comment in this same essay: 'We must begin to love in order not to fall ill, and we are bound to fall ill if, in consequence of frustration, we are unable to love' (Freud, 1914, p. 85). Later he described narcissists as 'seeking themselves as a love-object, and are exhibiting a type of object-choice which must be termed narcissistic' (p. 88).

Later theorists on narcissism

Herbert Rosenfeld, Ronald Britton and John Steiner are some of the theorists from the more recent British psychoanalytic tradition who described various conceptualisations of narcissism. I present them here briefly to engage in a dialogue interweaving their comparative discourse, accentuating the various approaches and generating reflection. They illustrate the destructive, singular, withdrawn and hidden aspects of the suffering of narcissism.

Herbert Rosenfeld (1971) addressed the destructive aspects of narcissism, conceiving it as a manifestation of the death instinct. He addressed internal and external destructiveness becoming split off and creating envy of others. These parts can become addictive and operate like gang warfare within a person. They attack the personality while holding out the promise to protect against despair and emotional pain. The resultant internal and external destructive impulses distort and poison any of the good elements in the self, in objects and any positive relationships between them.

As Rosenfeld wrote in his later work (1987), these states are destructive and create impasses in the analytical and therapeutic work, whereas seeking to make them conscious alters their hold on the personality. As Michael Rustin notes,

> Rosenfeld's work spoke to two different forms of narcissism. On the one hand, 'libidinal narcissism' is the condition of love directed away from others and towards the self. And on the other hand, 'destructive narcissism', in which the self becomes identified with a destructive part of itself dominated by hatred. It maintains itself not only in a state of self-sufficiency or indifference towards objects, but rather in a state of covert hostility or contempt towards them.
>
> (2017, p. 44)

In addition, Rosenfeld conceptualised two narcissistic types. One is called *thin-skinned*, describing people who are fragile, vulnerable, hypersensitive, easily hurt, find it difficult to deal with any trauma or failure. In contrast those called *thick-skinned* are oblivious to profound feelings, inaccessible and characterised by intense envy leading to a devaluation of others as well as a denial of dependency in any situation (Bernardi & Eidlin, 2018, p. 293). Both types have difficulties in interpersonal relations and a profound need for the other, albeit enacted in different ways, to reaffirm their shaky self-esteem.

Rosenfeld focused on narcissism in its destructive aspects with self-idealisation of the omnipotently destructive parts of the self playing a central role. These parts dominate the personality, eating up the good elements. They are

> directed both against any positive libidinal object relationship and any libidinal part of the self which experiences need for the object and desire to depend on it ... they have a very powerful effect in preventing dependent object relations and in keeping external objects permanently devalued, which accounts for the apparent indifference of the narcissistic individual towards external objects and the world.
>
> (Rosenfeld, 1971, p. 173)

Any separateness is prevented by the rigid nature of the internal organisation. The destructive part connects to the envy, threatening to destroy the person who is addicted to an omnipotent self-image. This imprisons the person in the false promises of a painless existence where they do not need others. In other words, a narcissist is locked alone within the misery of destruction with no way out.

John Steiner (1993) similarly described narcissism as associated with a destructive organisation within the personality functioning to deny dependence and at the same time expressing envy. Steiner is known for his concept of psychic retreat (1993) and its application to narcissism. There is withdrawal of energy from others following experiences of emotional lack and unmet needs. He commented on 'a cruel type of tyranny in which objects and the [person] are controlled and bullied in a ruthless way ... with a seductive hold on the person' (p. 12). The retreat occurs when reality becomes unbearable, a not uncommon position for the vulnerable narcissist. One remains out of contact with others, needing safety and propelled by the compensatory avoidance of being disliked or found amiss in any way.

Otto Kernberg's formulations are often juxtaposed with those of Heinz Kohut. Both present the concept that disturbances of the self experience are primary in narcissism (Mollon, 1986, p. 152). The greatest fear of narcissists is to be dependent on anybody else because to be dependent means to expose themselves to the emotions of hate and envy and the accompanied danger of being exploited, mistreated and frustrated (Kernberg, 1975, p. 235). Kernberg contended narcissism gets stronger with age. The tragedy increases as the person cannot deal with those who are real.

Overt grandiose narcissism was described by Kernberg (1975, p. 295) as the principal characteristic of pathological narcissism. He viewed the grandiose self as the main disturbance 'reinforced by early experience, the ideal self compensating for the severe frustration, rage and envy and the ideal object as an ever-loving parent in contrast to the child's experience as a devalued parental object' (pp. 265–266). Narcissism describes a sense of self lacking sufficient inner resources to give meaning to life. Kernberg's focus was on the individual's hostile feelings and envy towards others, marked by ethical disregard, inner emptiness and a sense of brokenness linked to violence and aggression. In Kernberg's view, narcissism is a defensive or deficit-driven psychological structure against the original parental abandonments (1975).

American psychoanalyst 'Heinz Kohut's self psychology provides a far-reaching new perspective on deeper understanding and at the same time prompting a rethinking of many aspects of theory and technique of psychoanalysis' (Mollon, 1986, p. 160). Kohut ascribed narcissism to the lack of empathic mirroring and relating from caregivers by which the child's positive self-image is reflected to them by the parent (Kohut, 1977). Presenting a more positive outlook than Kernberg, 'Kohut contended narcissism can lead to assertion of a firm sense of self-esteem feeling the balance of being in the world and separate from it as well' (Morrison, 1996, p. 444).

Heinz Kohut stressed the transformative potential of narcissism, whereas Kernberg emphasised the negative, destructive and controlling aspects (Schwartz-Salant, 1982, p. 31). For Kohut, empathy transforms narcissism. Empathy is the mode by which a person gathers psychological data about other people, and when they say what they think or feel, that person can imagine their inner experience (Kohut, 1966, p. 261). Through empathy we aim at discerning and recognising complex psychological configurations. A question remains if the narcissistic self is structured to defend the fragile core from attack or to maximise opportunities for self-enhancement or both.

Kohut stressed the lack of empathy especially as well as vulnerability and grandiosity as these verify the vital elements of the self. They are split off and unavailable and combine with a heightened sensitivity for environmental approval (Jacoby, 1990, p. 165). Kohut regarded the rage and envy of the narcissist as not fixed but attributed them to empathic failures and blocked development (Schwartz-Salant, 1982, p. 31). For Kohut, the self is not basically disturbed or distorted, as Kernberg assessed, but is basically sound and able to develop and use the innate talents and skills to express the basic design of the self. Kohut emphasised the immature character of pathological narcissism, and Rosenfeld and Kernberg focused on the aspects of the debilitating aggression (Bernardi & Eidlin, 2018, p. 292).

Narcissism develops from early deficient dynamics, which create future relational wounds. The craving for positive attention from others is to compensate for the nagging and lingering lack of parental warmth. However, there is another situation in which some parents are overly indulgent without limits, putting the child on a pedestal with unrealistic goals or abilities. The child can do no wrong and becomes a performer for the parents, a display object to gratify the parent to the world. For the narcissist, the resulting cycle of self-admiration and depreciation to others is another mechanism for eliminating dependency and verifying lack of trust in others.

Kohut extended British psychoanalyst Donald Winnicott's work in his investigation of narcissism and the false self, viewing narcissists as evolving a defensive armour around their damaged inner selves. Winnicott drew attention to the pervasiveness of the narcissistic processes of grandiosity and idealisation and how these affect one's perception of reality. He illustrated narcissism is not eliminated but rather transformed as it is part of life in both constructive and destructive aspects. In its destructive aspect we cannot ignore Narcissus being trapped by his reflection. He is mesmerised, staring into the mirror of the pool and unable to move. The situation is indeed deadly, as he is trapped in his own image. Narcissism is a painful and singular path.

Winnicott (1965, p. 142) quite famously popularised the term *false self*. Its function is to protect the true self from insult. However, it will inevitably begin to fail in reaction to environmental demands (p. 146). One of the elements Winnicott considered could be lost in childhood was what he called the sense of being a primary element with a sense of doing as a derivative. The false self hides the inner reality, and a feeling of non-existence pervades. Winnicott perceived the capacity for being or the ability to feel genuinely alive as essential to the maintenance of a true self. This true self feels real and is creative, coming from the aliveness of body and mind experiences. Without feeling real, one can hardly be present or entirely there, and the false self takes charge to protect the true self, lying in abeyance.

Noted for arrogance, haughtiness and coldness, narcissists are aggressive in their response to hurt and injury, operating with disdain to appear strong and impervious. 'The narcissistic person is one who loves himself well, but also one who loves himself poorly or not at all' (Grunberger, 1979, p. 3). Narcissistic people often are leaders who desperately need others to applaud and to bask in their admiration. The narcissist must keep out of awareness any information or feelings in any way diminishing their sense of self. Aloof, inaccessible, self-admiring, self-important, over-confident fantasies of omnipotence and omniscience are their defences against being average and engaging with reality. They indicate the inflation and aggression necessary to protect one's self-concept. The oscillations in self-esteem leave little tolerance for failure as the person quickly cycles from the grandiose to despair, unable to manage the fluctuations of daily life due to the emptiness and chronic hunger for admiration and excitement.

'As-if' personality interpreted

I explored this personality type and aligned it with narcissism and Jungian analytical psychology in my previous books (2023, 2024, 2020). Prior to this, British Jungian analyst Hester Solomon (2004) recognised analytical treatment as possible for the 'as-if' personality. She assessed they could accomplish internal development and were not merely superficial or beyond reach.

British psychoanalyst Ronald Britton (1998) discussed the 'as-if' personality, referencing its originator, Freudian psychoanalyst Helene Deutsch (1942). As Deutsch described, there is emotional capacity but in contrast to an apparent absence of inner experience (1942). She contended these people neither escape their minds through external reality nor withdraw to their inner world to avoid fears of the outside in the belief that real consequences will be catastrophic for them.

Britton ascribed

> a turning away from interest in external figures to self-preoccupation: I will call that clinical narcissism. Secondly the word narcissism is used to describe a force or innate tendency within the personality that opposes relationships outside the self. And thirdly it is used to designate a specific group of personality dysfunctional cases called the narcissistic disorders. Narcissism is used in the literature referring to a force in the personality opposed to object relations.
>
> (2004, p. 478)

He contended poor parenting experiences contributed to an ego-destructive superego or harsh ruling principle that led to narcissistic organisation and failures of emotional containment or relational issues. Britton defined these as thin-skinned or hyper-subjective people seeking to incorporate the other, also meaning the therapist or analyst into their subjective world. They try to eliminate any differences between the analyst and their interpretation of them because it is difficult to tolerate the other position of the analyst (Bernardi & Eidlin, 2018, p. 294). Britton emphasised the pervasive sense of unreality in relationship with the world and themselves (1998, p. 59). He also noted these people are terrified of both inner and outer reality, seeking refuge in the state of unreality characterising all relationships while their external perceptions lack significance and inner experience lacks substance (p. 59).

For example, a woman in childhood became lost in fantasy, creating her own world to escape her home life and create a safe place. To this day the world is not trusted; anything could happen. There must be enough money to avoid any catastrophe, and she must make sure to not reveal too much of herself. She has adopted an attitude towards others that all is fine to defend against anyone knowing otherwise. She anticipates adverse information will be used against her, and she will be vulnerable and open to emotional hurt. Astute and quick minded, she seems to know a lot about herself, yet she knows little, especially about herself with others. She always feels shaky and subject to rejection, or she anticipates the accusation of being too much, and then she withdraws.

The avoidance of psychic change indicates the anticipated, irreparably damaged internal objects that they expect to find devastated or horrifying (Britton, 1998, p. 60). In this kind of reservation about life, fear prevents intimacy and commitment and there is a turning away from love objects. Masking what is missing becomes the link between narcissistic self-regard and object hunger. 'Omnipotent fantasies are not so much the inner reality itself as a defense against the acceptance of it' (Britton, 1998, p. 16). This can be translated to apply to the fantasy of superiority as a singular position to protect the vulnerable and fragile narcissist.

The sadistic, abusive aspect of narcissism stems from the belief, often held unconsciously, that the separate subjectivity of the other is a threat to the survival, literally or figuratively, of one's own subjectivity – and the other must therefore be kept under control. The narcissist objectifies themselves and others, leading to the apprehension of being subjugated and they act without trust or appropriate dependency. This person is ruled by the feeling of exploitation and need for subjugation of the suspected exploitation, little realising it is mostly orchestrated by themself. This, of course, affects interpersonal and romantic relationships and the structure of subjectivity itself (Greenberg, 2016, p. 131).

The moment-to-moment sense of being has little relevance other than as a preparation for the next moment. 'Existence becomes either a search or a waiting period for that time not yet here when real life and true love will begin making the present always imperfect in and of itself' (Bromberg, 1983, p. 360). Our 'relentless need to validate the self as the goal of living may fascinate psychoanalysts in our time because the experience of meaninglessness may be the context in which the narcissistic form of personality most typically expresses itself in our time' (p. 363). Accomplishment is transformed into manipulation, exploitation and a vague feeling of fooling people. The self-contained existence where no stimuli from the outside can impinge supports the fallacy that they lack anything that is not contained in themselves. It is, in effect, 'a temporary unmasking of the illusion of self-sufficiency' (p. 365).

In analysing the omnipotent structure of the narcissistic state, Adam Phillips asked, 'What is Narcissus trying to escape from?' (2016, p. 214). He went on to describe the 'tyranny of the other' or the longing the narcissist has regarding the other. He described a conflict in this, the self-absorption and isolation, as tyrannical and without freedom, but running the personality. He called it a 'religion of closure' and the narcissist out of reach, stuck, keeping otherness away. The motive is to escape from reality as it is hard to accept. Yet, the person is immobilised, the life problems can neither be escaped from nor dealt with, so they isolate, stagnate, shut down and off. 'If external reality is unbearable, one needs the illusion of internal refuge' (p. 216).

Case example

A man in his thirties was quite intelligent but drinking and using drugs more and more, chronically obsessed with video games, using music to lull him away from living. His body physically hurt, but he distanced from it and ignored the problems. He wanted but could not maintain presence in relationships because he was bewildered and confused about what to do. Then quite suddenly he died early, like Narcissus. His inability to grasp life could be interpreted as a strange form of privacy, a singularity and hallmark of narcissism. Unable to be reached, telling no one about his confusion and misery, denying the issues or their severity, avoiding self and body, he was increasingly lost. He said, '*I had this dream once (this week) that everything I've been going through is stuck in a moment I can't get out of.*' How painful and prophetic this dream!

This man as a child turned away from reciprocal interaction with others to protect his growing implicit self from chronic disappointment, from experiencing powerlessness instead of agency, from feeling the absence of being met adequately by anyone in his world. The parental relationship was a mismatch with him and his intellect and the need to pretend took over. 'The infant feels that normal emotional needs are unwanted by the parent and therefore something to be ashamed of, an experience which leaves a deep narcissistic wound' (Knox, 2003, p. 218). The child becomes aware of shame and is rejected for their normal dependency needs when the parent cannot understand, give or is abusive. Turning away from the potentially frustrating interaction with significant others and opting for self-absorption in the accumulation of hampered development, aspects of the self become frail and self-regulation is dysfunctional. Jung commented,

> The careful consideration of psychic factors is of importance for the individual's balance as well as society's otherwise the destructive tendencies easily gain the upper hand as the atom bomb is an unparalleled means of mass destruction so the misguided development of the soul leads to psychic mass destruction.
> (1954/1969, CW 8, para. 428)

Good is turned to bad and destructive themes pre-empt any others. The response pattern of feeling of no value, ignored, even subject to elimination is unbearable. All this is revealed in the man's dream. His life became a sad story, revealed in his early death as potential unable to be realised or separated from its deep narcissistic wounds, leaving the trail of despair.

André Green – death and life narcissism

The concept and experience of the emotionally dead and absent parent was brought to the forefront by French psychoanalyst André Green (Kohon, 1999). He described what happens when a child experiences detachment through the absence of parental love and attention. 'The psychic abandonment affects access to the self' (Green, 1986, p. 153). Green emphasised this parental absence or emotional deadness is unconsciously transferred onto children. Lack, absence and depression have detrimental effects, creating an impasse and eventually leading the child to despair that can be masked with narcissism and grandiosity. The narcissist is left with many longings blocked by an impotence for living.

At the core of the dead parental complex is the sudden psychic loss of the caregiver, causing 'massive decathexis' leaving traces in the unconscious in the form of gaps, lacunae, which André Green termed 'psychical holes' (2001, p. 189). To mitigate this loss, the child becomes the keeper of the parent's tomb, or in a sense incorporates the parent cannibalistically to preserve and rescue them to stay alive. The absence is postponed, and a makeshift structure precariously protects the psyche from falling into emptiness. However, it means internalised unease and distance from the child's own supportive, life-giving feelings. They are preoccupied with death and absence, yet watchful to retain something of the parent with little energy left for themselves. Paradoxically Green noted, 'Absence is an intermediary

Psychoanalysis and André Green's life and death narcissism 107

situation between presence (as far as intrusion) and loss (as far as annihilation)' (1986, p. 50). He then went on to explain in more detail, 'In this context, absence does not mean loss, but potential presence' (p. 293).

Throughout his *Collected Works*, Jung repeatedly not only mentioned but also stressed that a parent's unlived life has the greatest psychological effect on their child. The parent, sad, preoccupied, self-absorbed, can leave the child in an unconscious identification with their emotional deadness, leaving in its wake lack, frustration and self-destruction. This means there is not a good match between the parents' and the child's temperaments. The parents discussed here do not see the separate identity of the child and are often narcissistically self-absorbed, depressed, preoccupied or otherwise emotionally unreliable and unavailable. The impression passed to the child was to need nothing and expect nothing, as they were to give to the parent. Their derailed identity and disturbed time sense combined with a shutdown of the attachment system are felt by the child and interpreted as the definition of love and relationship. When this is the case, a relationship feels neither safe nor fulfilling because it risks activating the loving desires the child learned would not be met.

Clinical example – Sharyne and the demon lover

Sharyne illustrates André Green's framework for understanding this melancholic attachment to the internalised absence and how it forms the reaction called *death narcissism*. The resulting destruction of the self is sometimes interpreted as an expression of the death instinct unconsciously enacted from the lack of sufficient love. Sharyne is an example of a person drawn helplessly into the clutches of the demon lover, describing a form of death narcissism. André Green refers to this as the dead mother concept although it is applicable to any caregiver. This creates a psychological need to understand the roots of the depression within narcissism and unties the destructive bonds so one can get into life.

Sharyne found herself repeating yet unable to combat or realise fully the deceptive internal state of emptiness. She could feel the dread creeping over her when she began something or started a relationship, apprehending it would all unravel. She felt she was in danger and a familiar coldness would come over her, terrifying in its clarity and finality. Was it the fear of her own destructiveness or the parental ties? In a state of darkness, she was left severely fatigued, without money, place or any security because she found herself repeatedly embroiled with partners whose energy was like the demon lover. In this enclosed space, she was entangled in the grip of death narcissism, drawn in and unable to move as the old energic drain and despair took over. Full of agony, anguish and depression, she was sucked in, helpless with no exit. Such death dealing was taken for granted, with no awareness of its serious intent to take her out of life.

The demon lover is a sadistic attachment. It kept Sharyne alone but shielded from accessing a separate identity. She suffered the absence of self-connection. She found herself encased in a bubble, unconscious of the damage, dead within, suffering the lack of grounding in her body and often feeling numb. The demon lover is an abandoning figure, bringing with it an attachment to various forms of psychological suicide, or what André Green referred to as death narcissism. Unable to connect with herself when attached to the demon lover, she could only merge in a slow insidious succumbing to the seduction and betrayal. The dance with death occurred so seamlessly because it was learned so early.

The demon lover, usually in disguise, is a figure of psychological guile. This figure does not always appear as ugly and fearsome, nor armed with knives and guns. Often, they are seductive, eloquent, offering everything we think we need and want. They seem accommodating, even marvellous. Abruptly Sharyne says one day in therapy that the fairytale of Bluebeard is hers. In the tale, Bluebeard lures in the young, innocent maiden, unprotected by her mother or sisters, like he has done with so many women before. There is no father figure mentioned in the tale. She marries Bluebeard.

At first, she does not realise succumbing to him means she will lose her soul and life. He leaves on a trip and gives her keys to the rooms of the house but warns her to not unlock the room at the end of the hall. Immediately curiosity and unease grip her, and she disobeys him, unlocks the door to the room and sees the blood and dead women piled up. She now realises he intends to kill her. He has killed each woman he previously married and put the dead bodies in this room. When she comprehends what is happening, she saves herself and he is killed by her brothers. No one else in the tale knew he was a killer, yet she finds the strength to recognise the situation and escape as so many before did not.

This tale is pertinent to our era when many are abused, destroyed by oppressive beliefs, lack of self, undeveloped, without chances to save or be saved. They remain emotionally avoidant, defensive, depressed, overtaken with self-doubt and with any aggressiveness stymied. The process of understanding the effects of the demon lover and extricating from this lover, as in the fairytale, parallels Jungian analytical treatment in the journey for recovery of oneself. It is a precarious journey *but is part of the process for release from death narcissism.* However, this has not yet occurred for Sharyne.

Sharyne is still caught. She had a dream years before, and it returns to her in the analysis. She wonders if and how it still applies. *There are two men, one old and one young, who she is carrying in a coffin. The deal is if they played dead, they could get away from the father. She accomplishes this, gets to the place, and there are ten other men who also escaped from him. She gets $200 for doing this and all are now free.* But are they, and what does the dream and its repetition in the present day mean?

Dreaming is central to life, revealing the struggles to be set free. Dreams provide guidance and direction and help us cope and establish an embodied existence. This dream is enlightening for Sharyne. Although upsetting, it helps put some pieces together and she begins the process of finding solidity within. In Sharyne's associations, she recalls the father in the dream who plays a cat-and-mouse game with her.

She always knew if she played dead in life, she could escape any entanglements with her father. It was an intricate dance, and the dream, although confirmatory, clarifies the conundrum in which she was immersed. She feels the only way to get out of these entanglements is to hide herself, remain on the surface, enact no intimacy and avoid entrapment by him.

She has become bewildered by the emotionally blank father, a man internally absent, no one home, and she is unable to read the cues of love. By trying to remain unseen, she avoided the expected condemnation from him, the absent, dead inside father, a man with the blank hole André Green described as the dead parent. However, this father was passed into her as a child. Like Narcissus in Ovid's poem, she had lived dead, unconscious and alone. Years later Sharyne finally realises the price she had paid was to go dead, and now she does not know another way to be. No wonder relationships feel like work and always involve harsh people and some form of abuse. The game of avoidance became an albatross of deadness enacted in Sharyne's inability to take hold and participate in life.

The persecutor, like Bluebeard and her father, is active inside her psyche, needing to be attended to but never satiated. Sharyne is confused and defended against what she wants and cannot complete what she aims for. She experiences disparity in yearning for the good she cannot attain, left empty by frustration, and she is continually exhausted.

She wonders why her dreams compulsively drew her to the childhood home. Sharyne recalls it was a place of early comfort, but then her father turned strange, and she was disquieted around him as she grew older. She called her mother an empty shell, yet she clung to her. Although she felt close when young, now she is confused. Mother became distant, jealous, and Sharyne did not understand. All this happened between the ages of 10 and 14. Sharyne was under pressure to comply with the parental need to act as

> ... a repository for the parent's intolerable emotions and states of mind and the child enacts this role. Children are vulnerable to this kind of pressure because they need to be loved by the parents even if the price is the development of a distorted sense of self as a result of the parental projections.
> (Knox, 2003, p. 221)

As a young teen Sharyne became active sexually, but each sexual encounter left her with a hollow feeling inside, a black hole she never fully understood.

She dreams, *The husband of my friend, an absolute narcissist and self-centred, only thinking of himself, was buying a house for him and me. We must have been together, but the house would be in his name, not mine. As I awoke, I thought he was just like my father, unable to consider anyone else, unable to give and just wore fancy clothes but did not share or care about anyone else.* The dream is like her real life in that she does not declare her ownership or, in fact, say anything to counter the situation.

The lack of her entitlement and her subsequent deadness and how she just went along is portrayed in the dream and reveals Sharyne's vulnerability and silent obedience. Bewildered and bright, Sharyne could not focus on school even though she was intelligent. In her late teens she became inexplicably tired and developed Epstein-Barr autoimmune disease. She recalls being confused about growing up but had no one to ask. Siblings were no help as they all were in the same bind of fearfulness and not knowing what to do.

What occurred for Sharyne is a typical reaction to unprotective, emotionally deadened parents sending messages of annihilation and fear, not providing safety or security for the child. The child cannot find or recover from this lack of love, nor can the child bring the parent to life, to awaken or animate them or make them kind and loving. This initiates a series of defences against loss and mourning and then unconscious identification with what André Green called the dead mother or father (Green, 2001, p. 178). The parental depression, emotional blankness and absence leave a child with a fantasy of domination by an internalised other with a malignant power denying love and relationship (Green, 1986, p. 168). This is replicated in the Bluebeard fairytale and in Sharyne's psyche.

Attempts to fill the void meet the internalised feelings of disintegration and disappearance. There is not enough space between the self and others initiating a withdrawal of contact and distancing mechanisms to protect oneself from falling into the anticipated blank, dead and black hole of the parental psychological and unconscious situation. André Green commented about this overwhelming and encompassing yet unconscious state as 'the subject fearing the utmost, either the ultimate loss of the object or the invasion of emptiness' (1986, p. 189). Sharyne recalls becoming invisible and increasingly bereft and tired. Now, years later, she is gradually beginning to put the pieces together.

At issue is leaving behind the psychic material laden with negativity and absence of connection from the severely wrong parental relations. Due to the many instances of disappointment and then despair, the cycle of destruction turned inward. For Sharyne, an ever-present fear returns with repetitive dreams of the father, overpowering and tyrannising the family. This is accompanied by images of the restrictive mother siding with him, pummelling her mind. She retains a sense of irreparable damage that continues to have a toxic effect upon her. Sharyne could proceed only so far in school and career, and although smart, she was without resilience or confidence to continue. Each job, schooling attempt and relationship came to a halt. The cycle of self-development remained incomplete.

Sharyne exhibits 'impotence to withdraw from a conflictual situation, impotence to love, to make the most of one's talents, to multiply one's assets, accompanied by a profound dissatisfaction with life as a whole' (Green, 1986, p. 148). She has longings but is insecure about life and lacks trust in herself or others. She internally tries to fight the depressive hopelessness; however, she does not feel and is numb. Enacted in a feeling of continual body dissatisfaction and disdain, she assesses herself as being too flabby and fat but has no other image of herself. This keeps her empty, unable to find pleasure within herself, devoid of self-connection. Something always tells her she is wrong, unattractive, not as effective as others. The deadness of depression seems to live in her bones, and she cannot overcome it or the empty feeling. She is fearful of the outside world and tends to have few relationships and seldom goes anywhere. Her traumatic early childhood full of emotional and physical threats and harm wrapped her in a blanket of aloneness that kept her from developing crucial areas of her heart and mind.

However, I do not find myself empty, depressed or without energy in the therapy sessions, although Sharyne recounts being numb and not feeling or reacting to much outside her. The therapeutic transferences seem positive with a consistent flow. There is life between us as we discuss the destructive inner voices, the persecutor who harangues, exposing the detritus of her personality left in its wake. The detrimental effects are strong and our efforts to break into the tenacious pattern difficult to penetrate. Meanwhile she remains attached to the destruction and the fears engendered from early in life, repeating the tragedy of the deadened parents with her depression and its unfillable lack or ability to access movement.

André Green characterised negative narcissism as the manifestation of the death drive, aiming for a total shutdown of the psychic system. He described death narcissism as the void, emptiness and destructive withdrawal with a masochistic quality. It disinvests from relationships. Green identified the destructive death narcissism as predominant in lives like Sharyne's, 'caught between two losses: presence in death, or absence in life' (1986, p. 164). Her life is stricken, and she is frail. The psyche is devoid of being loved. The aim is refuge in what is termed *narcissistic withdrawal* inside the narcissistic shield, with the fantasy this protection provides. The illusion is of autonomy, singularity, of needing no one. The situation is driven by undefined but palpable fears, lack of confidence, assumed failures and inability to launch.

André Green called life and death narcissism Janus-faced. He described *life narcissism* as the ego's unity while reflecting the 'antagonism between life and non-life ... For narcissism is bound, given its frailty, to the continuous threat of breaking up' (2023, p. 18). In positive narcissism, the aim is the illusion of self-sufficiency and to be free from dependency so they will never be frustrated or withheld by others. The attitude of life narcissism is characterised by an impoverished ego, limited to relationships without deep involvement while striving for the absolutes of certainty and singularity. The answer lies in the energy attained from accessing the unconscious elements and bringing unity and ballast to the personality.

The frailty of the narcissist arises from early parental and relational losses and manifests in melancholia or a dark sadness, like with Sharyne. It all seems daunting as the initial caregivers' emptiness seeps into the child, not as theirs but becomes theirs to answer. This results in the child being overtaken by something beyond who they are or what they can manage. As André Green noted, 'Narcissism is impenetrable to any relationship with the other. It is "closed off" like in melancholia, depression, marked by the self-destruction, devaluing, discouragement, apathy, withdrawal and the "intensity of unconscious hate"' (Green, 2023, p. 71).

As 'narcissism is a medium of illusion' (Green, 2023, p. 23) the natural state of neediness proves unbearable, intolerable and is experienced as loss of self-control amid the terror of dependence, resulting in tragic withdrawal and lack of intimacy. The narcissist cannot depend on others as there is distrust, and while the narcissist appears otherwise, their personality foundation is shaky. The tendency is to avoid and remain secluded. This preserves the image, although illusionary, of the self as not needy and self-reliant. The solipsistic attitude reigns and the narcissist has learned to be inviolate to maintain some form of identity.

In concert with this, Sharyne learned whoever she relied on disappeared and went away, so she must rely on herself. There had been no place to express the early grief or frustrated desire. She was not attended to by others. Being independent and self-sufficient began early, and she did not know another way. Sacrificed was the need for closeness and healthy dependency. It is the work of analysis to negotiate between the poles of omnipotence and self-disappearance, to find harmony between what is rejected or accepted, allowed to be recognised or not. Despite the wish to be close, this is too precarious to contemplate. Sharyne is alone inside even as the desire for connection longingly remains. As a result, few get close to her real self. But then, she hardly knows how to find or express her real self, having been numb to feelings and emotions for so long.

Effects of parental absences

The outer experiences of disunity and discontinuity as well as those outside of Sharyne's control became a source of distress. Narcissistic injury refers to the self as threatened and felt as deformed or inadequate in the image of the other. 'The intolerable experience of hostile caregiving forces this child to internalize aspects of the caregiver the child cannot then integrate' (Knox, 2003, p. 222). Distorted, the internalisation of any safety of being is absent, and intersubjectivity is not achieved. It is assumed the perspective of the other will take over and eliminate her. By default, there is only room for the singular. The addiction psychologically and physically is to the repetition of the black hole, the emptiness, the depression, and perverse commitment to the destructive state of mind enacted in the body.

Mother was described as insecure, and she relied on Sharyne during the divorce from father. She wanted to be close to mother and make her happy but recalls standing next to her talking after school and feeling her mother was not listening. She begged her mother to look at her. Sharyne finds some pictures of herself at age eight and describes how small she appeared with sad and unhappy eyes. She knew to not say or request anything and realised her mother was not focused on Sharyne, only on herself. Mother made lewd sexual comments as Sharyne grew and has continued being sexually inappropriate and intrusive. Meanwhile mother is shady and dishonest about money, feelings, relationships. Sharyne is frequently suspicious something is going on behind her back and she does not trust any of her partners nor does she feel safe in the world.

Father was depressed and leaned on her to verify him when she was young. The effect of his later indifference but also hostility to her development fostered a confused form of love. There was no real presence of an active or involved father, and she had little foundation from him to base herself upon. The lack or appropriateness of his response created fears of annihilation or psychological obliteration. This was compounded by his physical threats, violent behaviour and emotional abuse, alternating with his demands for her attention.

Predatory elements and demon lovers as well as the death side of narcissism are seriously dangerous. Sharyne is repeatedly attracted to those people incapable of connecting, thus leaving her in the familiar desert of longing and singularity, isolation and depression. As André Green enigmatically described, 'narcissism erases the trace of the Other in its Desire for the One' (2001, p. 86). Living in a painful self-conscious state left her without the ability to anticipate the consequences of her behaviour. Sharyne felt her parents and subsequent partners in adulthood negated her existence; all provided inadequate responses to her. She feels unseen yet safer but longs to be seen for who she is. Yet, here is the conundrum as she does not trust nor feel she can impose her wants and needs on any other. Her authentic feelings became emotionally cut off, detached, and she remains unable to think or decide what to do. She worries about making a mistake, changing ideas and career paths frequently. Alienated from her feelings, confused, uncertain about goals and stymied desire has left her on automatic pilot, without passion or energy.

Sharyne represents the quiet kind of narcissist, held within, having huge desires but silent about them. She assumes she cannot take up as much room as others and she is worried and needs to please them. In a repetitive dream *father is behind her, looming and she is worried he will critique her*. Sharyne continues to find partners who abuse or ignore her. She fears speaking out and lacks confidence. She wanted a mother who understood and saw her. This is encapsulated in *a recent dream when she is expecting mother to pick her up at the bus stop, but mother does not appear. It seems Sharyne has a car there and will go on her own. The mother, empty and absent emotionally, does not recognise who she is or the help she needs*. This scenario repeats in her life and with her various partners who never last.

Sharyne can starve herself or eat too much and not feel anything as her body is numb. 'The inability and refusal to take in food is anxiety and self-punishment. It is a feeding inhibition leading to a serious fate. The aggression and sadism are turned inwards with the self-destructive potential threatening the individual' (Green, 2023, p. 67). Sharyne hesitates to imbibe life, digest or feel as she has to suppress so very much. As André Green further noted (2023, p. 18), the life narcissism aspires to the ego's unity, and death narcissism serves a disorienting function, a death with zero degree of excitation, deadness as its essence. Sharyne worries about imposing, holds back, and fears rejection. She frequently goes numb, deadened within her death-in-life existence.

Winnicott (1967, p. 131) suggested that being seen and the feeling of existence comes from the child seeing their reflection in the parent's face. But this did not happen for Sharyne. Connection with people remains difficult as she is disappointed, wary, and something always seems wrong. Sharyne both defends against the deadness and at the same time holds onto it. She clings to her attachment to the bad objects because she views absence as intolerable while investing in her own psychic productions is also impossible. Indeed, it has felt as if there was no replacement for the emotionally dead parents, and she is unable to separate because she never had them close enough to begin with.

André Green's perspective on this absence, which he also called the negative, was a progressive loss of meaning due to holes in the psyche. Things fall out of holes; the container is not viable; the person feels lack and cannot imagine anything other than what was experienced. Nothing can refer to either 'having been so and being so no longer' or 'never having come into existence' (White, 1999, p. 1121).

The psychic holes are the unrepresented places developed as the home and the parents expose her to what is abusive, threatening, dangerous. The aim is not pleasure but finding refuge in narcissistic withdrawal and the fantasy of anaesthesia and inertia (White, 1999, p. 1126). It is a solution to the problem of destructiveness by dissociating from any aggression, even the healthy aggression needed for psychological movement. There is an inhibition of pleasure accompanying the rise of the death drive, ultimately abolishing experiences and feelings as she turns the aggression inward to destroy herself.

Sharyne dreams of being in the food market and sees men with their heads on stakes in the parking lot. She runs away, ending up in a small room, dark, and in so much fear she worries the dream will repeat. She often wakes up anxious like this and fearful of being alone and vulnerable. She is uneasy with people and filled with harsh, judgemental self-talk. She says this dream is another of the bad father dreams, sexual, where she cannot find herself. She wonders if there was too much damage and the destructive talk heard from her parents too internalised and entrenched. In the dream she is in a public place. We do not know if she has the food she needs as fear took over and she ran. The image could also be her fear of wanting to behead the father figure, an aggressive move she could not take. Instead, her aggression turns inwards, and she has nothing, no car, few clothes or anything of much value. She takes up little space and lives without definition. André Green described the disinvestment that wants to destroy connections and retreats inside the narcissistic wall (Green, 1975, p. 7).

> There seems no choice other than the flight towards nothingness. No way to find the state of peace and quietude following satisfaction as there is never peace or satisfaction. There is internal suffering of malaise … and she is progressively reduced in the direction of self-annihilation.
>
> (1975, p. 17)

Over time and in the midst of all this distress and the years of disappointment, *Sharyne has a recurrent dream in which she flies in the open sky without any mechanical means. She just spreads her arms as though they were wings and soars over a beautiful landscape of canyons and meadows, flying toward a beautiful sunset.* The recurrence of the dream gives her confidence and compensates the positions where she easily becomes disparaging about herself and even more withdrawn. The dream is powerful enough and with sufficient impact to keep her on the path of self-recovery. Sunk in death narcissism, recovery will take time, but she accepts this. Sharyne is beginning to imagine a way out of the morass she found herself in physically and psychologically. Sharyne has hopes, and the analytical process, although difficult, is part of what helps her out of the clutch of death narcissism.

References

Bernardi, R. & Eidlin, M. (2018). Thin-skinned or vulnerable narcissism and thick-skinned or grandiose narcissism: Similarities and differences. *The International Journal of Psychoanalysis, 99*(2), 291–313. DOI: 10.1080/00207578.2018.1425599

Bion, W. R. (1977). The past presented. In *A memoir of the future* (1991, pp. 219–426). Karnac.

Britton, R. (1998). *Belief and imagination.* Routledge.

Britton, R. (2004). Narcissistic disorder in clinical practice. *Journal of Analytical Psychology, 49*(4), 477–490.

Bromberg, P. (1983). The mirror and the mask – on narcissism and psychoanalysis. *Contemporary Psychoanalysis, 19,* 359–387.

Deutsch, H. (1942). Some forms of emotional disturbance and their relationship to schizophrenia. *The Psychoanalytic Quarterly, 11*(3), 301–321.

Engels, D. (2013). Narcissism against narcissus? A classical myth and its influence on the elaboration of earlier psychoanalysis from Binet to Jung. In V. Zaijko & E. O'Gorman (Ed.), *Classical myth and psychoanalysis* (pp. 75–95). Oxford University Press.

Freud, S. (1914). On Narcissism. In J. Strachey (Trans.), *The standard edition of the complete psychological works of Sigmund Freud: Vol. XIV. On the history of the psycho-analytic movement, papers on metapsychology and other works* (pp. 67–102). Hogarth Press.

Green, A. (1975). The analyst, symbolization and absence in the analytic setting. *International Journal of Psychoanalysis, 56,* 1–22. https://bgsp.edu/wp-content/uploads/2014/12/Green-The-Analyst-Symbolization-an.pdf

Green, A. (1986). The dead mother. In *On private madness.* International Universities Press.

Green, A. (2001). The dead mother. In *Life narcissism, death narcissism.* Free Association Books.

Green, A. (2023). *On the destruction and death drives.* Phoenix Publishing.

Greenberg, D. (2016). [Review of *Traumatic narcissism: Relational systems of subjugation* by D. Shaw.] *Contemporary Psychoanalysis, 52*(1), 130–177.

Grunberger, B. (1979). *Narcissism: Psychoanalytic essays* (J. S. Diamanti, Trans.). International Universities Press.

Jacoby, M. (1990). *Individuation and narcissism: The psychology of self in Jung and Kohut.* Routledge.

Jung, C. G. (1954/1969). On the nature of the psyche. In *The structure and dynamics of the psyche* (Vol. 8). Princeton University Press.

Kernberg, O. (1975). *Borderline conditions and pathological narcissism*. Aronson.

Knox, J. (2003). Trauma and defences: Their roots in relationship. *Journal of Analytical Psychology, 48*(2), 207–233.

Kohon, G. (Ed.) (1999). *The dead mother: The work of André Green*. Routledge.

Kohut, H. (1977). *Restoration of the self*. University of Chicago Press.

Kohut, H. (1966). Forms and transformations of narcissism. *Journal of the American Psychoanalytic Association, 14*(2), 243–272.

Mollon, P. (1986). Theoretical concepts: Narcissism. *British Journal of Psychotherapy, 3*(2), 151–161.

Morrison, A. ed. (1996). *Essential papers on narcissism*. New York University Press.

Phillips, A. (2016). *Promises, promises*. Faber and Faber.

Rosenfeld, H. (1971). A clinical approach to the psychoanalytic theory of the life and death instincts: An investigation into aggressive aspects of narcissism. *International Journal of Psycho-Analysis, 52*(2), 169–178.

Rosenfeld, H. (1987). *Impasse and interpretation*. Routledge.

Rustin, M. (2017). Narcissism and melancholia from the psychoanalytical perspective of object relations. In B. Sheils & J. Walsh (Eds.), *Narcissism, melancholia and the subject of community* (pp. 41–64). Palgrave Macmillan.

Samuels, A., Shorter, B. & Plaut, F. (Eds.) (1986). *A critical dictionary of Jungian analysis*. Routledge.

Schwartz, S. (2020) *The absent father effect on daughters: Father desire, father wounds*. Routledge.

Schwartz, S. (2023). *Imposter syndrome and the 'as-if' personality in analytical psychology: Fragility of the self*. Routledge.

Schwartz, S. (2024). *Exploration of the puella archetype in analytical psychology: Girl unfolding*. Routledge.

Schwartz-Salant, N. (1982). *Narcissism and character transformation*. Inner City Books.

Solomon, H. (2004). Self creation and the limitless void of dissociation: The 'as-if' personality. *Journal of Analytical Psychology, 49*(5), 635–656.

Steiner, J. (1993). *Psychic retreats: Pathological organizations in psychotic, neurotic and borderline patients*. Routledge.

White, R. (2017). Review of *The Work of the Negative* by André Green. Journal of the *American Psychoanalytical Association, 65*(6), 1119–1126. DOI: 10.1177/0003065117748551

Winnicott, D. W. (1965). *The maturational process and the facilitating environment*. Routledge.

Winnicott, D. W. (1967). Mirror role of mother and family in child development. In *Playing and Reality*. Tavistock/Penguin.

Chapter 8

Narcissism in Jungian thought

Jungian thought on narcissism explores the connection of self to others. For the narcissist intimacy is desired yet feared. Their internal world is a detritus of emotional distancing and dissociations. These are the unfinished areas of the personality, originating from early trauma, emotional neglect and negative parental complexes. These promote idealisation of others and can destroy initiative while feeding an internalised cycle of oppression, affecting creativity and the life force and compromising true self-love.

> Our consciousness is aware of resistances, because the other person seems strange and uncanny, and because we cannot get accustomed to the idea that we are not absolute master in our own house. We should prefer to be always 'I' and nothing else. But we are confronted with that inner friend or foe, and whether he is our friend or our foe depends on ourselves.
>
> (Jung, 1950/1968, CW 9i, para. 235)

The myth of Narcissus is a story of the self/Self. It is one of the defining characteristics of our era and highlights the ego in search of the Self. In Jungian thought this connection is necessary and enriches the personality. Although Jung rejected Freud's views on narcissism as a necessary stage of development, he said,

> If the soul image its projected, an immediate affective attachment to the object occurs. If it is not projected, then a rather unadapted disposition arises, partially described by Freud as narcissism ... The subject will be gradually submerged by unconscious material but as unable either to put it to use because of the deficient reaction to the object, or to assimilate it in any other way.
>
> (Jung, 1921/1971, 511ff)

The inner search of the narcissist, should they begin to venture forth, opens a door into the psyche imbued with beauty and strangeness, unlike what they knew previously. Like Alice in Wonderland, they go into the depths of the unconscious and encounter terror, longing, suffering and fulfilment, where things are both upside-down and right-side up and always changing. This is where the voice of the soul begins to be heard as a portal into a life larger, truer and more possible than imagined.

A man dreamt, *There is a red stockinged lady outside the bookshop in Zurich, where earlier in the day I had bought Jung's book* Modern Man in Search of a Soul. Here is the feminine other with an invitation to unite, a symbolic initiator in the guise of the prostitute as the entry into the soul and the Self. As Jung wrote, 'The image is a *condensed expression of the psychic condition of the whole*' (1921/1971, CW 6, para. 745). This quote addresses the psychological issue in the dream, opening from oneness to twoness, a union that includes the other who is yet unknown.

The past is activated by present experiences, although nothing overt might be occurring. It is the covert stirring of the unconscious and the Self asking to be accessed. When the complex narcissistic patterns are maladaptive, the necessary process of self-reflection is unable to occur. Dissociative defences arise against closeness, and the narcissist is unable to feel the reality of relationship, including in the analytical treatment. There is impairment of the intrinsic motivation to seek nearness and recognise the other as a subject. They find it impossible to value themselves unconditionally or ascribe value to others. All these aspects are obliquely yet prominently displayed in the dream.

The question is what the Narcissus myth means in terms of our psychic experiences and how it relates to love. The task is to reach beyond the narrow forms of narcissism into our more complete self (Jacoby, 1990, p. 29). The problem in the myth is that Narcissus sees his reflection as special, in need of no other, but he does not see it is himself. This sets up the need for the admiring other but one who he can never get close to, hold, or be held by. It is a love without consummation or acknowledgement of who he is. Self-love also needs self-awareness and self-reflection in terms of ego-fixation (p. 21). This means love of self is connected to the ego and each can feed into the other.

As Jung repeatedly commented, if a person is unconscious the world reflects their own face through their projections onto others, as they need the other to reflect their psychic contents. This is the narcissist who tends to create a sticky Velcro-like collusion with their partner, but this is not sufficient for growth as an individual. Jung said, 'Self-confidence ... conceals a profound sense of impotence, for which their conscious optimism acts as unsuccessful compensation; while the pessimistic resignation of others masks a defiant will to power' (1928/1969, CW 7, para. 222).

The use of the myth and its symbolism represents the archetypal dimension of Jungian psychology and expands beyond the personal. Jung contended 'there was an inner source, an internal organizing principle containing impersonal unconscious nodal points ... more in relation of the archetypes to objects formed in the ego' (Astor, 1995, p. 140). Through this process individual pursuits lead to transcendent elements as the mythological also symbolises an eternally timeless presence.

Jungian thought moves beyond the popularised and simplified interpretations of narcissism. There are unconscious parts that remain unknowable and illimitable, bringing together the various elements and dissociated functions of the personality. Some of these are connected to the hiddenness of narcissism. At the same time, narcissism leads to the self as James Astor, British Jungian analyst, explained, 'The self leads to the archetypal from the experiences extending beyond the ego' (1995, p. 151).

Narcissism has not been a centrepiece of Jungian analytical exploration, but the Jungian process of individuation brings focus to the Self as a basic concept. Yet, a caveat is due here regarding the definition of self or Self. It's specific use in Jungian analytical psychology is of import and magnifies the significance of this project. Self is not just ego or consciousness but includes the unconscious, the symbolic, the worlds we do not easily or quickly perceive or imagine. This is a unique concept expanding into the union of matter and spirit, body and psyche, personal and collective, the core and the whole. The Self gives a person's life direction, purpose, meaning, richness and fabric. It leads to emulsifying and differentiating psychological elements in a dynamic pattern without structure at the same time.

In terms of the Jungian approach to the psyche, to not attend to this and honour its presence or to not connect to its essence beyond the ego would be a rejection of the Self. It is the failure to live one's true pattern that leads to extreme forms of narcissism and what are now called *narcissistic character disorders*.

The Self reflects the totality of our being and the uniqueness of each person. It implies what is more than us, a spiritual approach accessed through dreams, psychological complexes, stress, war, life in average and extraordinary ways. As Jung said in one of his many commentaries on this concept, 'the self ... embraces ego-consciousness, shadow, anima, and collective unconscious in indeterminable extension. As a totality, the self is a coincidentia oppositorum; it is therefore bright and dark and yet neither' (Jung, 1963, CW 14, p. 1198, n66). Also, Jung stated, 'The Self is the total, timeless man ... who stands for the mutual integration of conscious and unconscious' (Jung, 1946/1966, CW 16, para. 531). Narcissism, while it can prevent connection, also holds the possibility of connection to Self.

A question is often asked about why Jung did not address narcissism. French Jungian analyst Ellie Humbert (1980, p. 241) contended Jung did not encounter it. Humbert's explanation of narcissism is that it is a phenomenon that strikes the observer from the outside. Narcissus does not tell his story, but a third or observing party does. If a person speaks of narcissism they take an outside view, becomes an observer of themselves and of relations with their own singular image. Narcissus turns the gaze upon himself as a psychic object and expresses attachment to the world with which he alone is identified (Humbert, 1980, p. 242).

The Jungian perspectives of Nathan Schwartz-Salant in 1982 and Mario Jacoby in 1990 stand out as Jungian writers on this personality type. There are others as well, which indicates the topic is massive even though its exploration is late in Jungian thought. Exploring the intricacies takes one into a labyrinth of possibilities and interpretations. Again, it can feel overwhelming and requires a circumambulation process as referenced in alchemy, circling around to amass and then entering.

This circling process gathers disparate elements of the personality, and, in doing so, inner solidity and the sense of self attain more foundation and structure. Movement jostles the elements while making the situation more distinct and, therefore, understandable and applicable to oneself.

However, the symbols of growth clash with the narcissistic reactions of withdrawal, creating a distancing and then loosening to bring knowledge for accessing the unconscious. This is one way into the search for what Jung called wholeness through the process of individuation or knowing the Self. It brings up fundamental questions like: Who am I? How do I know myself? Is this really me? Sometimes we have no doubt about our realness and at other times we do not know it at all. The journey is lifelong and the questions ever fungible, and the answers as well. Accessing our authenticity evolves and shapes what it is to be human and feel alive rather than numbed out. The work in Jungian analysis is about sorting and differentiating, finding the symbols and meanings that change through life. It is an ongoing, evolving and challenging experience.

Narcissism is recognised as being at the root of living. In essence all existence is narcissistic, for to live we need to protect, foster and embellish who we are. There are many avenues to find ourselves, to survive and to thrive in the descent into the potential of the personality, to find meaning and make sense of the trials and sufferings. As Jung said,

> Filling the conscious mind with ideal conceptions is a characteristic of Western theosophy, but not the confrontation with the shadow and the world of darkness. One does not become enlightened by imagining figures of light, but by making the darkness conscious.
>
> (Jung, 1954/1968, CW 13, para. 335)

The figure of Narcissus has fascinated for centuries and does so even more now. The figure of Echo not so much, exposing the lack of attention to the feminine and promoting a narrow purview reflecting the cultural and historical impress of masculine supremacy. This is the tragedy as portrayed in the myth as well as clarifying no one unites. The feminine aspects are ignored, and the myth reveals what happens when bodies shrivel up and disappear due to the lack of love, being acknowledged or adequately seen. Attention to the voice of the psyche in all its aspects means hearing the totality of the personality with its many sounds of desire and search for love and union. It means exploring the restlessness, conflicts and complexes clamouring for a voice and removing the obstacles for accessing our more complete selves. Postmodern fluidity presents the opportunities of other realities, rethinking and reenacting how to live true to oneself.

Puer and puella archetypes

Narcissism presents with a web of associations and interpretations in a shifting ground reflecting contemporary events. These appear in the Jungian archetypes of puella and puer, the eternal youth, and are more fully explored in my earlier books (Schwartz, 2020, 2023, 2024). These figures appearing in the personality coincide with many traits and characteristics of narcissism.

The intense energy and appeal of the puella/puer often masks a more fragile personality – unrealistic, fantasy driven, easily dissembled, immature, untouched. This person is blocked by a persona adaptation, obscuring their basic instincts. By looking into the mirror, we find our shadow selves through experiences of walking down personal and collective avenues. This is a pathway encouraging a deepening into what we have yet to discover about ourselves and relationships to others. The splits in the psyche and the dissociations preset us with the questions of how to relate to the otherness of the figures populating both out inner and outer worlds.

Puella/puer types are usually youthful, charming, appealing, seductive and part of what unfolds into the energetic, the unusual. Puella/puer leads to the creative, expressive, and the future, but if denigrated, distorted and disturbed, halts the psyche's development until addressed. Otherwise, these people can be dolorous, dejected, defeated easily and have little fortitude for actual working at being all they can be.

They hesitate to grow up, needing focus and attention, unable to commit to life, relationships, love or acceptance of self. A punishing core of inadequacy indicates a lack in the capacity for realistic self-reflection in which the ego is narcissistic and the larger self unable to be accessed. The narcissist avoids the present and is busy turning outwards, looking for an audience and an easy way through. Impatient, they live an ethereal existence while striving for immediate satisfaction and achievement.

As an eternal child, time becomes unreal for the puer/puella. In their partial world and ethereal place, they live within a revolving door of things, people, situations. They rush with no time to feel anything, much less love. There are vain and empty attempts in this provisional life; they are not yet really living, just waiting and feeling without enough mastery. Bogged down with a secret numbness and dead weight, their life zest is compromised and the full development of personality stunted. They embody the constructive as well as the destructive sides of life. This child also contains the universality of the human condition in the promise of new growth.

As an essential part of the psyche, Jung said,

> In every adult there lurks a child – an eternal child, something that is always becoming, is never completed, and calls for unceasing care, attention, and education. That is the part of the human personality which wants to develop and become whole.
>
> (1934/1954, CW17, para. 286)

These are called *threshold experiences*, new beginnings, an initiation into another phase to be reborn. However, the emotional portrayals can lead to failure to recognise the flattening of love interests and an inability to seriously devote themselves to the process. They can be fused with childlike unsteadiness and an incapacity for perseverance; they lack tenacity, giving up too soon. They are restless, inundated with ennui, bored but also comfortable in the waiting, entitled, while languishing as they waste time.

Unfortunately, many puella/puer types relate to the world through hiding, mimicry and adaptation at the expense of authenticity. The deep longing for connection has been hurt, cut off, afraid, damaged. The remnants of this tragedy are an inability to change; they are unmovable and present with an outer show of movement and flashy persona. They feel lost, stagnant and hide behind their appealing but elusive façade. Eventually, life is no longer sustainable in an illusionary world solely reliant on the ego and persona.

There is disembodiment and a psychological distancing that can be disarming (Chalquist, 2009, p. 170). The puella/puer can be inordinately identified with the persona and denies any shadow; their display can be superficial, and like the narcissist, this type is often mesmerizing. However, the basic instincts to perceive body and emotions as sources of information are lost in relation to others or oneself. The narcissistic personality is a defence against a primary depression. Distorted by an unusual degree of self reference (Belviso, 2020, p. 54), their presentation can be alluring while underneath they are cold, ruthless, restless and bored. They often do not trust the unconscious and assess only the more grandiose aspects, neglecting the vulnerable narcissistic traits.

Tending to be unrealistic, they aim high, will push, wonder and dream to make what seems impossible happen. At the same time the luxury of relaxing into just being is absconded by focus on the façade and the future with its flight from the present. Our technological world can reflect the same lack of balance with roots in avoidance of the real (Gosling, 2009, p. 148). This personality type compensates with narcissistic grandiosity. It is not easy to accept the loss to romanticised ideals, so they deny, jump over them, leave and do anything to avoid disappointment.

Existence is provisional. Combined with this, as Jungian analyst Marie Louise von Franz noted, is the person caught in a 'childish state of constant dissatisfaction with themselves and the whole of reality' (2000, p. 87). Although often highly creative, their interior support system is without foundation. Empty, feeling depleted, a puer type described his life and his feeling about it using these words: *I am finding that I can no longer garner the energy to keep cycling through the fruitless changes. The anticipation of more years of emptiness is intolerable. The exhaustion with this routine is translating into a deep, abiding urge to simply no longer be.*

Transformative potential of love

The underlying aspects of the narcissistic personality contain the desire to be comprehended. However, the cover of slick grandiosity and persona of self-reliance combine with the lack of healthy dependence to work against intimacy and love. A narcissist needs the defence of an impermeable persona to cover the fragile self.

When the unconscious is refused and kept hidden, many facets of the interior human experience become destructive.

Jungian thought deals with human suffering, with the search to find meaning, growth and expansion beyond a personality narrowed and stuck in singularity. 'This construction of narratives serves a protective and defensive purpose by ordering experience into patterns so that the world does not seem to be a place where dangers occur which the child can neither predict nor control' (Knox, 2003, p. 217). The work is to access the transformative processes, catalysing the creative impulses and bringing them into the world.

The narcissist is hemmed in by family, society, learned behaviours. They adapt themselves to be seen but not get close, to get by rather than expose the real. Nathan Schwartz-Salant (1982) went into detail on the Narcissus mythology and its symbolism with an archetypal/mythological perspective. Mario Jacoby (1990) presented the ideas of Heinz Kohut in alignment with other psychoanalytic thought. British Jungian analyst Michael Fordham said, 'There is a need for defenses against what is not-self as essential to health … little or no inner world can develop; the self-integrate becomes rigid and persists' (1985, p. 167). These writers describe the process of the narcissist in finding a way to the self. American Jungian analyst Patricia Berry (2008) wrote about Echo, reminding us of her presence in the psyche.

Marie Louise von Franz, well known for her work on fairytales, addressed the concept of initiation. 'Every dark thing one falls into can be called an initiation. The first step is falling into a dark place appearing in a dubious or negative form … or being possessed by something' (1972, p. 74). Writing on the puer aeternus and delving into this personality type, von Franz does not address puella or narcissism per se. She notes what is difficult, however, what is possessive and perhaps rigid, strangled in the hold of the complex and depleting energy. Yet the complex and the core of this myth also contain the possibility of growth and development as it initiates us into ourselves. Narcissism once made conscious can be a signal of what is needed for the personality to develop.

For example, *a woman dreamt she saw some shoes on the sidewalk. They were four-inch heels, decorated and fancy. Attracted to their unusual look and knowing she would be admired for wearing them, she was drawn to the idea of taking them. No one was claiming the shoes, and she waited until all was clear to try them on. They were too big in the heel. She could stand in them but not walk. She regretfully took them off and put them back in the middle of the sidewalk and went on, wishing they fit.* After the dream, she realised it meant she had not yet found the right fit to her own self and could not put on the identity of some random other person. As Schwartz-Salant described, 'The self-hate, hunger, secret stealing and lack of warmth' are aspects of the inner life of the narcissist and all these exacerbate the rule of envy (1982, p. 24). The quest to find herself would mean she would have to come to earth, be more practical and do the work and choose for herself rather than easily taking an identity from another. The fancy shoes will not suffice for the practical work needed for the process of walking to become who she is and get where she wants to go.

Narcissists need the perfect and ideal to compensate for their shaky self-image, creating a better one in the minds of others. They are propped up by the façade presentation. Appearing successful to others does not suffice nor fill the missing internal spaces from the narcissistic failure to link body, affect, soul and mind. However, the narcissistic personality structures defend against feeling depression and suffering. Unable to access the joy or keep hold of it, narcissists experience an unacknowledged interior accumulation of violence and hostility split off from libidinal and loving communication towards the self.

Schwartz-Salant (1982, p. 37) viewed the narcissistic tendency as something new trying to emerge in the collective, a new self-image arising from an archetypal situation attempting to come forth. He focused on the Self as numinous and beyond, more encompassing than the ego, but unable to be accessed by the power-oriented narcissist. The narcissist makes the deeper more grounded search for ego and Self connection seem a defeat to their grandiosity. 'The Self, the transcendent and the mystery, searches for and provides meaning by thoroughly living one's life not on the illusionary surface of existence' (p. 20). If stuck in self-hate, disgust, perfectionism, surface façade, fear, vulnerability, loneliness and feelings of not being understood, inner security and curiosity for the unknown remain elusive.

For Schwartz-Salant the archetypal dimension comes to ignite the conflictual impersonal powers with their greater energic contents moving beyond the roots of the narcissistic problems in the interpersonal and parental failures (1982, p. 37). When the outer structures are no longer holding, we are drawn into the archetypal realms where we can become either stuck or reborn to more complete inner and outer relationships. Schwartz-Salant noted narcissistic character structures can lead to the emergence of a new spirit as the grandiose self can transform into a positive spiritual form (p. 36). Yet, these also can forestall future growth if unacknowledged or misused to feed the grandiose cover. The narcissistic character compensates rather than struggles towards the Self by not living the experiment of life or is overcome by the feeling that life has turned negative. Schwartz-Salant (p. 120) noted that Jung involved the body because the unconscious is also evident in the physical way life is experienced.

The structures of narcissistic character are in withdrawal, 'as if the personality has gone on hold waiting for the right experiences and relationships to unfold' (Schwartz-Salant, 1982, p. 134). This person, no matter how it appears, feels themselves to be insecure and powerless, drained of spirit and without connection to the Self. Jung (1968, CW 12, para. 563) described this as follows:

> An inflated consciousness is always egocentric and conscious of nothing but its own existence. It is incapable of learning from the past, incapable of contemporary events, and incapable of drawing right conclusions about the future. It is hypnotized by itself and therefore cannot be argued with. It inevitably dooms itself to calamities that must strike it dead.

Hence the need for the narcissistic defences, rigidity and control. All serve to avoid the numbness and coming alive through recognising and taking in the unconscious information.

The narcissist carries within, an assembly of disturbing experiences, fantasies, secrets and wishful daydreams. Narcissists are depicted as subsumed in themselves to the exclusion of others, without empathy or giving so much as a glance to anyone else. When a person has been exposed to too much distress early in life, unmet sufficiently by caregivers, overrun by the traumas of war, displacements, shock, abuse, that person will learn to withdraw, put on a façade, not rely on others, and feel insufficient, depressed and saddened within their own being. The frantic reactions and inability to be content fuels the search for the ideal rather than the real. 'This is a narcissism that has to do with a forced power and is a grandiose copy of the real self' (Schwartz-Salant, 1982, p. 24). In other words, the narcissist must reach beyond the ordinary to compensate for the weightiness of painful experiences, and this is what leads to the extraordinary.

The problems and symptoms of narcissism are purposeful and highlight the transformation possible through accessing the unconscious. The self-regulating function of the psyche comes forth, compensating for the poor and inadequate mirroring, leaving the child without self-love or acceptance. The ability to face the world and to healthily depend on others becomes damaged. However, there are means for recovery.

Jung's view was stated in his seminars on Nietzsche's *Thus Spake Zarathustra* (unpublished lecture, quoted in Schwartz-Salant, 1982, p. 24),

> You see that degenerating sense which says 'all for myself' is unfulfilled destiny, that is somebody who did not live himself, who did not give himself what he needed, who did not toil for the fulfillment of that pattern which had been given him when he was born. Because that thing is one's genus it ought to be fulfilled and in as much as it is not, there is that hunger which says, 'all for myself'.

The adaptation suggests the narcissistic character gives rise to complexes or splinter psyches that become dissociated from each other. 'In dissociation both conscious and unconscious representations are kept separate from one another' (Knox, 2003, p. 211). The dissociation serves to fragment the painful and anxious experiences occurring in the realm of the unbearable. The distressing memories are assiduously avoided. From the extremes of abuse, neglect, lack of care, 'defended against by the elimination of thought itself Michael Fordham coined the phrase defences of the self' (p. 229). This need for defences results from the loss of a sense of self, a profound effect set early in life, hardening as the original offenses were so egregious they remained unthought and self-reflection was compromised in development.

Schwartz-Salant traced the defensiveness and seeming impenetrability of the narcissist to poor self-esteem and fragile identity.

> The masochistic development may ensue from the distorted parental response to the child's self ... the early experiences of the narcissistic character – and this is true to some degree for everyone – is that the self was psychically attacked. Consequently, the child's self withdrew and instead a more compliant and masochistic attitude developed. The self is suppressed and then hated forming apprehension and lack of knowledge of the venture into the depth of the self.
>
> (1982, p. 159)

Rather than viewing this person as unanalysable and untreatable, Schwartz-Salant perceived, along with others, that they could form strong transferences and gain identity and access to the deeper layers of the psyche, meaning the Self. This experience brings the kind of repair that facilitates increased openness and relatedness to self and others.

In addition, Schwartz-Salant highlighted that the narcissistic character has generally been subject to massive envious attacks in childhood. To avoid a repeat of that they 'hide any prize from others and from himself ... the chronic lack of mirroring, often stemming from parental envy... a disquiet due to the parents' discomfort with their child's uniqueness' (Schwartz-Salant, 1982, p. 48). Self-recognition implies owning their vulnerability and the harmful and shadow aspects of the personality instead of projecting them onto others. This becomes more complicated as the narcissist does not see what they are projecting. 'This narcissistic vulnerability is reflected in experiences of anger, envy, aggression, helplessness, emptiness, low self-esteem, shame, social avoidance, and even suicidality' (Pincus, 2013, p. 95). Narcissists are too self-involved and the self too inaccessible.

Human love based in reality accepts the ordinary, imperfect and often humdrum aspects of life with another and works to form a viable, caring relationship together. 'Human love affirms the person who is actually there, rather than the ideal we would like him or her to be or the projection that flows from our minds' (Johnson, 1983, p. 191). Others do matter and their relational value depends on the instrumental function they serve for the regulation of self-esteem. Narcissism as a psychodynamic function is motivated by the need for 'self-definition, self-development, self-organization, self-preservation, self-cohesion, self-enhancement, self-evaluation, self-regard, and self-esteem' (Meissner, 2008, p. 768).

Incoherence of self identity

For the narcissist the self is consciously experienced as consistently defective, headed in the direction of failure. They lack the capacity for self-soothing and they are invaded by an existential loneliness. Shame is associated with falling behind their expectations, which are driven by a harsh ideal and grandiose self. High levels of shame and anxiety accompany uncovering the implicit self as the narcissist is compelled to ward this off, thinking it defective. Likewise, the narcissist both over- and underestimates their effects on others. Characteristically, others are easily idealised or devalued excessively and usually inappropriately.

Narcissism makes us ponder the nature and structure of identity. Narcissism 'has a great attraction for those who have renounced part of their own narcissism and are in search of object love. The charm of a child lies to a great extent in his narcissism, his self-contentment and inaccessibility' (Freud, quoted in Jacoby, 1990, p. 90). The wounded and healing parts of the personality are split from each other, leaving deprivation and deficit. Mario Jacoby (1990) goes into detail describing Kohut's maturation of the self through the development of narcissism and aligns this with Jung's individuation process.

The impact of the postmodern Jungian approach is a willingness to question, to turn the ideas we have taken for granted inside out. It is a way of playing with what we believe we know and opening to what we do not. Without careful reflection, how we adapt to collective reactions, unthinking and going along, can insidiously seep in. Cultures are transmitted, become devoured and devouring, unconsciously idealised and interiorised by participants leaving, nothing clear or defined and yet altering how people show up in the world.

We have become collectively trapped in images, either of our own choosing or those imposed on us by others. The illusions of self can shape how we think, feel and behave and are seemingly necessary for our functioning in society. Placing narcissism in a historical and transcultural perspective leads to recognising the loneliness and loss of meaning characterising much of our world today. The current psychic spread of narcissism reflects cultures breeding emptiness and soullessness. The narcissism of aggression and rejection brings about loss of reality as the libido draws inwards, isolates, without relationship to others.

Narcissists become invested in their grandiose self-images, consistently sacrificing perceptions of truth and reality in the service of maintaining the fictious. In such states, they can become blind to both the subjectivity of others and to the deeper and more authentic aspects of self. Narcissism affects all human beings, and its thematic tentacles enter all forms of psychotherapy and relationships as we seek to increase understanding and bring focus on connection, intimacy and movements out of isolation.

However, for the narcissist differences are eliminated rather than honoured to satisfy the sameness of homogeneity. This standardisation, excluding anything else, supports the narcissist's identity and need for sameness. The overconsumption and generalisation of the term *narcissism* has led to its simplification and obscures the issues surrounding this personality structure. Although a normal stage in development, it brings to light the necessary dialectical movement between sameness and otherness. Jung commented 'The self is relatedness ... The self only exists inasmuch as you appear. Not that you are, but that you do is the self. The self appears in your deeds and deeds always mean relationship' (Jung, 1988, para. 73).

The myth of Narcissus illustrates the ego has been unable to manage emergence of the self successfully and individuation has become distorted and stuck. When there is an environmental or constitutional deficit, the self may feel unable, under attack from outside or within, too vulnerable and isolated. The defences of the self are mobilised, creating the narcissistic false self with its anti-individuation forces and the subsequent psychic retreat. 'Individuation is then nothing but ego-centredness and autoeroticism' (Jung, 1954/1968, CW 8, para 432).

Clinical example: Galita

Galita is in her early fifties, married but unhappy, no children, an accomplished professional. Her career was faltering and she was distraught. Her marriage felt rocky, and she did not know why. She decided to pursue the pathway of Jungian psychology to discover more about herself as she felt up against a wall of unknowing. It was a wall she recounted feeling at various times in her life, and it meant something different each time, but she had not gotten to the bottom of it – yet. Her outer appearance was stylish and trendy. However, she frequently commented on cellulite, weight, worried about her work, about her body not being good enough. Meanwhile every outer slight and rejection went to the core of a self-destructive abyss.

Galita tended to scorn her mother for being just a mother and mothering being a lowly rather worthless and old-fashioned role. The demeaning of mother represented her own turn from the maternal. Galita was rather harsh in her critique of mothering, and whatever mother denoted as feminine or masculine was deemed stereotypical and unpalatable. However, she bought into the part that said being a woman meant acting a charmer and seductive. To her father she was a darling who could do no wrong and she loved him dearly. She had a series of dreams revealing difficulty being in her skin, decisive, solid. She struggled with intimacy.

Galita presented the protection by her father and his all-encompassing goodness as different from her mother, who was assigned to be the bad one who did not understand and to whom she could not get close. She sarcastically joked hers was a typical Oedipal family as she emotionally aligned with her father and her brother was with her mother. The joking was no doubt a defence to hide her anxiety about the unconscious material immersed in this family.

Galita was sleeping in some way, floating and oblivious. Everything remained distantly charming, wishful, on hold, like she was a statue acquiring dust. Unable to awaken, her life stagnated and she could not form relationships of substance or consistency. She struggled to take herself seriously, refused the maternal ground of being, was insecure about her talent or ability to love. Galita, this puella-type figure with her narcissistic overlay, is in continual ambivalence about commitment.

In the Jungian process both unconscious and conscious dynamics intermix, influencing us in our daily lives, for example, decisions, expressions of emotion, our sense of identity and every other human characteristic (Silvestro, 2017, p. xi). Becoming aware or conscious of these dynamics lies at the heart of Jungian analysis and helps a person like Galita to undergo a meaningful transformation, a process often appearing in dreams.

Narcissism is a detachment from the true self as well as deeply disguised and unsettled despair and despondency. It creates a demand with no concessions, its terms unbending. Life must be lived in its service. A common element persisting throughout this complex psychological condition is identity and that is why it becomes so basic to the ego. However, the Self is regarded as both the centre and its surroundings, including the whole conscious and unconscious psyche. It is individual to a person and simultaneously a collective element connecting to others and beyond. It can be considered a blueprint of an individual's direction and meaning, illustrating simultaneously a critical social commentary.

No matter the psychological and analytical approach, narcissism is intriguing and requires expansion from oneness to twoness, benefitting person, culture, conscious and unconscious. Narcissus longs for a permanent relationship with the Self, which is symbolically evident when he finally meets his own reflected image in the pond.

Narcissism is also a seeking of fulfilment. Jungian analysis looks deeply into the Self without flinching, bringing out variations on universal themes. These include the joy of renewal and the pain and tragedy of the damage unable to be repaired. In the longing we regain the energy to proceed. 'By restructuring the ego and forming a relationship with the Self, the wounded individual can move into and beyond the feelings of emptiness and longing' (Silvestro, 2017, p. 5). In the words of Emily Dickinson, 'I'm Nobody! Who are you? Are you Nobody – too?'

References

Astor, J. (1995). *Michael Fordham: Innovations in analytical psychology.* Psychology Press.
Belviso, F. (2020). *Jungian reflections on grandiosity.* Routledge.
Berry, P. (2008). *Echo's subtle body: Contributions to an archetypal psychology.* Spring Publications.
Chalquist, C. (2009). Insanity by the numbers, knowings from the ground. In S. Porterfield, K. Polette, T. F. Baumlin (Eds.), *Perpetual adolescence* (pp. 169–186). State University of New York Press.
Fordham, M. (1985). *Exploration into the self.* Karnac Books.
Gosling, J. (2009). 'Protracted adolescence': Reflections on forces informing the American collective. In S. Porterfield, K. Polette, T. F. Baumlin (Eds.), *Perpetual adolescence* (pp. 137–154). State University of New York Press.
Humbert, E. (1980). The self and narcissism. *Journal of Analytical Psychology*, 25(3), 237–246.
Jacoby, M. (1990). *Individuation and narcissism: The psychology of self in Jung and Kohut.* Routledge.
Johnson, R. (1983). *We: Understand the psychology of romantic love.* Harper Collins.
Jung, C. G. (1921/1971). *The collected works of C. G. Jung: Vol. 6. Psychological types.* Princeton University Press.
Jung, C. G. (1928/1969). The relations between the ego and the unconscious. In *Two essays on analytical psychology* (Vol. 7). Princeton University Press.
Jung, C. G. (1934/1954). The development of personality. In *The development of personality* (Vol. 17). Princeton University Press.
Jung, C. G. (1946/1966). The psychology of the transference. In *The practice of psychotherapy* (Vol. 16). Princeton University Press.

Jung, C. G. (1950/1968). Concerning rebirth. In *The archetypes and the collective unconscious*. Princeton University Press.
Jung, C. G. (1954/1968). The philosophical tree. In *Alchemical studies* (Vol. 13). Princeton University Press.
Jung, C. G. (1954/1968). On the nature of the psyche. In *The structure and dynamics of the psyche* (Vol. 8). Princeton University Press.
Jung, C. G. (1963). *The collected works of C. G. Jung: Vol. 14. Mysterium coniunctionis*. Princeton University Press.
Jung, C. G. (1968). Epilogue. In *Psychology and alchemy* (Vol. 12). Princeton University Press.
Jung, C. G. (1988). *Nietzsche's Zarathustra: Notes on the seminar given in 1934–1939*. Princeton University Press.
Jung, C. G. (1921/1971). *The collected works of C. G. Jung: Vol. 6. Psychological types*. Princeton University Press.
Knox, J. (2003). Trauma and defences: Their roots in relationship. *Journal of Analytical Psychology, 48*(2), 207–233.
Meissner W. W. (2008). Narcissism as motive. *Psychanalytic Quarterly, 78*, 755–798. 10.1002/j.2167–4086.2008.tb00359.x
Pincus A. L. (2013). The pathological narcissism inventory. In J. S. Ogrodniczuk (Ed.), *Understanding and treating pathological narcissism* (pp. 93–110). American Psychological Association. 10.1037/14041-006
Schwartz-Salant, N. (1982). *Narcissism and character transformation*. Inner City Books.
Schwartz, S. (2020). *The absent father effect on daughters: Father desire, father wounds*. Routledge.
Schwartz, S. (2023). *Imposter syndrome and the 'as-if' personality in analytical psychology: Fragility of the self*. Routledge.
Schwartz, S. (2024). *Exploration of the Puella archetype in analytical psychology: Girl unfolding*. Routledge.
Silvestro, K. (2017). *Narcissism and sexuality: A self inflicted wound*. Cambridge Scholars Publishing.
von Franz, M.-L. (1972). *The feminine in fairytales*. Shambhala.
von Franz, M.-L. (2000). *The problem of the puer aeternus*. Inner City Books.

Chapter 9

The shadows of love in relationship

The phrase 'only the shadow knows for sure' reveals the underside of narcissism, a place for exploration but difficult for the narcissist to pursue. We are continually in the process of becoming ourselves, a moving target of various energies with a range from the awkward to the marvellous. This includes what we do not know of the other and the unexpected, challenging us to question and grow, letting in vulnerable and reflective aspects of ourselves and others. Love is not easy for a narcissist as it is hard to feel the reality of being present as themselves. In Jungian thought, this is comparable to recognising and accepting the shadow.

In this chapter the focus is on the shadow, which represents the unconscious, repressed or disowned aspects of an individual's personality that are typically hidden from consciousness. This aligns with the thoughts on love combined with the concept of the *abject*, or what we reject yet is a part of us, from Lacanian psychoanalyst Julia Kristeva. As Jung wrote, 'I falter before the task of finding the language which might adequately express the incalculable paradoxes of love' (1963, p. 353).

Narcissism denotes an exaggerated focus on oneself. The narcissist hides from the shadow with an inflated sense of self-importance and lack of empathy to self or others. These traits often stem from deep-seated insecurities, unresolved emotional wounds and disconnection from their own authenticity. The narcissistic story is a veiled struggle against meaninglessness and unworthiness. A protective system guards the self from the risk of anticipated and repeated experiences of rejection, humiliation and shame. The roots of the negative and internalised self-objects are deeply embedded aspects of the personality. Venturing towards intimacy arouses the doubt and self-hatred lying just at the surface.

The term *narcissism* comes from the name of a common flower, the *narcissus*, whose etymology is reminiscent of the contemporary word 'toxic'. The flower is poisonous, and its name derives from the Greek referring to deadness or numbness. The verb form of the word means to grow numb, and it is the origin of the word *narcotic*. The experiences of both numbness and toxicity replicate those of the narcissist.

The narcissist's overt presentation feigns bravado while covertly, they feel deflated, self-critical, depressed. Both past and present are filled with discomfort and poor self-feelings. The narcissist's past is fraught with perceived misdeeds and micro moments of experiences loaded with the residue of debilitating shame, anguish, despair. Surviving requires avoiding this self-knowledge, obstructing integration of the past to the present. Memory is assumed to have a function, in fact 'a purpose: that is, to release futures – the possible futures that are wishes and desires' (Phillips, 1996, p. 70).

However, the narcissist can be described as one for whom love has become estranged. In love relationships we discover the otherness within ourselves, yet we must be separate to unite. Both processes challenge and threaten the narcissist. Love and consciousness are material and spiritual endeavours and require the presence of self and the other. 'And we could, of course, say that Narcissus was in flight from self-knowledge,' as Adam Phillips (2002, p. 214) wrote.

The narcissist lives in an armoured selfhood, avoiding encountering any other who can possibly wound, limit, shame or reject. The object of narcissistic love feels oppressed and enslaved by the subject's demands and expectations (Knox, 2007, p. 544). Destabilised by the emotional wounds, an internal confusion plunges the narcissist into a longing for Eros, for relatedness and relationship. Yet, it feels impossible as the narcissist is trapped between sets of mutually exclusive alternatives of desire and rejection. The narcissist then exists in a hall of mirrors, a retreat where the self becomes distorted, disguised or shattered into slivers without a means for reflection.

Love

Love is basic. A need? An instinct? A life force? Spirit? Yes, love is all of these and more. In the *Purgatorio*, Canto XXIV (1892), Dante speaks of love:

> Count of me but as one
> Who am the scribe of love; that, when he breathes,
> Take up my pen, and, as he dictates, write.

Our lives involve us in a series of images individually and collectively about love. The mythology and psychology of love reveal the conscious and unconscious elements of relationships. Jung called the contents of the collective unconscious *archetypes*, referring to a prototype or a first model after which other things are patterned.

Love itself can be viewed as an archetype with its movement towards uniting spirit and instinct, self and other, body and psyche. The archetypal love patterns are endless and intriguing, catalysing numerous and unexpected encounters uniquely constellated for each person. Each of us is drawn to different forms of love, depending on our unique wounds and needs. Recognising the mythic dimensions at the basis of personal experiences unites us in the universal nature of what it is to be a human who gives and needs love. The myths recounting these stories are metaphorical representations, and following their narratives allows us to gain insight into the sources of our reactions, behaviours and perceptions. Myths are blueprints for handling situations experienced at each stage of our lives. As Jung (1963, p. 195) exhorted, find your myth and live it to the fullest. Here I've explored the myth of Narcissus and Echo and what it reveals about the singularity and obstructions in love and relatedness prevalent in current forms of narcissism.

Love catalyses the necessary range of elements, unifying what appear as opposites through the individuation process. For the narcissist, however, love does not come through as it remains unseen. The narcissist is absorbed in their own self-interest, or so it appears. The psychological work comes in opening ourselves to be in love, to be loved by someone who can be real. This person, although irritating and unthinking, marvellous and surprising, challenges who we are and changes as we do, naturally. It is these aspects that the narcissist rebels against and turns from. 'The narcissist strives to keep everything of value within the compass of himself because, paradoxically, he is plagued by doubt as to whether there is anything of value within himself' (Colman, 1991, p. 365). Life is not natural but must be controlled and managed.

There are various forms of narcissism, each one effective for interrupting relationship. For the narcissist, self-cohesion is disturbed, driven by vulnerability and fear of others due to the fragility of the self. The narcissist is not only grandiose but also has a personality composed of finely tuned projections. These are based on feeling small, inadequate and unable to let anyone in due to the shaky self. This manifests in an unrealistic appraisal of the narcissist's attributes. There is a limiting and harsh scenario run by internal saboteurs, demonic, operating against love and relationship, maintaining singularity as preferable and safer.

For the narcissist, self-representation – who I am – and the definition of their being are all unquestioned consciously. The anxiety about being seen heightens as relationships with others are assumed to be precarious and threatening. Underneath is an idealisation of others, making them feel powerless and unconfident, weak, dependent and insecure. As Marcel Proust opined in the late 1800s, 'The hard and fast lines with which we circumscribe love arise solely from out of complete ignorance of life' (1919/1957, part 2, p. 85).

This process is a road littered with the recognition of loss and melancholia, beginning with those originating situations that are still unconscious but tinged with suffering. Fragility indicates the cracked, dissociated parts and unmet narcissistic needs. Held within are these parts intensely calling to pursue the psychological depths and access love.

But living and loving means encountering the shadow. For the narcissist, examining self and relationships in ways that are unfamiliar, unsettling and difficult, destabilises, disrupts and challenges. Jungian psychology is founded on the recognition of these splits and dissociations in the psyche. When acknowledged they lead to union of self and other. Therefore, understanding and integrating the shadow is a crucial part of psychological growth and self-awareness. Jung noted,

> But if you hate and despise yourself – if you have not accepted your pattern – then there are hungry animals (prowling cats and other beasts and vermin) in

your constitution which get at your neighbours like flies in order to satisfy the appetites which you have failed to satisfy.

(1988, p. 502)

Arising from its matrix of complex bonds for begetting aliveness and expressing connection, love brings change. It is composed of many elements – illusions, limits, disappointments and idealisations, exposure, sufferings, failures and paradox. Love leads us into the roots of the psyche. The dimensions of otherness are interrelated and constitute the biggest threat and greatest opportunity to the narcissist.

Love is where truth appears, yet it can become a subject of self-idealisation, especially for the narcissist. Yet, as Julia Kristeva asks, 'How can I be without a border?' (1982, p. 4). This reminds us we are defined, not merged with others, and we are each separate with boundaries. Within our boundaries, we retain a sense of self-responsibility, choice and possibility. The way to accomplish this is without a delusion of unity but a primacy of self, including others. Love is fed by considering the heterogeneous in all its psychological, emotional and social aspects.

Julia Kristeva recognised the powerful and inextricable relationship between love of self and love of the other. Often self-love is perceived as pathology in our modern world where the paradox is that Narcissus represents both the fatal error and sublime value (DeArmitt, 2014, p. 54). Yet, narcissists are short-changing themselves. Instead of the total picture, they shut off anything outside themselves, refusing to turn towards the other and failing to love.

Love holds both the promise and abyss. The nature of love itself is a state whose very structure presupposes a disturbance of identity. The flexible and adaptable subjectivity is built on an unstable, ever evolving yet firm sense of self and other. Accepting and embracing this attitude disrupts the exclusionary tendencies of the narcissist. Julia Kristeva described love as absorbing 'my narcissistic needs, erotic desires, phantasmatic ideals ... also the place where stability carries within it the risk of dissolving ... and the risks of abandonment, separation or rupture' (2010, p. 162). Narcissus could not take these risks and could not go towards a true, loving recognition of Self, including its natural differences.

The abject

What Julia Kristeva called the *abject* represents a breakdown and has to do with 'what disturbs identity, system and order' (1982, p. 4). She noted the effect of the other as the catalyst for the return of repressed otherness, the abject, the human part in the self, often ascribed with disgust. The complex arena of the abject pushes beyond what are considered the safe and necessary margins, acknowledges something has happened, fallen, dissolved, decayed to its basic self. Kristeva described this as the 'corporeal embodiment of consciousness and constitutive ambiguity of perception and sexuality' (2010, p. 104).

When the psychic space is taken over by negative extremes, love may be associated with destruction. As Kristeva remarked: 'Narcissus in love hides the suicidal Narcissus. Left to itself, without the assistance of projection upon the other, the Ego takes itself for a preferential target of aggression and murder' (1987, p. 124). Inherently fragile, easily shattered, doubt, fear, regret, threatened by the less than perfect, the personal isolation of the narcissist inclines toward self-aggression. Narcissus was unable to distinguish between internal and exterior perception and unable to master these, he perished (Kristeva, 1987, p. 116). The persisting isolation and singularity of narcissism makes the narcissist into the living dead, unreal to themselves, depersonalised and enclosed in their own capsule. 'The self-love of the immature psyche is from the narcissistic wounds paradoxically constituting a scar at the suture of being and meaning' (Kristeva, 1992, p. 129).

The loneliness of the narcissist is profound while the effect of the other is associated with vulnerability to the self. Narcissists needs illusions to protect the fragile psyche. Their melancholy is a sadness bound with the loss of something that really occurred but in another and earlier form. Kristeva defines narcissism as 'a screen over emptiness' (1987, p. 23). Narcissism, according to Kristeva, is thus a defence against what would otherwise be recognising and enduring the emptiness of separation (1987, p. 3). One of the distinctive characteristics of the melancholic is they cannot find the words to adequately express emotional losses, and this prevents future love from being developed as the deadened past continues to haunt the present.

Kristeva defined 'the narcissism which imagines itself to be threatened, effectively turns into a "hatred of oneself" and withdrawal into a sullen, warm and private world, unnameable and biological, the impregnable "aloofness" of a weird primal paradise' (1993, pp. 2–3). She includes in this reference family, ethnicity, nation and race, all constituting and supporting a defensiveness, hatred and certainly a misunderstanding of those who are not the same. These insecure and paranoid aspects of narcissism fuel the obsessive worship of their own self while rejecting anything else. This describes the tendency to narcissistic fusion that denies the existence of otherness. The narcissist presents the dilemma of untangling the false from the real.

Julia Kristeva references this occurring in the analytical transferences, highlighting the borders of subjectivity sensitive to any disruption and causing destabilising effects (1991, p. 91). Narcissism resists and cannot take in the reality that love of self and other are enriched when together but need not be the same. Kristeva noted, 'We learn that the movement toward individuation, which can only take place through loving identification and transference, entails that the "I" lose itself in the Other and find itself (transformed) in and through this Other' (DeArmitt, 2014, p. 59).

The amatory discourse with its unconscious narcissistic foundations of self-love is necessary for there to be love of the other. This determines the choice of a love object and how one opens to the other. Love preserves the psychic life as the psyche renews itself from being open to differences.

Body abjection

Julia Kristeva's work links the body to the psychological, notably through her concept of the abject, considered a potentially harmful entity that is refused and cannot or will not be assimilated. Kristeva commented that this represented the secret and unknown wounds that can drive a person to wander (1992, p. 267). The abject signifies the foreigner within, referring to a person's sense of being that might also be unknown or unacceptable. Kristeva contended that what is foreign to oneself is a part of oneself that has been excluded and marginalised. Abjection in its psychological and physical form is the human reaction to a threatened breakdown, conceived as something that betrays, defiles, stigmatises and upsets one's sense of certainty. Kristeva further described the abject as something both terrifying and intriguing. Abjection is the phenomenon of tossing away what is felt to be the undesirable elements of life accompanied by the affective responses of disgust. Abjection is activated when the narcissist feels unable to incorporate experiences or symbolise them. However, ignoring the abject is a violence against nature because it is the natural expression of the personality calling to be understood.

Narcissus enacts the abject in his attitudes of rejection, not seeing Echo or others, ignoring their pleas. In reaction and sorrow, Echo's body gradually wastes away and disappears. This abjection is enacted in many forms of eating disorders and various narcissistic reactions to early emotional wounds. The figure of Echo, what she symbolises about the feminine, signifies her body then and now as abject. Echo lost her body from lack of love. She also colluded with her body regarded as abject, put aside, sacrificed and ignored.

The abject includes any entity compromising or threatening the existence of the self. Psychologically, physically and culturally what Julia Kristeva described as the abject are the unprocessed, rejected elements, the past traumas needing to be mourned. These reoccur in love relationships and need to be recognised consciously as they embody the potential of healing. When unrecognised they become destructive against love and loving. The concept is parallel to Jung's premise of the shadow representing the negated, submerged and denied aspects of physical and emotional life calling attention to be integrated. This reminds me of Jung's comment on the shadow, 'assimilating the thing a person has no wish to be' (Jung, 1954, CW 16, para. 470).

These are the strangers within we do not know, and we encounter them through love relationships. Both Jung and Kristeva acknowledge the outer as well as the inner manifestations of the disconnections when the unity of the self becomes splintered and fragmented, unable to connect to others. Julia Kristeva noted what is foreign to oneself is part of oneself. Jung's concept of the shadow comprises the parts resisted, the others awaiting integration, the unconscious personal and collective aspects, the multicultural nature of the psyche including the yet to be and still unknown.

Hints of these shadows are cast early in life, forming our vulnerabilities and wounds. Their unconscious memories create an estranged and melancholic language. Jung commented, 'To the degree [a person] does not admit the validity of the other, [they] deny the "other" within [themselves] the right to exist – and vice versa. The capacity for inner dialogue is a touchstone for outer objectivity' (1957/1969, CW 8, para. 187).

Narcissism is the search to be loved or admired, the sole object of attention, surrounded with those who see the narcissist as perfect or ideal. The narcissist doesn't love themself in what is misapprehended as self-sufficiency; they seek to procure an image of superiority. Narcissism aims to 'be loved as the idealization normally given to the object is usurped and one becomes one's own ideal' (Freud, 1914, pp. 74–75). In other words, the love for the other is transferred into themself in a move towards isolation and singularity. The superiority the narcissist expresses through the perfected image betrays the inferiority they feel. Depersonalised, lacking self-love, they are without their own good thoughts, body or feelings.

The confrontation with the unconscious, the shadow or the abject brings about a relative dissolution of the ego and its reconstruction in which both the conscious and unconscious play integral parts. However, the narcissist only loves the images or sensations derived from looking inwards and those focused on grand objects, owing to their inner demands for perfection. The ego feels anxiety while the defences and projections are enacted from the fantasised experience of external space demanding to be filled with eternal adulation. Narcissus is desired by Echo and others, yet he remains completely unobtainable and unreachable – as if he wishes to retain all his desirable qualities for himself. He drowns in this desire but remains unconsciousness it is for himself.

Crime to oneself

The following is a common dream. Is it a surprise? No. So many people become performers, acting against themselves, unreal; narcissists frantically need something, but they do not, knowing what it is, therefore nothing fulfils. As Jung said, dreams are

> pure nature; they show us the unvarnished, natural truth, and are therefore fitted, as nothing else is, to give us back an attitude that accords with our basic human nature when our consciousness has strayed too far from its foundations and run into an impasse.
>
> (Jung, 1934/1970, CW 10, para. 317)

For years Peter has a repetitive dream he commits a crime. Initially the crime is indistinct. The dream bothers him. *In time the dream escalates from his being an accomplice to a murder to becoming the main killer.* The reasons for this are never given in the dream. Who and why is he killing? Again, no reasons are given in the dream. The shock upon awakening is the acknowledgement he has done the crime. 'Oh, no,' he would exclaim in dismay. He is not conscious the crime is still going on and becomes upset by the dream message. The dream image portrays avoidance of self-responsibility and reveals his self-betrayal and lack of self-knowledge.

Rather than listening and reflecting, however, he tries to escape the dream, often not mentioning in therapy the dream's recurrence and the degree to which it upset him until later. He resists attending to his unconscious, not listening to the voices within. This attempt to remain unconscious is also part of the crime noted in the dream. And it is part of what makes it difficult to deal with and sometimes even to work with narcissists in psychological treatment. Like Peter, they do not appear to value the relationship and might behave with dismissiveness in therapy, creating chaos or boredom rather than interaction. Peter is not curious about any views other than his own and finds them hard to accept.

And then Peter's dream abruptly stops. Now he associates the dream to the harshness of his work, the deception and high-powered force he must muster; even though, he now realises this does not reflect his real self. When he stops being under the gun of this part of his personality, the dream desists. Over time, he becomes what he calls softer, more open, a yoga person and less the politico. He likes the yoga part but says it does not make money nor manifest in the aggressive push he needs, although the yoga aspects are better for forming relationships. Yet he remains alone, without love, fearful of intimacy and needing control, all signalling narcissism.

When in a relationship, Peter is subject to losing the Psyche side of himself, and Eros is only functional as erotic, not relational. Peter, like Narcissus, refuses the sensuous and spirit of Eros. He turns from the appeal of Echo; even though, he says he wants and desires a relationship. Peter is aware enough to observe love translates into his loss of self. But he can do nothing about this. He jumps into the other person and, because of separation anxiety, ends up being demanding, possessive and manipulative. He describes the bottom going out of his personality, and he distrusts the connection. As he feels so precarious, attention and love must always be on his terms, and he buys love through expensive presents, showering lovers with attention to get what he wants yet remaining in control, and watchful as it can all fall apart. Peter is envious of his current partner possibly turning to any other and needs constant attention to reassure himself of his value. For him, the affects take on a 'primitive, powerful, archetypal form because they were known, humanized, and managed by the ego. It is vital these elements are owned rather than denied, or they wreak havoc on the personality' (West, 2008, p. 378).

Peter's actions are typical of one who fears intimacy. Once his emotions are aroused, Peter reacts, anticipating love will disappear. And here is part of the significance of the crime dream. Emotional relationships are uncomfortable, and Peter panics as he cannot manage the intensity or threat of intimacy. He internally decomposes and falls apart. Therefore, he cannot give up control and kills the connection. To avoid any fragility being exposed, he just leaves when disappointed. Disappointment cannot be seen, and dependency is impossible as he needs to just be adored all the time. He remains torn between his desire for closeness and his fear of losing himself in the relationship. So he tries to possess the other, yet he remains with a gnawing insecurity no matter what. Despite his wish for relationship, he did not know what to do with intimacy besides have sex. He does not know Eros in relationship other than the erotic. Not speaking of love, he says he can turn the sex switch on or off. Confidence and trust, Psyche and Eros, Narcissus and Echo remain separate, yet undifferentiated.

He appears fickle as he goes from one relationship to another, searching. Something is always unsatisfying. He has to be right, and the other person never gives him enough. Peter tries to turn inwards but is easily deflected from himself. He struggles to face what he does not want to know. In the analysis nothing seems meaningful except his own words, and the rapidity of his speech masks his feelings of emptiness, void and the threat of disintegration. The analytic relationship itself must be held at a distance as it too carries a threat of him disappearing into what he cannot trust with another person.

In another dream, the pharmacy will not give Peter a prescription for pain because he lacks the correct government identity. He wonders whether he has ever been himself, what his self is and who he is. Behind him is a voice saying and repeating, 'The shadow knows'. The dream is quite direct about what he needs – an identity, including the shadow. And it also implies he cannot avoid feeling the discomforting process of self-discovery through taking medication. There is no quick fix.

Peter is a man in his forties with a history of lack in attachment beginning with parental figures. In his family, mother was the star, and he was a star to her. Mother adored him, thought he was better than anyone, and this encouragement seemed to inflate his personality but created an unreality within him and perpetuated a distorted and superior view of himself. Mother had been so available; he was used to getting attention all the time. He could not deal with disappointments and took them as rejection. He was his mother's favourite and was encouraged to believe he would one day be important in the world. The sense of omnipotence was prominent, and he believed he could have whatever he wanted and on his terms. Father was present, but only vaguely as a background figure who showed little emotional reaction and worked at a managerial-level job. Peter did not respect him and tended to dismiss he could have any effect from father. His goals and needs were grander. The representation of father as a solid and supportive figure bypassed Peter who staunchly denied being at all like his father. Peter never explored the obvious tie with mother and rejection with father as part of his inability to form a lasting relationship. Yet, like any aspect of narcissism, this could be too easy of an answer, although it could lead us into the complexity the narcissist represents.

Wanting to appear better than he feels, Peter lies. His sense of inner inadequacy propels his lies and self-deceptions. Not realising this, a narcissist desperately covers any assumed flaws and the lies only make the situation worse. He learns to repress, not emote, but then how can he love? Where is his centre? How can he see himself if he was unseen and continues to repeat this familiar scenario? The psychological harm magnifies; the power positions ossify; the flexibility of personality is sacrificed. When in a relationship, Peter pursues various modes of emotional protection and avenues of psychological escape. His inner dilemmas heighten in intensity, creating upset and resulting in more insecurity. He fears the demise of the false coverings and cannot chance exposure of the real, so Peter uses his wealth to deny, control and ignore his self. Money and power cover his insecurities. And his lies.

Peter unconsciously is enacting 'an aggressive aspect of the narcissistic self-state achieved by killing any loving dependent self and identifying almost entirely with the destructive narcissistic parts of the self which provides them with a sense of superiority and self-admiration' (Bollas, 1992, p. 198). This represents an incomplete and divided self composed of myriad different voices in a repetitious process leading nowhere. The transgressions are against any self or movement towards change. Peter was like Sisyphus in the Greek myth where he pushes the rock up the hill only to have it roll down again and up and down over and over – no change, no growth, no other path available.

The crime dream, like in the Greek myth of Sisyphus rolling the rock up and down the hill, shocks Peter and the dream's repetition will not let him go, insisting on gaining awareness. The dream illustrates he is betraying himself but is unconscious of this travesty against his personality. But Peter listens to no one. Needing to be in control he hardly stops talking in the therapy. I have to interrupt his monologue many times. The problem for Peter, as for many narcissists, is to find safety with self and others so he can emerge from the defensive shell protecting his insecurities and be seen intimately, letting in others.

Peter, unbeknownst to himself, is reacting to the environmental and constitutional deficit he experienced early in life. The learned reaction is to cover his fragility while being protected and adulated. Here is where the defences of the self begin in earnest. This narcissistic and false-self organisation are the façade, contributing to the 'as-if' personality formation. Peter experiences yet denies his dependency, vulnerability and loneliness that expose the need for others. To feel otherwise is obviously fallacious. Rather, it seems Peter cannot admit the needs of a precarious self. This is reinforced by ejecting and abjecting any vulnerable feelings, or anything and anyone reeking of any failure.

In adulthood, the defences fail against the depression, and vain attempts at reparation do not work while feelings of impotence become dominant. The thing that endures is a dull psychic pain, characterised by the incapacity to attach. 'In all, the subject's objects remain constantly at the limit of the ego, not wholly within, and not quite without ... for the place is occupied, in its centre' (Green, 1986, pp. 153–154). In Peter, I find the narcissistic defence against difference. It creates adhesive identification serving the avoidance of reality (West, 2010, p. 479). At root is the mental pain of the self refusing the other. The failure is the narcissist does not find the other in love while love is seeking the other as equal, not as a minor character in their story.

'Seeking the Self too quickly, unable to handle depth or approach the unconscious, there is little containing capacity' (Beebe, 2008, p. 11). The narcissist struggles, deprived of the means to access the wisdom in the Self. The process of individuation means working with the foreign, repressed and projected material formerly separating self from other, body from mind. Avoidance of the shadow or any difference is threatening and can erupt in creating a façade, a fascination to deflect the envy, repulsion, shame, strangeness felt acutely by the narcissist. Although in the analysis Peter verbalises wanting love, it seems an impenetrable issue. There is a frantic flurry of activity, glitz of trips, buying objects, anything to shore himself up and get attention from whoever his current partner is. Then he destroys it all with his fearful yet controlling ego force, leaving the deeper connection to the self dangling.

The narcissistic wounds are fragmentations in the mirror reflecting a fragile sense of self-worth and promoting the need for fantastic performances. The idealised self is stored away in deeply private places and a substitute self is put in its place. One becomes less present. Peter has trouble being authentic, loathe to relinquish the need to perform, dropping the façade and being real. For Peter, the task is to acknowledge the despair and find dialogue between his mental life and his body made abject and imprisoned without tenderness.

The narcissist represents the tragic condition of many people lacking love. 'These persons' real symptom is being lost in the "narcissism of small things", overfilled with everything superfluous yet lacking substance. They are also uprooted from any existential, spiritual meaning by the negative and centerless feeling' (Carta, 2015, p. 743). Narcissists like Peter come into analysis because they are beginning to feel something missing from their lives. They cannot name it, as the malaise is all-corrosive, imprecise and alienating from themselves. 'The melancholic patient is hounded by his constant self-accusations, depressed moods pressing the person into the cold depths of the psyche' (p. 744).

Even so and regardless of how hard it is for Peter to let anyone in, gradually through psychological treatment, words emerge to express the underlying chaos and disruption. From acknowledging and bearing with myself as the therapist, together we face the challenge of consciousness and the evolution of his psychological rebalancing towards love. The journey is not fast or easy and takes much patience by both of us as we stay on the pathway towards his Self.

Psychic wounds

In the myth of Narcissus, the blind seer Tiresias tells his mother Narcissus will not live if he gets to know himself. The message in this myth is present in the unconscious of us all, to some extent. It implies knowing oneself and opening to the other. Emergence involves death and change from the former emotional experiences with imprints and wounds to the psyche.

> Certain complexes arise after painful or unpleasant experiences in the life of the individual. They are personal experiences of an emotional nature, which leave lasting psychic wounds behind them. A bad experience of this often crushes valuable qualities in an individual. All these create unconscious complexes of a personal nature ... A great many autonomous complexes arise in this way.
> (Jung, 1954/1969, CW 8, para. 594)

These are the obstacles and openings to psychological development into the unknown and new, the different and other, departing from what was familiar and imagined to provide comfort but did not.

These restrictive isolated attitudes and emotional lacks pass down through the generations. Though appearing confident, inwardly narcissists are stuck and lost. The lack of healthy reflection interferes with the ability to form a relationship with the Self, although the longing to do so persists (Silvestro, 2013, p. 5). However, Narcissus is empty. The myth portrays Narcissus's inability to feel much emotion for anyone, revealing the destructive, numbing quality of narcissism. He can see in the pond where he gazes but cannot embrace what he sees. All is watery, ethereal. The Narcissus myth provides a rich symbolic meaning of the psychological complexities, the lack of relational authenticity and the pain and longing afflicting everyone touched by this dynamic (Silvestro, 2013, p. 15).

Narcissistic mother and a daughter's disappearance

In the presence of her narcissistic mother, Aziz described knowing she could not appear too much and was to melt into the wall – a child without needs or wants. There was just no room allotted to her. Striking in demeanour and appearance, Mother was like a diva, a grand person, wanting all the attention. As there was no way to be seen, Aziz adopted an attitude of being low maintenance. She was raised to serve and care for family from her Middle Eastern cultural heritage. In all relationships she complied to please the other and asked for nothing and no attention. In this scenario, her needs were unmet by anyone but herself and she knew to not expect anything else as she had no other experience. Consequently, as an adult she had an emotionally empty, long-term marriage without intimacy. How could she want what she had not experienced or knew existed?

Although close to her father and recognised by him, he relied on her to love him unconditionally. Through his affairs and mercurial business dealings, she remained loyal to him. He supported her independence and her professional endeavours, her ability to make money so she could help support the family. He was special to her, but she did not confide her unhappiness to him. Father was preoccupied with work and affairs, rarely seen with mother, unless for public show. In her mind he was better than mother and gave more. Her heart and soul seemed lost or perhaps just undeveloped with either parent because there was little modelling for the expression of affectionate love. As Aziz explained, she was not used to being seen and did not know it. She did not realise this until recently. And she did not see herself that she had been hiding; she had not thought of it. Her avoidance of being seen led to inner and outer effects and of all this she had been unaware.

In her dream a woman appeared wrapped in a veil. She was naked and both seen and unseen as her figure behind the veil was indistinct. The veil was not only significant in her culture but also represented the estrangement Aziz felt within it. As Aziz grew, she found herself ambivalent to cultural dictates. Aziz interpreted the veil as an image replicating how she felt, wrapped up and alone, her body, mind and soul veiled and protected, seen but unseen. This veil protected her body and her psyche. She did not easily share emotionally, and the dream was a statement about the emotions kept within, veiled. Her heart and mind were secluded from others. The veil was transparent but simultaneously opaque. This is how she learned to be in her family where both the narcissistic mother and equally, although differently self-absorbed father did not really see her. In the dream no face was perceived, and no words were spoken. In addition, the veil can also be an image of herself to herself, seen and unseen at the same time.

Aziz explained this dream figure was like a guardian angel, directing and supporting but not talking, no overt affection or reaching out, a distant but reliable figure. She took the veil to represent her struggle for women's rights, a position exposing her to danger in her culture. This symbol carried many meanings for her and connected her to roots she wanted to sever yet were integral to her identity.

Aziz's mother was unreachable and self-absorbed, unable to see or appreciate her daughter's nature. The self had to be veiled because being seen met with competition from mother who did not understand her emotional or attachment needs. Mother was just not present as she was absorbed in taking all the attention; she was cold, like an ice queen, disparaging, ignoring and lacking affection. Aziz has few memories of encouragement from mother or anyone else although she said she felt loved. Mostly she was to keep everything within and do it all on her own.

Aziz was to remain small, without needs. *Her dream themes often showed her with a woman in the distance whose back was turned from her. The other woman says nothing. There is no touch or affection displayed. She is just there. Sometimes there is a girl and woman but again no verbal or apparent communication.*

She learned to keep everything precious to her secret and safely tucked away within. No one knew the whole story. She could not afford to trust. However, her prolific dream life is restoring her. She is now beginning to access the imaginal world she developed as a child. Over time, and slowly, slowly in dream after dream the woman began coming towards her. By sharing these dreams in analysis, their value multiplied with our interest in exploring her inner and outer world. The dream dramas unfolded to reshape her personality. The dreams freed her to experience the many layers of her being, the parts of the self previously isolated within. She was gradually coming to less self-abjection, which coincided with more honesty with her partner and less avoidance. It remained unclear how much love and intimacy could evolve for her or between them, but she was more open to the possibilities.

An imbalance in a person's psyche is often related to the underdevelopment of the true self. Distress emphasises transformational needs and potential renewal. Beneath the anxiety and fears, a tenderness towards the self is needed to mediate contact with reality, to waken from the frozen torpor of the near-living or half-death of narcissism. Rather, by pursuing the meaning in the isolation and apprehension of love, the narcissist can become unblocked, opening to the capacity for the owned, embodied and cherished vulnerability. Along with this is release of the potency of the unconscious emerging into love in conscious life.

Narcissism and love demonstrate everything is interrelated and contextual and enact how reality is constructed. Characters and their realities function within the scenes of our lives and frequently shift. The challenge of love for the narcissist becomes how to open to and express this reality. The psyche is not static; it is always transient, interconnected, full of paradox, morphing between thesis and antithesis, operating within a larger system of the unconscious layer under the surface.

'Borges and I', a classic page-long story by the Argentine writer Jorge Luis Borges (1964), illustrates this process and presents the conundrum within it. How are we to distinguish between Borges, the living, breathing human being, and the affected and somewhat dandyish persona depicted in his writings? It raises questions about the difference between self and persona, who we truly are and who we pretend to be. The story reveals a way to capture the whole of reality in a single page. Although the two characters share certain tastes and characteristics, it's 'the other one' who has a 'perverse custom of falsifying and magnifying things. ... Thus, my life is a flight and I lose everything and everything belongs to oblivion, or to him' (Borges, 1964, p. 246). Ultimately, the author concludes the writer's projection of himself is the one who will endure. In the paradox defining this story the question is also of shadow and abject, self and other, as Borges concludes, 'I do not know which of us has written this page' (p. 246).

References

Alighieri, D. (1892). *The divine comedy: The vision of hell, purgatory, and paradise* (H. F. Cary, Trans.). Cassell & Company.

Beebe, J. (2008). Attitudes toward the unconscious. *Journal of Analytical Psychology*, *41*(1), 3–20.

Bollas, C. (1992). *Being a character: Psychoanalysis and self experience*. Routledge.

Borges, J. L. (1964). 'Borges and I.' In *Labyrinths* (J. E. Irby, Trans.). New Directions Publishing.

Carta, S. (2015). [Review of the film *Melancholia*, directed by L. von Trier]. *Journal of Analytical Psychology*, *60*(5), 741–751.

Colman, W. (1991). Envy, self-esteem and the fear of separation. *British Journal of Psychotherapy*, *7*(4), 356–367.

DeArmitt, P. (2014). *The right to narcissism: A case for an impossible self-love*. Fordham University Press.

Freud, S. (1914). On narcissism. In J. Strachey (Trans.), *The standard edition of the complete psychological works of Sigmund Freud: Vol. XIV. On the history of the psycho-analytic movement, papers on metapsychology and other works* (pp. 67–102). Hogarth Press.

Green, A. (1986). The dead mother. In *On private madness*. International Universities Press.

Jung, C. G. (1934/1970). The meaning of psychology for modern man. In *Civilization in transition* (Vol. 10). Princeton University Press.

Jung, C. G. (1954). The psychology of the transference. In *The practice of psychotherapy* (Vol. 16). Princeton University Press.

Jung, C. G. (1954/1969). On the nature of the psyche. In *The structure and dynamics of the psyche* (Vol. 8). Princeton University Press.

Jung, C. G. (1957/1969). The transcendent function. In *The structure and dynamics of the psyche* (Vol. 8). Princeton University Press.
Jung, C. G. (1963). *Memories, dreams, reflections.* Vintage.
Jung, C. G. (1988). *Nietzsche's Zarathustra: Notes on the seminar given in 1934–1939.* Princeton University Press.
Knox, J. (2007). The fear of love: The denial of self in relationship. *Journal of Analytical Psychology, 52*(5), 543–563.
Kristeva, J. (1982). *Powers of horror: An essay on abjection* (L. S. Roudiez, Trans.). Colombia University Press.
Kristeva, J. (1987). *Tales of love* (L. S. Roudiez, Trans.). Columbia University Press.
Kristeva, J. (1991). *Strangers to ourselves.* Columbia University Press.
Kristeva, J. (1992). *Black sun* (L. S. Roudiez, Trans.). Columbia University Press.
Kristeva, J. (1993). *Nations without nationalism.* Columbia University Press.
Kristeva, J. (2010). *Hatred and forgiveness* (J. Herman, Trans.). Columbia University Press.
Moi, T. (Ed.). (1991). *The Kristeva reader.* Columbia University Press.
Phillips, A. (1996). *On flirtation.* Harvard University Press.
Phillips, A. (2002). *Promises, promises.* Basic Books.
Proust, M. (1919/1957). *Within a budding grove: In search of lost time, part 2.* Chatto and Windus.
Silvestro, K. (2013). *Narcissism and sexuality.* Create Space Publishing.
West, M. (2008). The narrow use of the term ego in analytical psychology: the 'not-I' is also who I am. *Journal of Analytical Psychology, 53*, 367–388.
West, M. (2010). Envy and difference. *Journal of Analytical Psychology, 55*(4), 459–484.

Chapter 10

The analytical bridge to Self through cultural diversity

In a Chinese legend 'The Cowherd and the Weaver Girl,' the Cowherd and the Weaver Girl will meet on a bridge of magpies across the Milky Way once a year. The story tells of the love between Zhinü (織女), the weaver girl who symbolises the star Vega, and Niulang (牛郎), the cowherd who symbolises the star Altair. Because their love was forbidden, they were banished to opposite sides of the Milky Way. Once a year, on the seventh day of the seventh lunar month, a flock of magpies form a bridge to reunite the lovers for a single day. There are many variations of the story; however, the earliest-known reference to this famous myth dates back more than 2600 years to a poem in the *Classic of Poetry*, the oldest collection of Chinese Poetry (Schomp, 2009, p. 89).

This chapter explores the clinical issues encompassing complex therapeutic problems relating to contemporary Jungian analytic theory and practice. It includes transferences that expose the issues of aloneness and the pathways to relationship integral to analytical work. The process weaves in and out of the myriad unconscious and conscious communications of both participants, opening to the Self as the fuller composition of the personality with all its light and shadow. As poet Stanley Kunitz writes, he wandered through a dark night of the soul and a voice told him to 'live in the layers' (2002). The analytic contract issues from 'the inevitable discontent a person feels arising also from the inability to find a discourse for love or to speak with a lover's discourse' towards themselves and others (DeArmitt, 2014, p. 56).

Clinical example: Lin

The composite clinical example is a woman I will call Lin, a woman of mixed cultures, Chinese and American, pulled between historical and contemporary clashes. The tale of 'The Cowherd and the Weaver Girl' symbolically enacts traversing the bridge of Lin's own lived experience within the mixture of cultures as both a minority and a woman, and the forces – personal, collective and unconscious – propelling her. The cultural devices link to the unfolding self in the analytic process. The narcissistic aspect is the singularity of Lin, her hiddenness and struggle to be seen, for authenticity and intimacy. As André Green described, 'The analytic situation reveals meaning ... It brings from absence to potentiality, and then makes it actual' (1986, p. 293).

How we define both self and other shifts when portions of self are forbidden in one culture but not another. This affects the physical and emotional, subtle and incompatible as a person enters into relationship both with other people and themselves.

Raised by Chinese parents who left China years ago to reside in the USA, Lin was continually in conflict with their differing cultural values and ways of life. *In a dream she and her current dating partner, a white American male, are crossing a bridge. He is the driver, and she does not know where they are going.* The dream repeats. Although brief, the dream itself is a bridge, and it is unclear where they are coming from or where they are going.

The meeting with the other is crucial for encountering one's narcissistic defences. Arrival and erasure, promise and excuse constitute two sides of the same oscillating aporia of self-cancelling and self-discovery. 'The narcissistic omnipotent object relations are partly defensive against the recognition of the separateness of self and object' (Colman, 1991, p. 359). From the stance of narcissistic singularity, Lin asks, 'What is this other? What does the other have I don't? What do I want?' Lin is in conflict about loving herself with appreciation and acceptance. Future growth and fulfilment will entail feeling centred, rather than off centre, and cohesive rather than split, full rather than emptied, confident rather than fearful of internal and external connections.

From the lonely position of the narcissist, the world is difficult; the fear of challenge from others and the need to be loved by them is paramount. All these are ingredients for the analytical journey, but the question is how to access the trust needed for entry into the personality. Failure to grasp these sensitive and hidden dynamics may lead therapists to miss the opportunities to assist their clients in the meaningful unfolding of their life and destiny. This can subtly perpetuate the series of unconscious and perhaps tragic cycles and patterns. Believing they know another culture can be a fiction therapists cling to in the face of a schema reflecting their assumptions, their own insecurity or even lack of curiosity.

Symbolically, the bridge in Lin's dream anticipates traversing the road of the personal and cultural influences. This will mean encountering shadows from the past bleeding into the present and future. It implicates the differences explored for deepening mutuality and uncovering the dissociations and disconnected complexes of her personality. These attitudes hold implications for developing the sense of self as gained through the Jungian process of individuation. The concepts explored are the transference, the shadow, complexes and healing through the transcendent function as it is activated in the therapeutic and analytical relationship.

Like Narcissus, who could love no other than himself, the narcissistic individual is self-absorbed and defensively involved with themselves. There are no bridges across which to relate or value others. Such narcissism is a compensation for early and deeply harming narcissistic wounds obstructing and often destroying the bridges to a true Self. The individual is left with an idealised and illusory self, but it has become rootless and fragile. Thus, the narcissist lacks bridges to their own Self or to other persons or groups. They remain vulnerable, isolated, feel insubstantial and without reliable guidelines or the understanding to steer relationships towards the intimate connections between self and others. This can be acquired in the therapeutic and analytical relationship.

The process involves investment in the capacity to question, decompose and bring together the personality into another form. The symbolic events and dreams provide the inner and outer process of analytical work, imaging access to the transcendent function as the bridge to the more complete Self. The symbol is a 'use of metaphor to transfer meaning and serves as a bridge between domains of experience, creating a novel route for their re-combination' (Winborn, 2022, p. 89).

The analyst might feel the process is blocked and going nowhere, as time after time any small moment of insight or of affective contact gained in one session might disappear by the next, sucked into a whirlpool of stasis and nothingness. In this mire both analyst and patient can become 'frozen in an indefinite and futile waiting in which the failure of the process becomes masked by an idealization of analysis and an inflated over evaluation of its possibilities' (Connolly, 2007, p. 43).

This situation refers to the need for the analyst to provide a temporary psychic skin to metaphorically hold the patient. British Jungian analyst Bani Shorter said individuation is a 'movement through liminal space and time, from disorientation to integration... What takes place in the dark phase of liminality is a process of breaking down... in the interest of making whole one's meaning, purpose and sense of relatedness once more' (Shorter, 1988, pp. 73, 79). This liminal space, between conscious and unconscious, is as full of creative potential as it is of disastrous ruin, the stuff of madness, spiritual realisation and artistic inspiration.

As Jung said, 'The patient needs you (the analyst) in order to unite her dissociated personality in your unity, calm and security ... The patient will get out of you what she needs' (Jung, 1929, pp. xxxii–xxxiii). Although paramount, the narcissist has difficulty recognising the subjectivity of the analyst. In the confrontation with otherness, the meeting with what we do not know of the other or of ourselves, entangles us in desire and lack, and this initiates a skirmish for recognition. Although desired, it is difficult for the narcissist as envy, jealousy and passive aggressiveness are common reactions. The person quickly 'intuits their own deficiency, one sidedness, singularity, threat and it seems there is something which although it belongs to its own essence, it lacks' (Mills, 2019, p. 7). This defence, although maladaptive, becomes erected against registering the full impact of the core issues and what seem to be their problematic solutions. Having gone on for so long, it is not unusual for the narcissist to hesitate to move beyond what substituted for the truth of themself.

Lin is questioning who she is authentically. Analysis helps break down the restrictions, the façades of persona and complexes stifling language and imprisoning understanding. Complexes are either the cause or the effect of the conflict whether internal or external, the vulnerable points carrying truths perhaps unknown or even unwanted. The transferences illustrate these conflicts arising from the unconscious.

They become conscious so Lin can move beyond the voices clashing loudly from her mixed cultural background. She wants to belong but not lose her identity.

She has felt a lack, an uncertainty, a split into multiple roles. The analysis builds a bridge between new and old attitudes for rescuing her beleaguered self. Cultural conflicts create mental conflicts exacerbated by the desire to divest herself of ancestral claims and assimilate into the dominant culture. This creates separation anxiety, guilt and unstable self-esteem. 'We find our truth in the face of others in the dynamics of absence/presence, existence/non-existence' (Lanfranchi, 2018, p. 547). Images arise from the ancient and deeply personal centre of her personality, exposing the tensions from inner and outer issues, yet these also function as the bridges for transformation.

'The aims of psychoanalysis to produce a story of the past – a reconstructed life-history – that makes the past available, as a resource to be thought about rather than a persecution to be endlessly re-enacted' (Phillips, 1994, p. 69). The Jungian therapeutic process promotes psychic activity, including tolerance for contradiction. The paradoxes and the back and forth, the psyche with its principle of synthesis and balance bring forth the submerged parts of the personality. Therapy explores losses and woundings of all kinds, internal and external, acute and cumulative, personal and collective. 'The fragmentariness of his or her associations entails the making of links; a psychoanalysis is as much about the making of gaps as about the making of links' (Phillips, 1994, p. 68).

Part of this involves Lin encountering the traumatic dissociated aspects of the feminine inherited from her parents' Asian perspective, made stronger due to their cultural displacement (Ghate, 2018, p. 150). In the US they experienced cultural rejection and prejudice against the Chinese. Lin turned from the traditional role for Chinese women as submissive to family obligations and was keen to embrace the Western identity into which she was born. Yet, she continually felt two ways about many things. She is responding to the cultural fragmentation and the fracturing from the complexity of the personal and transgenerational wounding that paradoxically also carries the potential for healing.

Lin strongly felt and reacted to cultural ties she could neither negate nor leave. It takes much effort to make sense of painful formative and transgenerational experiences affecting us at visceral and raw levels. These are the ingredients and the emotionally interactive dynamic of conscious and unconscious processes from which the transcendent function forms. Jung described, 'From the activity of the unconscious there now emerges a new content, constellated by thesis and antithesis in equal measure and standing in complementary relation to both' (1971, CW 6, para. 825).

As Andrew Samuels questioned, how do we recount ourselves to others? 'The phenomenon of difference brings forth the social and cultural structures erected on the basis of the difference, including what difference is like, what the experience of difference is like and how it becomes distorted' (Samuels, 1989, p. 97). This raises questions of identity within the collective culture and within oneself. Defences of the self become mobilised to enact the narcissism of façade and falsity. These can be associated with anti-individuation forces creating psychic retreat while the developing self is driven by the sense of something dire needing to be addressed. Pain and resistance accompany breaking from the old even as steps are taken towards movement and change.

The experience of alterity disrupts the former coherence. We can never return to how it was prior to a particular interaction with anyone or anything. As a result, we change fundamentally and irreversibly from interactions with others. Cultural differences bring out the awareness of each participant in the analytic couple to social class and culture with implications and impact on the transference and countertransference (Kiehl, 2016, p. 467). Lin brought to analysis her current experiences of prejudice and projections, especially during and after COVID-19 pandemic, as well as transgenerational issues. Although hard to accept, if the therapist is ignorant with set assumptions, the necessary spaces of examination close and emotions are unexplored, shutting the patient down consciously and unconsciously.

What is significant for change is the relationship and dialogue in a back-and-forth dynamic. This only occurs if we lean into the inner voices, asking ourselves who or what is this other. If we listen, the conversation can become a living dialogue in which identity is enhanced. The need together 'to build a dialogue and a relationship with her to create a safe framework from within the painful material can be explored. It creates co-operative meaning making in the intersubjective relationship' (Knox, 2011, p. 346).

Cultural exclusion

Jung commented, 'As far as we can discern, the sole purpose of human existence is to kindle a light of meaning in the darkness of mere being' (1963, p. 326). Various forms of psychological and cultural wounding and exclusion come from the lack of belonging to family, partner, social group or self. We are inextricably embedded in and constituted by our relations to others, and this is fundamental to establishing our subjectivity. Without others, a person can feel erased, non-existent. Here resides despair, hopelessness, longing and mourning for what was and was not. Analysis traces the social and psychological conditions under which people are left out and the scripted shaping of acceptable selves performing to survive. Traumatic events, attachment failures and systemic oppression, both historical and current, powerfully influence expectations of ourselves, others and how we take our place in the world.

Because existence is confirmed by the 'acknowledging look of the Other' 'true subjectivities come to flourish only in communities that provide for reciprocal recognition' (Butler, 1999, p. 58). Feeling excluded a person learns to become an image, maybe even a caricature and not the real self. These reactions contribute to depression, anxiety and the creation of a narcissist actor with a façade but not an authentic self.

In Jungian psychology the process of individuation or becoming oneself involves accessing the bridge to the unconscious for personality development. Experiences of loss and separation are characterised by the desire to unite, indicating a move towards individuation, meaning and value. The process opens possibilities for re-patterning and increased consciousness. The desire to understand, to be surprised, to listen and bear witness to others are elements facilitating psychological growth and development. Lin illustrates how difficult it is to muster defences and heal from the losses engendered by personal, cultural and intergenerational wounds. This includes the shadows disowned and denied in the family and cultural lineage but also enacted in the culture of the United States of America.

The ancient Greeks called the act of being reached out to as *philoxenia*, or friendship with the strange. The stranger and the immigrant symbolise those unfamiliar parts of the personality we try to deny or negate while their recognition and inclusion enhance personal and cultural growth. However, the faces of those considered strangers too often evoke fears of the unknown and create threat rather than openness. When this happens, energy recedes into the unconscious, fostering a climate of separation and exclusion or a situation of we versus them. Remaining unconsciousness truncates and throws a person into chaos whereas reflection and connection foster strength of self.

Retaining the illusion that we are all the same or should become the same feeds the fantasy a group can achieve its own completely secure and harmonious existence. This is a dangerous fiction of purity predicated on the annihilation of difference. The identity and narrative of those outside what is considered mainstream too often are ascribed as other, needing to be distanced and relegated to the outskirts.

For example, identity and pride are for Lin a road littered with apprehension and trauma. She is the oldest child in the family, but female. In the Chinese tradition of her parents, the girl is to care for them and the family as well as excel in school but not rebel or authentically separate. The parents' love was conditional as Lin is the child who is supposed to gratify the parents and their cultural expectations. This laid a burden both conscious and unconscious upon her. Jung commented,

> But are we really free? We are weak and unimportant and we try to be so; our style of life is narrow and our outlook hampered not only by ordinary hills but by veritable mountains of prejudice against anything and everybody that exceeds our size.
>
> (1976, CW 18, para. 1338)

Belonging and attachment are key elements in living and their absence can lead to spiritual and personal crises. Contiguous to the sense of estrangement, depression, unconscious complexes and psychological splitting can predominate. In the search for understanding, disruptive inner and outer emotions are aroused from the lack of belonging, creating many factors contributing to personal and cultural complexes. These complexes influence the course of life and are replicated in psychological treatment.

This subject of the cultural complexes is significant as more and more people suffer migrations and war accompanied by being othered, rejected and abandoned, with consequences binding the past to future and the narcissistic actions of self to others. We are not isolated, but exist in multiple, shifting relationships and conscious and unconscious interactions. Cultural identifications define the personality and hinge on emotional connection and attachment with others as established through cultural religion, language, history, customs and so on.

The loss, threat or attack on a set of beliefs forming the basis for a person's ideals and behaviours can provoke helplessness, depression and alienation. They become an illusion living within a society of illusion and distance from the inner world of the Self. Defenceless and imprisoned at the same time, they feel unaccepted for who they are. This rupture indicates the intricate dialectical tension between inner states and outer social realities.

For example, Lin struggles against the imposition and dehumanisation from the socio-cultural impress of being othered. She struggles to be noticed in her career, and is thwarted in filling the healthy narcissistic needs to be recognised for her achievements. Life can become desiccated from the past cultural traumata, and the memories and their severity stored in the psyche and body often emerge years later. Like Lin, we can be haunted by these past ghosts dragging their luggage of trans-generational trauma, yet they provide guidance when addressed.

Personal complex

Identity brings with it the realisation of psychological and cultural complexes and how they become powerful enough to autocratically rule the personality. During times of transition and change, the loss of self is magnified and access to familiar cultural signifiers of identity and belonging is blocked. Amid the diversity of changing populations and beliefs, people are disconnected and estranged from what they knew previously. The world becomes disorganised with social and psychological immersion in the unknown and unfamiliar. People feel adrift in a sea of insecurity and ambiguity with no way for navigating the storms. This creates a type of loneliness that can escalate into a psychic terror creeping inexorably under the skin.

When identity becomes negated it introduces the question of where and how a person belongs to both self and others. When excluded from society and without its holding and containing qualities, a person becomes vulnerable, fearful and insecure. They learn rigidity, to maintain omnipotence and control, develop an unwillingness to express their total selves and experience shame over their reality. As with narcissistic make-up, the dependent self cannot come forth. However, the rejected, uncomfortable material maintains its pressure and, if not integrated consciously, manifests in various physical and psychological symptoms as with the narcissistic defence. The psyche continually, in one way or another, seeks to be known to establish a healthy equilibrium.

'There is an inner displacement in the self due to a dramatic change in the interplay between inner and outer worlds that profoundly alters the previous organization between the ego-complex and other autonomous complexes' (Luci, 2020, p. 269). Over time, sometimes after a long time, we become increasingly conscious of the burdens we carry psychologically from our socio-historical experiences and those remaining unaddressed by previous generations. Samuel Kimbles, American Jungian analyst writing on cultural complexes, described the intergenerational transmissions of cultural complexes through the 'persuasive unconscious stories or phantom narratives embedded in the collective cultural traumas' (2014, p. 12).

Lin's emotional wounds were suffered as an adult and replicated events in childhood, originating with parental lack in attachment. Lin's father was a strict, depressive man, emotionally distant and authoritarian; whereas her mother was highly anxious. Although both were educated professionals in their Chinese culture and generation, the mother, as the woman, was regarded as less than the man. Lin was to conform to this traditional way, but it conflicted with that of the US where there was more individual independence and choice. Having escaped China, both her parents were preoccupied with acclimating to the USA. They felt prejudice and remained within the known and safer family circle outside the general US culture. Mother was poorly attuned to Lin, unable to empathise accurately with her internally and certainly unfamiliar with her external experiences. Unable to get close enough or feel securely accepted, Lin did not know how to make time for herself. Nothing really goes away but there comes a time when the old defences become unbearable, are unchanging and no longer controllable (Singer and Kimbles, 2004, p. 85). Many feelings were stored in Lin's body and psyche as unassimilated material clashing with the need to prove her value through continual achievements to satisfy her parents.

Although a university professor, Lin constantly puts others and their demands before her own as she unconsciously enacts the servile role of the female in Chinese culture. For Lin the paternal lack of emotional relating and the Chinese cultural rules so opposite those of the US adversely affect her security and ability to share with spontaneity, enthusiasm or assertion. Lin looks for approval, forgetting or fearful to focus on herself and worried she might be asking for too much. So busy looking outward and taking care of others, her emotional needs remain unseen, unheard, abandoned. She is masterful at her own self-deception. This results in her professional advancement lacking focus as well as her partnerships being fractured and unsatisfying. She has found one self-centred person after another to whom she gives herself emotionally but with whom she is incompletely met, leaving her in stress and loveless.

Shaken by parental neglect and absence the 'often perilously obtained clinical experience and information along the hazardous journey is difficult and requires much patience on the parts of both participants' in the analytic treatment (Solomon, 2004, p. 635). Therapy requires the type of waiting and surrendering that can be difficult for the scared person who clings to external demands. The ego wants clarity and guidance, a sure path and the suffering to stop. The patient needs 'presence combined with early experiences of appropriate absence to form thoughts and make creative use of the symbolic and the imaginal' (Colman, 2007, p. 266). The unconscious and cultural shields erected for protection can obstruct in-depth examination and self-reflection.

For example, Lin worried that I would say her father did his best. She thought I would defend him, like she and everyone else had done her whole life. Father respect and deference is part of Chinese tradition, no matter how the father acts or what he does. Typical of his culture, this father did not show overt care or emotional affection. When he disapproved of Lin's life choices, he cruelly ignored her and withdrew financial support.

In a recent dream he does not pick her up when she falls. She is bleeding and the blood spreads up her arms. Her hands are shaking like they used to as a child with him. She is upset and quite uneasy following the dream. Now she remembers why. She was quite alone in her family and imaginal as a child, and her unemotional, detached father said children were to obey. She knew she must put herself aside and not communicate emotional needs. This strict traditional father kept to himself, any emotions icy and layered with harsh tones and disapproval.

A bejewelled dagger occurs in many dreams. Not knowing why it is there, at first, she just acknowledges it. What it means or how to interpret it is a mystery, nor does she initially value its symbolic significance. The dagger is old, Chinese, with emeralds and rubies on the handle, precious. When researching this symbol, she realises the dagger is a token of authority and dignity, honour and strength. The dagger, because unknown and held in the unconscious, represents the special parts of which she was previously unaware. The emergence of the self into consciousness in its symbolic form is highly valuable. Dream symbols tend to act as focal points for integration, fostering a sense of pattern and meaning. These experiences are unknown to her. Jung called them the uniting symbols (Colman, 2010, p. 91).

In therapy immersion in the uncomfortable, in searing and painful material reconciles the unaddressed, unconscious personality components. The therapeutic relationship becomes the vessel to slowly take down the defensive walls and build patterns of relatedness. Therapy evokes many feelings, including repressed expectations, yearnings, love and hate, bringing a patient up against the formerly negated and avoided, including persecutory aspects as well. In addition, dependency needs denied and refused are the very ones evoked in the context of the therapeutic transference.

Therapy includes the naked moments of being seen, acknowledged and accepted while the person retains a mask until it feels safe to take it off (Bromberg, 1983, p. 379). The process occurs slowly as it can be discordant to the controlled and watchful self. This is difficult if the limp personality, even if seemingly alive, is internally deadened with assertion inhibited as the parent was unrelated, preoccupied and not expressive in love.

There is need for acceptance or else we feel lonely, depersonalised. This can escalate to 'a void of futility, meaninglessness, feeling deadened and numb while at the core resides the dependency needs propelling the search for connection' (Ashton, 2007, p. 21). This may be the very place where Lin can recover, and the analytical, intersubjective experiences foster self-development and the capability for transformation. Concerning

[early] relational trauma it is the containing relationship in psychotherapy making it possible to dream what was previously the undreamable. It is a prelude to becoming able to think the unthinkable, and as a foretaste of creating experience, not in terms of the historical past, but in terms of the relational present.
(Wilkinson, 2006, p. 54)

The recognition of belonging and not belonging occurs in psychotherapy and is exposed in the transference and countertransference. The therapy situation ideally provides enough security for the self to unfold in its authenticity (Solomon, 2007, p. 240). This helps re-negotiate the wounded places, dismantle the defensive strategies, connect the dissociations, and in the process also reveals the psychic panic. The interpretations and rhythms of analysis, as we uncover the symbols and unhook the complexes, break into the tenacious chain of self-persecutions and denigrations. Jung opined, 'In any effective psychological treatment the doctor is bound to influence the patient; but this influence can only take place if the patient has a reciprocal influence on the doctor' (1929/1966, CW 16, para. 163).

The therapeutic process of questioning and self-exploration dredges up elements of desire, passion and suffering – all ingredients for renewal to the psyche. The therapist provides a place to bear the wounds in the unfolding narrative in which the unthinkable, awesome, empty spaces can be contemplated. The process of self-awareness means uncovering the denials guarding against truths, the protective fantasies and the bonds retaining old inhibiting roles. This work disrupts memory, disturbs the ego's status quo and pierces the psychological complexes.

The shadow is a moral problem that challenges the whole ego-personality, for no one can become conscious of the shadow without considerable moral effort. To become conscious of it involves recognizing the dark aspects of the personality as present and real. This act is the essential condition for any kind of self-knowledge.
(Jung, 1968, CW 9ii, p. 14)

It means becoming conscious of and grieving the losses and developing an independent self by reigniting desires and passions.

The narcissistic personality has a lingering absence of passion from early toxic and disjointed experiences, which originally forced the self into hiding. Integration is difficult for this person living in a state of singularity, with unease with the other, a body separated from psyche and fantasy replacing the real. Green (1986, p. 42) explained this as a person needing the container of the therapist for the content to be presented. It is a self-to-self interweaving, a mutual steeping in the issues. Jung commented, 'Individuation involves the transformation of the analyst as well as the patient, stirring up in his or her personality the layers that correspond to the patient's conflicts and insights' (1966, CW 17, p. 172).

Through the dynamism of the therapeutic interplay are the tasks of linking the known and unknown, conscious and unconscious, and balancing the tension between them. In Jungian psychology the principle of holding the tension of these opposites is essential for bridging the gap between ego consciousness and the unconscious. If the tension can be sustained without succumbing to the urge to identify with one side or the other, the third and completely unexpected image unites the psychological elements in a creative new way. The psyche is fluid, multi-dimensional, alive and capable of creative development. The challenge is to emerge from the conflicts, find authenticity and intimacy with self and others. The task delves into discovering what is called in Jungian psychology the 'treasure hard to attain' or the knowledge residing in the unconscious, the body and the discovery of Self.

To become conscious of prejudice reveals a powerful cultural complex with its capacity to contaminate the personal and collective psyche.

> The re-occurring trauma experienced as a racial complex moves with the self and the shadow. This relationship creates anxiety and a fear specific to the trauma that initially caused such a complex to develop and becomes repeatedly realized through the generations.
>
> (Brewster, 2020, p. 22)

Personal and social identity denotes the fact that a person or a group has certain particular and characteristic qualities marking them as separate and distinguishable from others. The post-Jungian concept of the cultural complex refers to active unconscious elements in the psyche presenting therapeutic challenges, combining with the awareness necessary for continued growth.

Transcendent function

The concept of the transcendent function introduced in Jung's 1916 essay marked his break with Freud. Jung described this function as guiding the psyche towards individuation. He said, 'Unlived life is a destructive, irresistible force that works softly but inexorably' (Jung, 1927/1968, CW 10, para. 252). The transcendent function addresses the unknown energy reaching beyond the predicable and the rote quick fixes. This distinctive process helps heal the injuries to restore healthy self-love and self-esteem.

The transcendent function bridges the border between self and other, psyche and body. The word *function* derives from the Latin verb *fungere*, to perform. *Transcend* is a compound of two Latin words, the prefix *trans*, 'beyond, across', and the verb *scandere*, 'to climb'. When something transcends it goes above, beyond or below. It is an active confrontation between conscious and unconscious, resulting in the emergence of new symbolic forms. The unconscious memories form into an estranged and melancholic language and provide a crucible for mourning and for healing.

These transcend the internal conflicts and lead to increasing psychic connections. If the mediatory product remains intact, it moulds the raw material for a process, not of dissolution, but of construction, in which thesis and antithesis both play their part. In this way,

> [it] becomes a new content that governs the whole attitude, putting an end to the division and forcing the energy of the opposites into a common channel. The standstill is overcome and life can flow on with renewed power towards new goals.
>
> (Jung, 1971, CW 6, para. 827)

Dreams, complexes and dissociations of the psyche reveal the transcendent function appearing in therapeutic work. The transcendent function moves the psyche, yet it depends on the ego's ability to hold the opposing forces and sustain their dynamic interaction. In the process of the old breaking down, there is pain and resistance even as the steps are taken towards movement. Jung described, 'The tendencies of the conscious and the unconscious are the two factors that together make up the transcendent function. It is called transcendent because it makes the transition from one attitude to another organically possible' (Jung, 1957/1969, CW 8, para. 145). The paradoxes and processes of going back and forth from the varied positions in the unconscious bring the psyche out of polarisation and oppositional states. The transcendent function emerges as a catalysing force and the synthesis for repair, rebalancing and regulation of the psyche.

Lin dreams she is looking for a bathroom in a hotel, which has previously appeared in several dreams. In every dream she has to go all over to find a clean and private bathroom. Then she encounters a large figure – heavy, dark colour and androgenous. Suddenly, a silver bullet hits her in the vagina and a pulsating penis emerges. She is not frightened but intrigued. She feels the figure, although in many ways grotesque, is an omen of the unexpected. What she retains is the fact of being hit but unhurt. The strangeness of the dream accentuates her desire for change and transformation. She feels it is shocking with its insistence but not overwhelming. She can handle the force of the impact. As an inner image I interpret this as a symbol indicating the transcendent function with its possibilities and surprise. It hits but does not hurt. From its power will come something, but what it is yet unknown. And it includes transformation with the male and female elements united in her psyche as she becomes both energetically and psychically more than she was aware of previously.

Lin begins therapy at a loss: about what to do, what to feel, what to think. What is her purpose? The therapeutic work consists neither of releasing nor repressing, but of holding and working with the psyche to uncover the internal and external complexes, challenges and the blockages. Through therapy she will make conscious the issues appearing in dreams, thoughts and feelings, affecting relationships with self and others.

The self is supported in its development through the symbolic nature of the transcendent function so the creative resources residing in the unconscious become accessible to consciousness (Solomon, 2007, p. 244). The unconscious influences are found in their constant intrusions in daily life, often without consciousness. Analysis can bring these to awareness and free the psyche in a readjustment of the psychological contents. The process includes regression to former times, experiences, memories. This does not imply illness but occurs because there is an inherent impulse towards a unitary psyche. Once pieces fragment and dissemble, they will begin to reassemble. Because of this impulse, a disintegrated psyche spontaneously attempts to reintegrate. Regression activates the impulse towards reintegration and is facilitated through dreams, the therapeutic relationship and other life events.

The narcissist often does not realise how much the unacknowledged elements control freedom of expression, confidence and ease in being. However, the transferences can be difficult and often trying with a narcissist as this person allows no other, only the same, no separation, and there can be an inability to symbolise. The narcissist can obstruct the relationality of the analytical process.

Here lies the uncomfortable gaps between self and others, the idealisations, need for defence – all emerging in the therapeutic relationship. These are the communications oscillating in unspoken ways for both participants to dialogue with and expose the relational wounds. The psychological life is complex, as even in therapy a narcissist fights against exposing their desires and repressed dependency needs.

Deprived of the alchemy of engagement long ago, Lin drew a magic circle around herself to appear self-sufficient. Bringing this to consciousness will include the unexpressed grief and mourning over what she missed.

> The therapeutic situation is the only place explicitly provided for in the social contract in which we are allowed to talk about the wounds we have suffered and to search for possible new identities and new ways of talking about ourselves.
> (Kristeva, 1988, p. 6)

However, comfort with self and others is not easily acquired. It requires getting to know oneself outside the boundaries of cultural upbringing. There is no simple solution or a predictable recipe to this complex process. The personality expands as the conscious and unconscious form a dynamic relationship rather than being stuck in old emotions, discontents and stress to create new visions and opportunities. It is a circuitous process taking perseverance and time.

We go beyond recognition of the familiar to encounter what is unknown. 'The unknown information is a feature functional for emergence of the therapeutic third, a jointly created unconscious life from the flow between the therapeutic pair' (Colman, 2010, p. 292). This psychological work brings us back to the suffering experienced in interpersonal relationships. Wounds and blows to the heart signify the past, the un-mourned grief and loneliness, and the deconstruction and reconstruction of the self for finding meaning and value. In reference to this Green stated,

'The mind has the capacity to bring something back again which has been related to an object, without the object being there' (1979, p. 30). This refers to the psychological capacity for renewal, transcending the limits of time and space.

Transference and the symbolic

Jung suggests:

> To the extent that the transference is projection and nothing more, it divides quite as much as it connects ... because relationship to the self is at once relationship to our fellow man, and no one can be related to the latter until he is related to himself.
>
> (1946/1966, CW 16, para. 445)

We make sense of ourselves through the webs of meaning supplied by our personal and collective social, historical and symbolic systems. A relationship means being seen in the multiplicity of selves making up the totality.

> Analytic work encompasses relational as well as interpretive agents to bring about the integration and increased connectivity between and within both hemispheres of the mind-brain leading to a change in the nature of attachment which will then permit the self to emerge more fully through the process of individuation.
>
> (Wilkinson, 2006, p. 113)

From staying with this process, symbols arise to move the personality from previously constricting situations. The symbols and metaphors are central to the unconscious becoming conscious. 'The psyche accomplishes its transformation through the creation of symbols which are capable of bringing together opposing aspects of the self' (Solomon, 1998, p. 227). Symbols are also impersonal metaphors, sharing meaning from past and current conventions, myths and cultural artefacts, a medium of communication revealing our inherent intersubjectivity. 'The self is supported in its development through the symbolic nature of the transcendent function and the creative resources residing in the unconscious that become accessible for the conflict to dissipate and the energy reorganise' (Solomon, 2007, p. 244).

The differences in culture between analyst and analysand are recognised in the transference and countertransference. 'Culture is a deeply imbedded structure that underlies the perception of our self, our reality, and the ways we become individuals' (Mattoon, 1992, p. 124). To meet with an open frame of mind the analyst will be faced with the intrinsically unknown feeling of being limited by their own culture. It requires not assuming the cultural themes and social trends the person identifies with or what they are moving towards. 'The political and social isms of our day preach every conceivable ideal, but, under this mask, they lower the level of our culture by restricting or all together inhibiting the possibilities of individual development' (Jung, 1950/1968, CW 9i, para. 617).

Awareness of the contents of the personal unconscious, including our cultural backgrounds, entails also accessing the layers of images and motifs comprising the vast cultural array along with the hauntings of transgenerational tragedies. 'A much greater part of our personality than we generally believe is collectively determined' (Alho, 2006, p. 662). This is the collective unconscious reflecting many of our deepest human instincts like love, fear, social projections, sex, wisdom and good and evil. Embodying a psychological attitude includes acknowledging the universal longing for acceptance and value. The understanding of this also means awareness of our tendencies for polarisation, the shadow of blame, shaming, bullying, rejection and receiving differences, or not. All this requires thoughtful reflection and response to the personal and cultural tapping into the past, changing the present and leading to a more fulfilling future. We explore these layers for connection, sustenance and meaning. 'This widened consciousness ... brings the individual into absolute, binding, and indissoluble communion with the world at large' (Jung, 1928/1969, CW 7, para. 275).

Our existence is fundamentally interpersonal. Human beings are not isolated, free-floating objects, but subjects existing in perpetual, multiple, shifting relationships. Life is defined by these myriad interactions – by the push and pull of intersubjectivity in overt and covert social contracts. However, many people experience helplessness, powerlessness and the resultant loneliness as one of the most painful experiences of human existence. Everybody experiences loneliness, but they experience it differently. It can radically cut people off from human connection, creating a kind of wilderness where a person feels deserted and abandoned. When experiencing too much loneliness, we lose the ability to expect anything else and new beginnings seem daunting. As soon as we begin to talk about loneliness, we transform one of the most deeply felt human experiences into an object of contemplation, reflection and ownership.

This means we feel the gaps from abandonment and lack of development. 'There are positive forces that seek to move the psyche into the future, there are powerful retrograde forces that seek to prevent such movement.' (Solomon, 1998, p. 226). In analysis we make space to open encounters with others, both inner and outer, so the transformative spirit may emerge. The past and the present become contiguous. Lin says she must break the inner lock and write her book. Doing so could express the heart and emotions she put away years ago that now want to be expressed. For the narcissist all this is complicated because the inner world of the self has been kept away from feeling defenceless and imprisoned as it seems impossible to be accepted for who she is.

Analysis deals with these dissociative mechanisms of defence. This situation requires the therapist's capacity to resonate with the multiple and sometimes contradictory threads of the person's narrative in the co-construction of symbolic space. The analyst's search for unconscious meaning in the patient's communications becomes an agent of change. Taking the other perspective is necessary to resolve conflict, whether inner or outer, as conflicts can arise and be perpetuated from adopting a single perspective. In the analytical relationship patient and analyst come to engage each other more fully. As more of the analyst and patient find access to an increasingly enlivened form of engagement, both begin to change in ways that transform and transfigure how the work is experienced by each of them. Each analytical journey has a unique cast, as the qualities both patient and analyst bring to the work shape the proceedings.

The discovery of the Self occurs through this minutely reflective process integrating both the chaos and order of the psyche. *Lin dreams she is in a large room with light shimmering through the windows. She takes a step and abruptly falls to the next floor. She is unhurt and looks up to see two people dancing together.* The dream leaves her with a feeling of peace, not knowing who the people are but it does not matter because their dance together does.

Conclusion

American writer Susan Griffin queried,

> How old is the habit of denial? We keep secrets from ourselves that all along we know ... For perhaps we are like stones; our own history and the history of the world embedded in us, we hold a sorrow deep within and cannot weep until that history is sung.
>
> (1992, p. 48)

Possibilities for the future emerge through the symbolic capacity of the transcendent function. The alliance between therapist and client secures trust and evolves through the relationship as it is dependent on separation and connection between both participants. This process requires the capacity to recognise and gather the multiple personal and collective threads. Through the analytical work the analyst can perceive the moments when the analysand emerges from their narcissistic psychic retreat of singularity. Faced with the anxieties and recognising the damage done, the repair becomes possible through the dialogical analytical relationship.

> We can only live this experience in the form of an aporia ... where faithful interiorization bears the others and constitutes him in me (in us), at once living and dead. It makes the other part of us, between us – and then the other no longer quite seems to be the other, because we grieve for him and bear him in us, like an unborn child, like a future. And inversely, the failure succeeds: an aborted interiorization is at the same time a respect for the other as other, a sort of tender rejection, a movement of renunciation which leaves the other alone, outside, over there, in (her) death, outside of us.
>
> (Derrida, quoted in DeArmitt, 2014, p. 113)

Meanwhile, the conscious awareness of the emotional wounds arouses the disillusionment, the profound disappointments and the means to cope. Facing illusions becomes restorative and needs both participants to be active in the interplay of the unconscious processes in the consulting room. Hopelessness and impasse then can shift and create space for hope and movement.

The psyche looks to complete itself, to manifest in higher modes of consciousness, to fill the lack and unify the disparate. Its quest is for truth and fulfilment in an organic, developmental and relational process. Doing so makes it possible to repair the losses, yearnings, needs, anxieties. Lin attends to the psyche but, at times, pulls away. There is a sense of immobility, powerlessness and yet the search for development continues. The psychological process had been previously held in abeyance, defensive but unaware, stagnating attempts to engage thoughts but isolated from the affects.

Despite her fear and anxiety, through the clinical work the unconscious is made conscious and puts into verbal expression what was not allowed previously. This becomes a container in which to grow beyond despair to foster hope. Analyst and patient stand together in the space between realities where what seemed unimaginable becomes possible. The emphasis is on the co-creation of meaning in this interpersonal space. From the perspective of Jungian analytical psychology, the self seeks union of unconscious to conscious, personal to cultural. This acknowledges the longing for connection, a sense of belonging and identity. The engagement with others gives voice to many selves for expression and increased consciousness and inclusion rather than foreclosing on the different.

Lin comes from a culture based on values different from the independence and narcissism of the US and the Jungian analytical process of individuation is a coming to herself. 'Self love and love of the other is a process of self-organization and a source of renewal and creativity' (Kristeva, 1983, p. 24). Engagement with the other brings about recognition of the self, reconciliation and mutual understanding evolving from a sense of personal and collective belonging and pride in identity. Personality transformation occurs, fulfilling the basic longing for inclusion and acceptance. The integration results in communication between self and others, the shadow and the stranger. Herein lie the reasons for the continual crossing of the bridge. In the words of Nikolai Gogol, 'I saw that I'd get nowhere on the straight path, and that to go crookedly was straighter' (2011, p. 378).

References

Alho, PM. (2006). Collective complexes – total perspectives. *Journal of Analytical Psychology*, *51*(5), 661–680.

Ashton, P. (2007). *From the brink: Experiences of the void from a depth psychology perspective*. Routledge.

Brewster, F. (2020). *The racial complex: A Jungian perspective on culture and race*. Routledge.

Bromberg, P. (1983). The mirror and the mask: On narcissism and psychoanalytic growth. *Contemporary Psychoanalysis*, *19*(2), 359–387. https://doi.org/10.1080/00107530.1983.10746614

Butler, J. (1999) *Subjects of desire*. Columbia University Press.

Colman, W. (1991). Envy, self-esteem and the fear of separateness. *British Journal of Psychotherapy*, *7*(4), 356–367.

Colman, W. (2007). Symbolic conceptions: The idea of the third. *Journal of Analytical Psychology*, *52*(5), 565–583.

Colman, W. (2010). Mourning and the symbolic process. *Journal of Analytical Psychology*, *55*(2), 275–297.

Connolly, A. (2007). Frozen time and endless analyses: A response to David Tresan's 'Thinking individuation forward'. *Journal of Analytical Psychology*, *52*(1), 41–45, 47–49.

DeArmitt, P. (2014). *The right to narcissism: A case for an impossible self-love*. Fordham University Press.

Ghate, A. (2018). Traumatic dissociation of aspects of the feminine: An Asian cultural perspective. *Journal of Analytical Psychology*, *53*(2), 150–165.

Gogol, N. (2011). *Dead souls*. Vintage.

Green, A. (1979). *The tragic effect*. Cambridge University Press.

Green, A. (1986). *On private madness*. International Universities Press.

Griffin, S. (1992). *A chorus of stones: The private life of war*. Doubleday.

Jung, C. G. (1927/1968). Woman in Europe. In *Civilization in transition* (Vol. 10). Princeton University Press.

Jung, C. G. (1928/1969). The relations between the ego and the unconscious. In *Two essays on analytical psychology* (Vol. 7). Princeton University Press.

Jung, C. G. (1929/1966). *The collected works of C. G. Jung: Vol. 16. Practice of* psychotherapy. Princeton University Press.

Jung, C. G. (1946/1966). The psychology of the transference. In *The practice of psychotherapy* (Vol. 16). Princeton University Press.

Jung, C. G. (1950/1968). A study in the process of individuation. In *The archetypes and the collective unconscious* (Vol. 9i). Princeton University Press.

Jung, C.G. (1957/1969). The transcendent function. In *The structure and dynamics of the psyche* (Vol. 8). Princeton University Press.

Jung, C. G. (1963). *Memories, dreams, reflections*. Random House.

Jung, C. G. (1966). *The collected works of C. G. Jung: Vol. 17. The development of personality*. Princeton University Press.

Jung, C. G. (1968). *The collected works of C. G. Jung* (Vol. 9ii – *Aion.*) Princeton University Press.

Jung, C. G. (1971). *The collected works of C. G. Jung: Vol. 6. Psychological types*. Princeton University Press.

Jung, C. G. (1976). Psychology and national problems. In *The symbolic life* (Vol. 18). Princeton University Press.

Kiehl, E. (2016). 'You were not born here, so you are classless, you are free!' Social class and cultural complex in analysis. *Journal of Analytical Psychology*, *61*(4), 465–480.

Kimbles, S. (2014). *Phantom narratives: The unseen contributions of culture to psyche*. Rowman & Littlefield.

Knox, J. (2011). Dissociation and shame: Shadow aspects of multiplicity. *Journal of Analytical Psychology*, *56*(3), 341–347.

Kristeva, J. (1983). *Tales of love*. Columbia University Press.
Kristeva, J. (1988). *In the beginning was love*. Columbia University Press.
Kunitz, S. (2002). *The Collected Poems of Stanley Kunitz*. W. W. Norton & Company, Inc.
Lanfranchi, A. K. (2018). Intimacy, the drama and beauty of encountering the Other. *Journal of Analytical Psychology*, *63*(4), 546–549.
Luci, M. (2020). Disintegration of the self and the regeneration of 'psychic skin' in the treatment of traumatized refugees. *Journal of Analytical Psychology*, *65*(2), 260–280.
Mattoon, M. (1992). *Understanding dreams*. Spring Publications.
Mills, J. (2019). Recognition and Pathos. *International Journal of Jungian Studies*, *11*(1), 1–22.
Phillips, A. (1994). *On flirtation*. Harvard University Press.
Samuels, A. (1989). *The plural psyche: Personality, morality & the father*. Routledge.
Schomp, V. (2009). *The ancient Chinese*. Marshall Cavendish Benchmark.
Shorter, B. (1988). *An image darkly forming: Women and initiation*. Routledge.
Singer, T. & Kimbles, S. (Eds.). (2004). *The cultural complex: Contemporary Jungian perspectives on psyche and society*. Brunner-Routledge.
Solomon, H. (1998). The self in transformation: The passage from a two- to a three-dimensional internal world. *Journal of Analytical Psychology*, *43*(2), 225–238.
Solomon, H. (2004). Self creation and the limitless void of dissociation: The as if personality. *Journal of Analytical Psychology*, *49* (5), 635–656.
Solomon, H. (2007). *The self in transformation*. Karnac.
Wilkinson, M. (2006). *Coming into mind*. Routledge.
Winborn, M. (2022). Working with patients with disruptions in symbolic capacity. *Journal of Analytical Psychology*, *68*(1), 87–108.

Chapter 11
The nigredo of now

I'm in a dusty, desolate, drug-ridden and drab place. A place of ashes. A place where the children are grey and emaciated. I am walking on a hiking path, and I encounter two Latino gang members. I'm wearing a Bulls' tee-shirt, and I become worried that will make me a target. They start yelling at me, and I keep walking while putting my hands in the air. They continue to yell in English, telling me to keep walking, and asking me how I have the gall to come around here like this. One of them fires his gun at me, and I shiver in fear. The bullet hurts me, even though it doesn't hit me.

Later, I find a disintegrating, nearly burnt-to-the-ground hovel on flood stilts. I ascend the stairs. Inside are ashen-faced children. They must be in both deep poverty and deep mourning. They have a frail grandfather living with them. I find a giant egg (larger than an ostrich egg) in my hands. I somehow drop it and crack it on the floor, making a bunch of drinking glasses shatter on the floor at the same time.

The man who had this dream said, 'It has been a long odyssey, and I have been alone and aware of this fact, unable to sink into my real self, be silent, and open or honestly related.' In the absence of self-appreciation or regard, this dreamer has attempted to preserve a semblance of control in his life. Meanwhile the dream reveals the former illusion of the integrity of his self is collapsing. The dream demonstrates he is lacking inner stability as he drops the egg and the glasses shatter. What is the dream exposing? There is no holding of the glass container, and the potential in the egg symbol is also crushed. The link between his sense of personal agency and the self is weakened. Does he know how it could be strengthened? Can he repair it?

The dream image of this man reflects a vision and internal echoing of disjointedness. It illustrates an aspect of a narcissist who has shaky self-worth and is threatened by the world. The idealised and illusionary supersede the real as the narcissist assumes the real will be disappointing combined with an underlying morass of sorrow and disillusionment. His remarks reveal the many negative, interfering inner thoughts of harsh and critical self-evaluation, judgement and pressure. Sadly, the dream comes true as he cannot put the pieces together, find his own truth or live according to it.

The narcissist is often preoccupied with illusions, dependent on retaining youth, unable to access maturity, needing adulation, but unfulfilled as the wishes for

DOI: 10.4324/9781003463290-12

being seen, also by themselves, remain unrealised. Through therapy these issues can become conscious as they appear in dreams, thoughts and feelings, affecting relationships with self and others. As Jung noted, the aim is also to elicit from the unconscious the meanings relating to future attitudes (1971, CW 6, para. 702). Within this the search is to find one's true and more complete self.

> Such a man knows that whatever is wrong in the world is in himself, and if he only learns to deal with his own shadow he has done something real for the world. He has succeeded in shouldering at least an infinitesimal part of the gigantic, unsolved social problems of our day.
> (Jung, 1938/1969, CW 11, para. 140)

Nigredo

The alchemical stage called nigredo is apparent in feelings of dissolution and decomposition. This stage represents the unseen well of the unconscious containing the lesser known or accepted parts of the personality. Jung perceived the medieval science of alchemy as revealing a symbolic process illustrating the transformation of human consciousness. It begins with the raw material of the personality, called in alchemy the *prima materia* or *basic matter*. This refers to the base and lowly substances, the less developed, vulnerable, often unacceptable aspects of the self. The point is these can be transformed into the gold of creativity and personality expansion. 'Jung saw in alchemy a symbolical imaginal world whose aim was to promote psychological and spiritual development through the contemplation, exploration and development of its very rich and elaborate imagery' (Colman, 2007, p. 568).

The nigredo represents an encounter with the suffering that eventually leads to personality assimilation and synthesis. It requires intense feelings and emotional reactions to constellate an emergence into the light of consciousness. Yet the beginning is the blackening depression, the shadow, melancholia, a time of slowing down amid the need for examining life in therapy and analysis. Acknowledging pain is difficult for the narcissist who desperately seeks attention from others. Repair can begin, however, through facing reality with its many unexpected layers to traverse for personality development.

The nigredo exposes not only the personal but also the baseness, the bare bones within our contemporary culture and ourselves. Personal and cultural fluidity and rigidity is combined with confusion and disintegration. Discontinuities are fraught with social unrest and worldwide challenges to our quality of life. This is defined by our computer era that tends towards isolation and the rise of narcissism. People feel disconnected, secluded behind screens; they communicate virtually and are only partially seen. We learn to not show up as real, compromising intimacy, and accepting the lack of meaningful connections.

The magnitude of uncertainties and transitions humanity is now undergoing indicates a particularly challenging and even despairing time. The effect is apparent worldwide with cultures lacking sufficient regard for others, exhibiting the isolation of narcissism and the decline of the planet's health. Yet, in comparison to the current global and societal crises and movements, it may seem contradictory to pay attention to this personality type often associated with superficiality and self-centredness. However, both indicate the need for a serious psychological approach to the deeper issues. The purpose of exploring narcissism is to nurture awareness of what can be replenishing and regenerative for each person and culture.

Although the narcissistic personality type can manifest in different forms in each culture, its psychological structure remains similar. By exploring this personality with its fractured bits and pretence, we are dealing with some of the most diverse and complex issues of our times. The search into narcissistic personality complexities guides us towards new ways of resolving conflicts and dissensions and broadens the circle of comprehension and connection to reality and the self. The nigredo is not only the beginning but also a continual stage of development.

In Jungian analysis and psychological treatment, the nigredo states of chaos and darkness occur as therapist and patient find themselves immersed in feelings, opposites mixed and inextricably entwined, such as trust and suspicion, hope and disillusionment, liking and aversion, a desire for progress and fear of change. However, in analysis the transference might become stillborn, despite the analyst's efforts to help or even to provoke its appearance. The analyst can feel caught in the patient's network of mummified objects, paralysed and unable to stimulate curiosity in the patient. 'The analyst might be excluded with a multiplicity of defence mechanisms against the regression' needed for pulling the person inward (Green, 1975, p. 4).

The difficulty for the narcissist is admitting they are hiding in the unreal. This is compounded by the narcissist wanting to be seen by others yet always feeling unseen, unrecognised, desirous of unending approval. Known for a slickly contrived persona/ego image, the narcissist lives in fantasy, preferring the illusionary. The issues affect intimacy with themselves and others and include not belonging, the cultural influence of social media, body image and split, dissociated selves. This personality type reflects the cultural tendencies for coverup, superficiality and the search for easy fixes, especially for those found on the internet. Accessing wealth and knowledge in the unconscious allows the narcissist to incorporate the inner dissociated parts into a more unified self while simultaneously reflecting the multiplicity of the psyche.

There are many internalised and conflicting components within the narcissist. Among them are envy and low self-worth, denial of the shadow, an appealing yet elusive persona but with the lack of self-connection. The narcissist's high levels of distress perpetuate the many attempts to escape any underlying disappointments and heaviness. All these aspects are promoted by the culture of social media where the lines between reality and illusion easily become blurred. However, the psychological isolation of this personality type also contains the yearning for self and other to find intimacy in relationship.

Paying attention to this personality type brings out the deeper individuation urge within it, opening to creative and authentic expression beyond the intriguing façade. 'Oneness is also other, self is also non-self' (Marlan, 2020, p. 3). Integration occurs through addressing the throes of mourning, acknowledging losses and depression, and bringing forth the formerly untouched, unacceptable and unknown aspects. Being real is a process of release and emergence from the inner emptiness of narcissism. It means facing the unrecognised and unmourned grief and loss to ignite desire, curiosity and aliveness.

Blackness as the starting gate

The alchemical nigredo represents the psychological encounter with suffering that eventually leads to its understanding and meaning, assimilation, synthesis and transformation. The ignored shadow needs awareness to constellate its opposite. 'I begin with nothingness ... Nothingness is both empty and full' (Jung, 1963, p. 379). In alchemy it is the blackness that is the beginning of whiteness (Edinger, 1985, p. 149). This process starts with the prima materia, the raw and essential basic matter described in alchemy as black on the outside and white on the inside. Light and dark are linked, illustrating the conscious and unconscious engagement with each other. The multiplicity of the psyche is challenging, opposing, yet pulls towards unification and 'catalyzes a symbol-making process' (Marlan, 2020, p. 2).

Only when things are torn apart, the elements separated and destroyed, do new ones develop and reunite (Edinger, 1985, p. 157). Symbols of the blackness appear in overflowing toilet dreams, worms burrowing in the earth, so on. For example, the I Ching, the Chinese Book of Wisdom hexagram #18, uses the character *ku* to indicate a bowl in which worms are breeding, signifying decay as part of the transformative process. The conscious endurance of this process requires holding the tension of the opposites to eventually nourish the self. Meanwhile, the ego dies to re-create and establish a more encompassing and expanded form.

However, the narcissist denies all these possibilities through glitzy presentation, insisting on the superficial while belying an impoverished or absent emotional and physical relationship to the world. They report internal emptiness, disillusionment, anxiousness, confusion and alienation, most of all from themselves. Appearing successful to others does not fill the missing internal spaces.

The narcissist is hiding, feels unreal, unable, unworthy. The complexity behind the masks and illusions and the attempted dissimulation works to mystify and deceive themself and others. A woman described, 'Today I had a moment of feeling real. Usually, I am somewhere else. But now I caught it and could tell the difference for the first time.' She narrates a story of personal and collective history composed of secret vicissitudes occupying her personality. This personality has a penchant for illusions and poses, an imposter with a shaky foundation based on inner distress and psychological confusion (Schwartz, 2024). The person clings to a precarious pretence of self-sufficiency to defend against feeling helpless and powerless, forming a swarm of instability and reflecting the pain of their existence.

The perfect body image and narcissistic showiness are desperate, compensatory attempts central to maintaining the persona façade. All must look light, shining, no blemishes, hiding what is considered flawed. The narcissist seeks to be loved, admired, to be the sole object of attention. These people surround themselves with those who see them as perfect or ideal. The shaky self-image compensates with attempts to manifest a grand image in the minds of others that props them up. The outward focus covers the belief in inner lack. The narcissist doesn't love themself in a way that means self-sufficiency, but they love an image dependent upon how others view them. Narcissism in this sense is not self-love but rather the intense need to be loved by others.

Freud contended, 'The idealization normally given to the object is usurped and one becomes one's own ideal' (1914, pp. 74–75). The superiority the narcissist tries to express through a perfected image betrays the inferiority they feel, originating from the absence of love. They don't love themselves but present the image that, parasitically, must be hosted in the minds of others for them to feel some worth. There can be an 'inability to contain and reflect upon affective experience, not having internalized a process of containment of affect. Such [people] can experience some of their affect but cannot form a representation. There (might be) no ability to symbolize and develop meaning' (Willemsen, 2014, p. 699). They suffer failure in the linkage between body, affect and mind.

Body

There is a loss of investment in the body, leading to disembodiment or depersonalisation bringing about alteration in the perception or experience of the self. To be separated from the body objectifies it and consequently separates it from the self. The deeper regions of the psyche remain elusive, and without touching the centre nothing fills. The lack of vitality and emptiness means that 'in more severe instances there are pervasive and overpowering feelings of psychic deadness accompanied by the conviction all is without meaning' (Connolly, 2013, p. 640).

The British Jungian analyst Michael Fordham said, 'There is a need for defenses against what is not-self as essential to health ... little or no inner world can develop; the self-integrate becomes rigid and persists' (1985, p. 167). This leads to the accumulation of violence and hostility split off from any libidinal and loving communication towards the self. American psychoanalyst Michael Eigen stated, 'More people than in the past seek help for feeling dead. Although feeling dead is a central complaint of many individuals, it is not clear where this deadness comes from, or what can be done about it' (Eigen, 1995, p. 277; quoted in Connolly, 2013, p. 640). Such people live numb, as if deadened, without desire, self-care or relatedness to self or others. All is kept emotionally distant. They are uncomfortable in their skin; they feel as if they do not really exist. There is an invisible barrier between them and other people, and the effort to broach this barrier seems insurmountable. They heartlessly abuse themselves in various ways – with food, by starving, with body alterations, addictions driven by the inner denigrating thoughts that tear them apart.

Such people lack empathy towards themselves. They are profoundly detached from their bodies, which they treat not as living entities but rather as inanimate objects to be manipulated to fit a look or design. In many personal scenarios there are various addictive behaviours accompanied by rote, monotonous routines and thoughts. A man told himself he could 'get away with it', meaning not attend to self-care. This lack of care had gone on so long, by now he could hardly be motivated otherwise and continued maltreating his body. The harmful effects did nothing to dissuade him to change. Another person is emotionally removed, distant, attacking herself with food as if it does not matter. She feels nothing while the self remains disconnected and she is lost in misery, defeat, despair. 'The feelings of not really being alive are linked to the fact she has no inner representation of her face or body' (Connolly, 2013, p. 641). Yet, she spends hours on makeup, hours upset about her clothes, feels she never looks right, and nothing ever fits. Piles of stuff collect in her house, no one enters, and life continues, a flat line of dissatisfied routines and distress with no end in sight, little opening to the world and a life shaped by fear of demise, yet no one knows.

Melancholia of nigredo

'The nigredo not only brought decay, suffering, death and the torments of hell visibly before the eyes of the alchemist, it also brought the shadow of its melancholy over his solitary soul' (Jung, 1970, CW 14, para. 493). When the original primary caregivers do not model a sense of self for the developing child, psychic wounds accumulate, and loss from the psychic trauma can remain as a potentially destructive undertow. The need is to escape the unbearable and the child, now adult, is dysregulated by continued fears of annihilation. They become wired, anxious, worried they are not good enough, found wanting, insufficient, fearing exposure. For example, Lyran experienced such distressing and empty spaces from being raised by blank, emotionally bankrupt parents, leaving her to retreat inside. Alone she had to make sense of a world without feelings, reactions or emotions. The parents' emotional absence along with their physical presence was profound, multilayered and couched with secrets, feelings unexpressed, generations of family lies and facts altered and hidden.

She clings to a precarious pretence of self-sufficiency, an illusion to defend against feeling helpless and powerless. As a child Lyran was left alone a lot, too much. In time, it became the aloneness rather than people who supported her. She created a better world in the backyard of her childhood, remaking her imaginative, emotional and creative life. The backyard became a place to deal with the overwhelming intensity of lack and absence to master experiences she was too young to master. The self-authored story made her feel able. This was also the fuel for the later images in dreams and active imaginations with their metaphorical power and capacity to facilitate emergent processes more appealing than the outer world.

She was told in a dream the ghosts were still there. She was unconsciously living with them as well as the nonverbal yet powerful early messages to not trust, talk or emote about her sorrows and lack of attention. She learned to mask all this and focus on others. The family atmosphere was weighed down with the deadness of flattened emotions. The parents' inner life was shrouded in the façade of appearing socially acceptable. Lyran had no choices available outside of the paternal rule prominent in family and culture. Mother was silent, uninvolved, a singular person wanting obedient and quiet children.

It was the lack of presence, the blankness of the parental connection to her or to each other that spurred Lyran's personality disappearance in favour of inner retreat. The emotionally dead family, the parental repressions, the weighty sorrow of unrequited love, the transgenerational following of tradition but without meaning created in her feelings of internal flaws. As far as relationships, she experienced temporary, fleeting attachments. She experienced no safety in being seen and thought the only option was to remain sexual but invisible.

The concept and experience of the emotionally dead and absent parent was referenced by André Green (Kohon, 1999). Details of this are found in Chapter 7, describing what happens when a child experiences detachment from the loss of parental love. The parent is too sad, preoccupied, self-absorbed, emotionally dead to attend to the child. Yet, the child can remain in an unconscious identification with the emotional deadness. These psychological attempts to preserve some relationship leave in their wake lack, frustration and self-debilitation.

Lyran entered Jungian analysis after a long-term relationship breakup. She was surprised to realise her consciously held former self-image had now become outmoded. She no longer knew where she fit. Old habits did not guide any longer as she was at a crossroads. She felt separated from the self she had been and was facing unfamiliar compositions of her identity. Like the alchemical state of nigredo, the psychological dissolution coincided with and required immersion in the unknown. Essentially, ego consciousness had yet to work out a new relationship with the unconscious.

She had never been in therapy previously, yet she took to the inner work. She journalled; active imaginations came easily as well as associating to the symbolic material abounding in her dreams. She had not known to care about the inner world just as she had not learned to care about herself except for her athletic and sexual prowess. Nothing else was noticed. She knew to look compliant, please others, not ask and surely not express her emotional desires.

It is a form of death to a child who identifies with the lost and depressed parent as the child cannot bear the depression, tries to heal the parent, but the task is too much. 'Dissociation is the consequence of disturbing experience undergone at a time when there was not sufficient access to a containing mind within which to process and integrate it' (Meredith-Owen, 2021, p. 853). In the need to escape the emotional emptiness, lack of mirroring and overload of unexpressed feelings, Lyran did not realise she was secretly depressed. She assumed no one cared.

Lyran spent much emotional time avoiding what she anticipated as the intrusions of others, needing to hide her personality by assuming compliance with their demands. The need for hiddenness meant she listened to others to gauge the expected response so she could avoid any critique. Much as she needed attention, such adaptations contributed to her formation of psychic retreat.

Warren Colman noted the gap between what is present and 'the imaginative capacity to defend against aspects of reality concerned with absence and loss [is] felt to be intolerable' (2006). The nigredo state can be described as the psyche suffering, a destruction to the soul, the body in the shambles of distancing, denial, pain – a war waging within. Lyran portrayed this as bleak, unpleasant, full of confusion and bewilderment, disorientation, a sickness of spirit.

From a young age, Lyran's continuity of being was either ignored or blatantly interrupted. She had little opportunity to gain solidity, as she felt constantly bombarded by the disturbing energy in an ostensibly placid home. Heavy shadows lay underneath the façade and the falsity became the paralysis of her self-connection. This psychological response arose from the early narcissistic wounds and missed parental emotional response. 'The trauma in the parent functions as a disorganizing force which transforms the parent into an unpredictable adult who cannot think and feel and has no capacity for containment and empathy' (Cavalli, 2012, p. 601). The child deprived of sufficient early experiences for finding their own mind in the mind of a devoted other is left without an authentic or vitalised sense of self. The response of shutting off, defensiveness, emotional distance becomes the central organising factor in the personality, needed as the world seemed to her a potentially wounding place.

Lyran learned there was nowhere to attach, and although it has been a lonely existence, it was all she knew. Being home alone was a safe and familiar place while the outer world was fraught. The psyche in a narcissistic split develops a self-encapsulated system and the splits from reality allow in little that is new. This can signify states of breakdown, a place where understanding ceases and feelings overwhelm. Lyran retained shame about exposing foibles or fears as she worries that she will be rejected. Meanwhile, she remains at an impasse, as the unknown seems a venture too frightening.

Lyran kept ideas and thoughts inside, organising them before each therapy session so she would not make a mistake. For a long time, she avoided exposing any emotion, fragility or vulnerability, even in therapy. This behaviour mimicked when she had to be strong and perfect as a child in the presence of her authoritarian father. *She had a dream in which someone said she had to take care of him.* She did not know what this meant but knew it brought uncomfortable reactions. The dream could imply care of him meant her true and total self was preoccupied with him. This meant she was sacrificed and her emotions unacknowledged. The resultant split within the self caused psychic numbness, a loss of passion, an inability to share enthusiasm openly, feelings of grief and distrust of others. Therefore, she had to attend to him in her psyche, how he had influenced her dissociative responses and how she can care for herself now. Jung commented,

As a result of some psychic upheaval whole tracts of our being can plunge back into the unconscious and vanish from the surface for years and decades ... disturbances caused by affects are known technically as phenomena of dissociation, and are indicative of a psychic split.

(Jung, 1934/1968, CW 10, para. 286)

Fragility and self-attack

Jung commented at some length on the 'inner emptiness' that 'conceals just as great a fulness':

If you will contemplate your lack of fantasy, of inspiration and inner aliveness, which you feel as sheer stagnation and a barren wilderness and impregnate it with the interest born of alarm at your inner death, then something can take shape in you, for your inner emptiness conceals just as great a fulness if only you will allow it to penetrate into you. If you prove receptive to this 'call of the wild', the longing for fulfillment will quicken the sterile wilderness of your soul as rain quickens the earth.

(Jung, 1970, CW 14, para. 190)

The nigredo stage was known by the alchemists to be dangerous as poisonous vapours of lead and quicksilver (mercury) were generated and the patient required patience for the work to proceed. It is a trying time, and the patient feels lost although energy releases when no longer clinging to the old patterns and habits. The encounter with the shadow aspects must be confronted and assimilated into consciousness. The feelings of guilt, worthlessness and powerlessness are suffered and worked through. As a prelude to resolving conflicts between the warring elements in the psyche, a cleansing process is required, involving the examination and withdrawal of projections.

Lyran dreamt she was running and fell into a puddle, got up, was alright and went on. The scene repeated several times and each time she slowed down but kept going. Then there appeared a woman covered in a dress of white jewels who moved towards a huge oak tree with seven roots, and she laid down in a puddle at the base of the tree.

In discussing the dream, the components of slowing down, falling and getting up and ending at the roots with immersion in the puddle seemed to indicate the nigredo and the up and down process of the analytical work. The white of the dress, although in the mud puddle, was not soiled. The white and the mud were opposites yet neither ruined the other. The number seven represented change emerging from the roots of the oak, an old and sturdy tree. The tree was a symbol of strength, indicating growth and ability to withstand regardless of the father influence putting her down.

The absence caused from fractured parental bonds results in the need to bolster the fragile defences of the self. Lyran felt emotionally fragile and the nigredo came in various forms of her self-attack, despair and narcissistic hatred. These fed an internalised cycle of oppression from relational neglect, abandonment and emotional rigidity, making it difficult to love or care for herself.

The body is a storehouse for emotions, but when denied and too separated can develop psychosomatic symptoms. A cloak of invisibility through a showy exterior deflects from the emotional wounds forming the relational complexes.

There is 'inability to contain and reflect upon affective experience, not having internalized a process for containment of affect. Such patients can experience some of their affect but cannot form a representation. There is no ability to ... develop meaning' (Willemsen, 2014, p. 699). A protective shell forms and underneath the person remains dead, a frozen presence, the interior at a standstill. At some point, life catches up to address the emotions and needs formerly denied. The narcissist has yet to travel the road inwards, faced with the truths they know unconsciously, including the discontinuity and dissociations. The courage it takes is part of the process evolving from the fog of denial and invisibility to the experience of presence. This is a journey inwards to evolve outwards.

Jung termed this as movement towards the Self in the process of individuation. 'Any symbol which is greater than the individual may be a symbol of the total self' (Jung, 1970, CW 14 para. 232). Jung took the term not from its customary usage in Western psychology but from the Hindu notion of the Self or 'Atman', that aspect of divine power which resides in every individual as a source of being. 'The self is the totality of the psyche, the self as an archetype and the self as a personification of the unconscious' (Colman, 2000, p. 1).

Shadow

The nigredo is also referred to as the putrefaction, the stage of confession or catharsis, burning away the dross accumulated over the real personality. Putrefaction is the rotting necessary to destroy the old personality formations taking the form of dead bodies. It 'transmutes them into a new state of being as everything that has life, dies; everything that is dead putrefies and finds a new life' (Edinger, 1985, p. 148). Through the process of burning away former ideas and beliefs one gains clarity about oneself. To sort out Lyran's present life, the analytical and therapeutic work involved understanding what qualities of herself were unaccepted and undervalued and how these beliefs shaped her life choices.

To become conscious of the shadow requires effort and brings forth increasingly human qualities and responses. As Jung writes,

> When one tries desperately to be good ... and perfect, then all the more the shadow develops a definite will to be black and evil and destructive. People cannot see that; they are always striving to be marvelous, and then they discover that terrible destructive things happen which they cannot understand, and they either deny that such facts have anything to do with them, or if they admit them, they take them for natural afflictions, or they try to minimize them and to shift

the responsibility elsewhere. The fact is that if one tries beyond one's capacity to be perfect, the shadow descends into hell and becomes the devil.
(1998, p. 569)

The shadow is substantive as it encompasses more than the repressed and includes the unconscious, both personally and collectively. The impact of denying and disguising ourselves from the personal and cultural shadows keeps us narrow, ignorant and trapped within limitations. The shadow exerts itself in the person who looks a part and functions outstandingly according to others, yet often feels nothing is meaningful, and without meaning the experiences of life are reduced to nothing (von Franz, 2000, p. 148). This is what Lyran learned very young: She did not count, was difficult, too intense, leaving her both intimidated by others, needing to please and still unloved. An antidote for all this can be found by descending into the shadows and facing the nigredo, abandoning the persona assumed to be necessary for protection.

The shadow produces chaos and melancholy and is felt as a dark time. It is a difficult task of separation from what was, facing oneself without coverup, and accepting the reality of what is. Jung described,

> It is no reckless adventure, but an effort inspired by deep spiritual distress to bring meaning once more into life based on fresh and unprejudiced experience. Caution has its place, no doubt, but we cannot refuse our support to a serious venture which challenges the whole of the personality. If we oppose it, we are trying to suppress what is best in man – his daring and his aspirations. And should we succeed, we should only have stood in the way of that invaluable experience which might have given a meaning to life.
> (1932/1969, CW 11, para. 529)

Although this process can be accompanied by moments of despair, encountering the shadow is a requisite for self-fruition. The shadowy recesses reveal the parts calling for re-cognition, accessing the core, exploring yearning, desire and melancholy. However, the narcissist tries to escape the shadow aspects, the depression and anxiety through flights of imagination and outer displays of grandiosity. The discomfiting but necessary awareness of the shadow represents a coming to earth necessary for actualising creativity and life (von Franz, 2000, p. 128).

The tension between ego and self, surface and shadow are part of forming an identity in which the various selves can co-exist in their logical, imaginative or material forms. There is a

> unity in convergence, that is, a 'falling together' ... a unity geometrically conceived, but without quantity ... It is a unity of substance without mingling and without obliteration of either party or substance ... The coincidence of opposites is beyond the reach of discursive reasoning and is a unity to which neither otherness nor plurality nor multiplicity is opposed.
> (Bond, 1997, p. 28)

The psychological process takes patience as the unmasking and moving into reality connotes a threat to the ego/persona that until now has been tightly relied upon. The need for unconditional love and anxiety about being refused had been the norm for Lyran. Behind the well-calculated front portraying intellect, aloofness and sophistication lay a tender, repressed vulnerability.

In a dream Lyran sees a white clawfoot tub like the one in my office bathroom. She looks and there is red in the tub, not blood but the colour. Then a woman emerges from it in a red flowing dress. She gives Lyran the shard of a mirror. Lyran looks in the shard and sees an eye. It is not hers, and she does not know whose it is. Is she looking at a part of herself yet unknown, emerging from the tub of colour?

The red is different from the black of nigredo and a favourite colour of hers. She emerges in the form of another woman from the tub full of her colour. Perhaps it is the fire of energy and passion now able to be put on for herself. The dream images refine the imaginative, emotional and spiritual to bring forward the intelligence in the body and feeling in the mind. 'Every psychological expression is a symbol if we assume that it states or signifies something more and other than itself which eludes our present knowledge' (Jung, 1971, CW 6, para. 817).

The mirror becomes restorative in analysis through the participants interplay of unconscious and conscious processes in the consulting room. Hopelessness and impasse then have a possibility to shift to hope and openness as we are moved and illuminated by dreams. 'The dream provides perspective on the personal unconscious and life circumstances, and because personal complexes have roots in archetypal images, dreams are also windows into the collective unconscious' (Henderson, 2018, p. 208).

Deadness

The dead parent referred to by Green is when a child experiences detachment from experiencing the presence of parental love and intimate relatedness through no fault of theirs. 'Subsequent to an event unknown to the child, [the parent] lost the lust for life' (Green, 2023, p. 71). However, due to the basic needs for care and love, the self-identification attaches to the deadened parent to preserve some sort of connection to them, but this severs connection to the self. The crucial rupture remains in the unconscious and is re-enacted towards themself in various destructive and negative ways. A protective shell forms and the child cannot feel alive due to the frozenness caused by the absence. There is emotional standstill. The lack is often somatised through weight loss or gain, illnesses, lethargy. In psychological work the analyst, if aware of their own deadness, can help bridge the discontinuity to use the deadened state as a resource rather than a drain.

The transformative dynamics of psychic life seek release for the fractured ego. This will lead to the breakdown of defences to push into the core of the voidness (Marlan, 2005, p. 73). The psychological descent feels like death. However, it expresses a radical shift in consciousness. It is part of the process of transformation in which symbolic events can be recognised. The self is discovered through the *mortificatio* process of burning away the nonessential and signifies a radical shift in consciousness. The 'abyss is black, containing everything and nothing ... and represents not a stage but a part throughout life' (Marlan, 2005, pp. 95, 190). It has a purpose to warn and dissolve in the continuous deconstruction leading to psychological change and construction.

Nigredo also marks the time drawing one towards introspection. As in the alchemical processes, it is through dissolution that new life is possible (Marlan, 2005, p. 66). This is the psychological descent into the *massa confusa* necessary for the old patterns to fall away and then reform. The processes begin with the nigredo, the despairing time when life feels lost, unpleasant, full of confusion and bewilderment, disorientation, sickness of spirit, bringing forth confrontation with the shadow. It is at this stage that Lyran became depressed, melancholic and deeply restless. This is the time when the question of meaning or purpose becomes central for the individual and is often triggered by feelings of dissatisfaction, unhappiness, frustration and inability to identify the source or cause of these feelings. The narcissist emits their elements of dysfunction in either relatedness to others or to themselves. Certain habits or defensive mechanisms developed in early years are no longer aiding the individual, but instead are hampering the ability to lead meaningful and fulfilling lives. The impulse to break out beyond this bleakness is a dynamic narcissists face on the individuation journey. Yet, they have difficulty staying with the unease, anxiety, discomfort of the old falling away and the new reforming. It takes time.

However, in therapy and analysis talking about things formerly not spoken of, but without the pressure for immediate solutions, can be comforting, sparking creativity and new ways of perceiving. Self-identity occurs through exploring one's subjectivity and imagination. In a broad sense 'modern humanity's great adventure is to ... plumb the depths of the human soul ... to open completely new dimensions' (Guggenbühl-Craig, 1999, p. 142).

The analytical process involves two people, with the new material emerging from the space created between them consciously and unconsciously. In-depth psychological work constellates self and other, patient and analyst, depicting together the movement of the psyche. The analyst's challenge is to assist the patient in finding her unknown aspects so she can escape the limits unconsciously adopted. 'In the final analysis, the therapist must always strive to constellate the healing factor in the patient' (Guggenbühl-Craig, 1999, p. 92). The therapist provides a mirror for the patient to perceive what she could not previously due to the arrested development of a starved psyche.

Lyran, a highly creative woman, was born to a family demanding compliance to their form of normality. She was outside of that box and got no reinforcement for her need to contradict their way of living. It was so false for her and could not fit. Her deviation from them into her specialness brought the revelation of her truths. Through the analytical process Lyran rediscovered her creative, artistic self. She voraciously read the favourite books she had put away years ago. She began to register feelings, at first with discomfort but gradually with appreciation. She was shedding the formerly dead layers, and her life desires were expanding and new vistas opening. Lyran began to find purpose and meaning and more sharply sense her own uniqueness.

The first hexagram of the I Ching is The Creative and illustrates the following:

> The hexagram is consistently strong in character, and since it is without weakness, its essence is power or energy. Its image is heaven. Its energy is represented as unrestricted by any fixed conditions in space and is therefore conceived of as motion. Time is regarded as the basis of this motion. Thus, the hexagram also includes the power of time and the power of persisting in time, that is, duration. The power represented by the hexagram is to be interpreted in a dual sense in terms of its action on the universe and of its action on the world of men. In relation to the universe, the hexagram expresses the strong, creative action of the Deity. In relation to the human world, it denotes the creative action of the holy man or sage, of the ruler or leader of men, who through his power awakens and develops their higher nature.
>
> (Wilhelm, 1977)

In the search for understanding, the disruptive inner and outer emotions arouse unexpected factors constellated in the psychological treatment. Through the dynamism of the therapeutic interplay are the tasks of linking the known and unknown, conscious and unconscious, and balancing the tension between. Jung said holding the tension of the opposites is essential for bridging the gap between ego consciousness and the unconscious. If the tension can be sustained without succumbing to the urge to identify with one side or the other, the completely unexpected images unite the elements in a creative new way.

The psyche is fluid, multidimensional, alive and capable of creative development. The challenge is to emerge from the narcissistic position and find authenticity and intimacy with self and others. The task delves into discovering what is called in Jungian psychology the 'treasure hard to attain' or the knowledge residing in the unconscious, the body, admitting and using the shadow responsibly for the discovery of Self while connecting us to others.

> Psychotherapy is at bottom a dialectical relationship between doctor and patient. It is an encounter, a discussion between two psychic wholes, in which ego knowledge is a tool assisting the goal of transformation. This is not one that is predetermined, but rather an indeterminable change, the only criterion of which is the disappearance of egohood. No efforts on the part of the doctor can compel this experience. The most he can do is to smooth the path for the patient and help him to attain an attitude which offers the least resistance to the decisive experience.
>
> (Jung, 1939/1969, CW 11, para. 904)

The unconscious is not linear but loops back to re-incorporate the sentient and imaginative in newly emergent ways. Revisioning ourselves and life is the act of looking back, seeing with fresh eyes, and acknowledging the assumptions blocking us from ourselves. Perceiving the past with a wider lens reassembles the material rather than passing on traditional or unconscious ways of being. By attending to the inner world, the self can be healed, bringing unity between body and mind, becoming active with a sense of purpose and meaning.

Jung commented, 'Relationship to the self is at once relationship to others, and no one can be related to the latter until he is related to himself' (1946/1966, CW 16, para. 445). This is a gathering of the multiple personal and collective threads, the social and historical forces conditioning our existence. To see one's life as a kind of palimpsest reinforces taking the risks to take off the cloak of 'as-if'. Unmasking the issues both personally and culturally leads to hope, unties the constraints and creates new ways of being throughout life. Out of the depths of the nigredo emerges one's individual and unique self.

> Tell all the truth but tell it slant –
> Success in Circuit lies
> Too bright for our infirm Delight
> The Truth's superb surprise
> As Lightning to the Children eased
> With explanation kind
> The Truth must dazzle gradually
> Or every man be blind –
> (Emily Dickinson, 1890)

References

Bond, H. L. (1997). Introduction to *Nicholas of Cusa: Selected spiritual writings*, by Nicholas of Cusa (H. L. Bond, Trans.). Paulist Press.

Cavalli, A. (2012). Transgenerational transmission of undigestible facts: From trauma, deadly ghosts and mental voids to meaning making interpretations. *Journal of Analytical Psychology*, 57(5), 597–614.

Colman, W. (2000). *Jungian thought in the modern world*. (E. Christopher & H. Solomon, Eds.). Free Association Books.

Colman, W. (2006). Imagination and the imaginary. *Journal of Analytical Psychology*, 51(1), 21–41.

Colman, W. (2007). Symbolic conceptions: The idea of the third. *Journal of Analytical Psychology*, 52(5), 565–583.

Connolly, A. (2013). Out of the body: Embodiment and its vicissitudes. *Journal of Analytical Psychology*, 58(5), 636–656.

Dickinson, E. (1890). *The Project Gutenberg eBook of Poems by Emily Dickinson, Series One*, edited by Thomas Wentworth Higginson and Mabel Loomis Todd. https://www.gutenberg.org/ebooks/2678

Edinger, E. (1985). *Anatomy of the psyche*. Open Court.

Eigen, M. (1995). Psychic deadness: Freud. *Contemporary Psychoanalysis, 31*, 277–298.
Fordham, M. (1985). *Explorations of the self.* Routledge.
Freud, S. (1914). On Narcissism. In J. Strachey (Trans.), *The standard edition of the complete psychological works of Sigmund Freud: Vol. XIV. On the history of the psychoanalytic movement, papers on metapsychology and other works* (pp. 67–102). Hogarth Press.
Green, A. (1975). The analyst, symbolization and absence in the analytic setting (On changes in analytic practice and analytic experience). *International Journal of Psycho-Analysis, 56*(1), 1–22
Green, A. (2023). *On the destruction and death drives.* Phoenix Publishing.
Guggenbühl-Craig, A. (1999). *Power in the helping professions.* Spring Publications.
Henderson, D. (2018). *Depth psychology and mysticism.* (T. Cattoi, and D. M. Odorisio, Eds.). Springer International Publishing AG.
Jung, C. G. (1932/1969). Psychotherapists or the clergy. In *Psychology and religion: West and East* (Vol. 11). Princeton University Press.
Jung, C. G. (1934/1968). *The collected works of C. G. Jung. Vol. 10. The meaning of psychology for modern man.* Princeton University Press.
Jung, C. G. (1938/1969). The Terry Lectures. In *Psychology and religion: West and East* (Vol. 11). Princeton University Press.
Jung, C. G. (1939/1969). Foreword to Suzuki's 'Introduction to Zen Buddhism'. In *Psychology and religion: West and East* (Vol. 11). Princeton University Press.
Jung, C. G. (1946/1966). The psychology of the transference. In *The practice of psychotherapy* (Vol. 16). Princeton University Press.
Jung, C. G. (1963). *Memories, dreams, reflections.* Random House.
Jung, C. G. (1970). *The collected works of C. G. Jung. Vol 14. Mysterium Conjunctionius.* Princeton University Press.
Jung, C. G. (1971). *The collected works of C. G. Jung: Vol 6. Psychological types.* Princeton University Press.
Jung, C. G. (1998). *Visions: Note on the seminar given in 1930–1934.* Princeton University Press.
Kohon, G. (Ed.) (1999). *The dead mother: The work of André Green.* Routledge.
Marlan, S. (2005). *Black sun.* Texas A&M University Press.
Marlan, S. (2020). *C. G. Jung and the alchemical imagination.* Routledge.
Meredith-Owen, W. (2021). Alchemical dragons: Winnicott's reaching towards the objective psyche. *Journal of Analytical Psychology, 66*(4), 848–873.
Schwartz, S. (2024). *Imposter syndrome and the 'as-if' personality in analytical psychology: Fragility of the self.* Routledge.
von Franz, M.-L. (2000). *The problem of the puer aeternus.* Inner City Books.
Willemsen, H. (2014). Early trauma and affect: The importance of the body for the development if the ability to symbolize. *Journal of Analytical Psychology, 59*(5), 695–712.
Wilhelm, R. Trans. (1977). *I Ching.* Princeton University Press. (No page number available.)

Chapter 12

Where do we go from here? Can Narcissus and Echo bloom into love?

An image from Zen Buddhism #10 of the Ox-Herding Picture Series depicts a meaning of psychological and physical integration. The commentary reads, 'He comes into the market bare-chested and barefooted: Though covered with dirt and dust, his face beams with delight. He doesn't use magic like a legendary wizard. But he makes dead trees bloom' (Stein, 2019, p. 16).

We are always hungry for stories of change and growth. And as in the previous commentary each story contains a mystery. The character is not beautiful or decked out glamorously but has the inner power for enhancing and giving life. On the other hand, the story of Narcissus and Echo is about unrequited love that does not grow and is based on exterior image. Narcissus remains in his personal shell, a world protecting the self from disappointment, uncertainty, risk. Echo is a figure of desire unmet, frustrated. Neither is satisfied and the ending sad and lonely with each trapped in deathlike states. If we dream this myth onward, it indicates the only way forwards is change. The form of love based on narcissism becomes stuck and will only get loosened with shifts and alterations if the characters find ways to communicate honestly and from the depths of the soul. Like the extreme of narcissism with no change, only death and demise occurs in this myth. Love remains undone. Death, the unconscious and loss are prominent as in the myth every symbol and word expose what is absent in the object, the subject and the lack of relationship between them.

However, the absence between Narcissus and Echo signifies space for the return of the object and subject. By filling the absence, it is transformed. This describes the psychological process of self-discovery where the capacity for curiosity, connection and change flourishes with in-depth explorations. Creativity releases by unwrapping the layers of narcissism. Through this journey inwards and its effects, we discover patterns in the myth applicable to ourselves and our culture.

This is the hope and attraction to narcissism. But is it impossible to break into this tightly wound personality type? Are we lured to a dead end? Will lack remain or can the narcissist learn to encounter themselves and others by unwrapping and accepting the plurality of the personality? This requires a polysemic approach to the psyche. It means being real. This recognition moves beyond the confines of the singular into the expansive and receptive, to the multiplicity of the psyche. In analysis there is movement to sustain and enhance life. The malleability, lessening of the strictures and becoming open can be both exhilarating and terrifying. The psychological constellation of qualities being revealed begin to fill personal and collective reactions, fears and traumas with joy and hope as new pathways are formed.

The narcissistic problem is the refusal of any pluralities as they entail the unfamiliar. It means acknowledging what seems like the virulent strain of psychic pain lodged deep in the soul. Love and narcissism return us to what we do not know about ourselves and others. As Jung said,

> In order to have a clear picture you must hold thesis and antithesis ever before your eyes, the two things that constantly work into each other or influence each other and then try to separate them. But it is really difficult.
>
> (Jung, 1989, p. 856)

The narcissist tries to escape reality although reality is integral for gaining consciousness of relationship with self and others. To look in the reflecting pond, unlike Narcissus, means moving beyond oneself and embracing the formerly refused. Love means finding oneself in another, the truths both ugly and beautiful and accepting the intimacy of change. It contains restless ambivalence, differences and embodies the paradox of losing the false security of being alone while simultaneously discovering oneself by growing with another. The figure of Echo reminds me of the traits and characteristics found by reaching out to love, filling the desire for the world to expand. Echo makes it possible by saying it again and again, her rhetoric containing the hope and the power to encourage and unite. Echo persists to be open and creative in her ways of emoting desire and love emitted from the words of the one she loves, Narcissus.

Narcissism and love

Exploring the topic of narcissism and love from the perspective of Jungian analytical psychology brings this personality, attitudes and traits out of the pathological into the symbolic and meaningful. The aim is to free the human soul from the constriction of rigid, fear-based and narrow defensive structures. The idea propelling inner work is to find the gold in the unknown, to unearth the personality from its layers of disguise and to break the shackles of isolation into expansive and varied relationships. Love itself is the unknown and the mystery, especially for a narcissist.

In general, the ego does not experience a feeling of being narcissistically wounded, but is unable to reach its ideals, with vague experiences and specific longings. The outwardly ambitious, success-driven narcissistic person has a poorly integrated, grandiose self-concept. These exhibitionistic proclivities arise as this person is prone to shame. Understanding the grandiose and vulnerable aspects, arrogance and envy brings these pieces together in a process of learning to listen to the unconscious.

It also involves a falling apart, as James Hillman noted, 'the psyche's autonomous ability to create illness, morbidity, disorder, abnormality, and suffering in any aspect of its behavior and to experience and imagine life through this deformed and afflicted perspective' (1975, p. 57). The narcissist must descend into the despair, depression and loss to recover the deeper and multiple layers of the personality. Instead, the narcissist often ends up killing their more complete self and identifying almost entirely with the superiority and their false, ego-driven needs for admiration. As Jung said, 'The unrelated human being lacks wholeness for we can achieve wholeness only through the soul, and the soul cannot exist without its other side, which is always found in a "You". Wholeness is a combination of I and You' (1946/1966, CW 16, para. 454).

Narcissism when examined is part of what can bring us into the reality of the psyche with its complexes, impasses, anxieties and defences. Its solutions derive from reflection and attention to the voices of the Self, the larger personality guiding life and extending far beyond the smallness of the ego. This is where we encounter the transformative mystery of love and gather its potential emerging from the narcissistic clutches. As Jung commented, 'Mighty is he who loves. But whoever distances himself from love, feels himself powerful' (2009, p. 253).

Love is a mercurial agent activating the erotic and relational energies. The eros of relationship involves getting to know the unseen desires. Eros is the yearning for relatedness and interaction with others, to fill the emptiness signalled by anxiety, despair, loss of meaning and proclivity to various addictions. As Jung said, 'Eros is not form-giving but form-fulfilling. It is the wine that will be poured into the bottle, it is not the bed and direction of the stream but the impetuous water flowing into it' (2009, p. 365).

In the Jungian psychological/analytical process unravelling narcissism and its obstructions to love, psychic and somatic factors are made conscious. These factors urge an increase in consciousness as the narcissist encounters their projections onto others and simultaneously discerns the primal source within themselves. In *The Red Book* Jung said,

> Just as you become a part of the manifold essence of the world through your bodies, so you become a part of the manifold essence of the inner world through your soul. This inner world is truly infinite, in no way poorer than the outer one. Man lives in two worlds.
>
> (2009, para. 64)

Narcissism can be construed as an integral part of the striving for knowledge of self and world. It requires a union of differences, opposites, surprising elements arising from the unconscious to consciousness.

Narcissism plunges us deeply into the psyche. The inner divisions discovered as we investigate our own reflecting pool mean examining what is found there in both the ponderous and light shadows within the matrix of the self. The differences provide the opportunity to explore shared ambitions, desire, experiences, affections as analysis looks deeply into the self. The pain and tragic forms of damage are not entirely able to be repaired, yet in the process the analysand discovers joy and renewal. The energy and instincts to save the day aim to recover what seems to have been unavailable. The search for fulfilment brings out the displaced elements as the narcissist searches for identity. This means recognising the self-destructive bits and areas of resistance but doing it anyway rather than submitting to closing off alternatives. It is facing the need to recognise they were mistaken, and this refusal has prevented the space for growth from opening.

However, the narcissist has become emotionally detached and threatened by others inside and out with their defensive posturing and entitlement manifested in the body and psyche. These were needed as a narcissist assesses themselves as deficient. Their singularity reflects a deep-seated belief there is nothing within or there is nothing there of value. The need to be recognised also derives from the disconcerting sensation of feeling invisible, insufficient, unnoticed and unimportant. Yet, the narcissist trembles at being seen up close. Desires to be centre stage can threaten control and exert pressure to present the perfect image adored by all. To be seen for who one really is also entails being seen for its opposite, who one is not.

The beliefs

'The language of belief is clearly cast in the language of a relationship' (Britton, 2015, 82). Beliefs offer a point of entry into the internal world and its myriad figures as reflected by others. Yet, narcissistic singularity defensively wipes out others in its destructive swash. The Self is distanced, and the personality weakened. For the narcissist, the ego fails to live up to its ideals, leaving them with a highly complex, dreaded, but misaligned relationship to the Self.

The narcissist struggles to gain internal purchase, desires yet refuses love and intimacy while needing control to hold onto power. Behind the front of bravado and braggadocio this person is sad and alone, but no one knows this nor the depth of their confusion and despair. This becomes apparent as the narcissist reaches the same point of intimacy with every partner and then backs off. They do not see the pattern. Missing inner connections means no outer connection can penetrate. This indicates an emotional injury, mental pain and distress in relationships to self and others, appearing in numerous isolating behaviours. The narcissist is awash with the feeling of self-alienation, unsure of anything let alone themselves. The question is how entrenched these traits can become and how resistant the narcissist is to hear the echo of the other. Some just cannot do it.

Narcissism is a part of emotional development and is alive with both destructive and constructive elements and possibilities. It entails actively wrestling with what it means to become a person in the world, to deal with loneliness yet not exclude others and to answer the feeling there is something more inside oneself. What does it mean to become a somebody rather than a nobody, to find the true authentic self? How do we combine our specialness with the common ordinary aspects of being human? It means existing in the unknowable, to be imagining and reimagining who we are and engaged in the process and possibility of becoming throughout life. Narcissism grows by moving from the predicable to the uncertain and unknown mystery of being. Grappling with the disharmony within, the conflicts and tensions lead to movement towards individuation.

The quest for meaning includes the shifting grounds of mental and emotional pain from the personality imbalances and conflicts in the psychic structure. Narcissism can bring thoughtful reflection or keep a person stagnate. It requires a pause, being present and aware of the absence rather than running from it. As Jung commented, it requires 'an empty stillness which precedes creative work followed by the release of the dammed up energy' (Jung, 1946/1966, CW 16, para. 373). Analysis means considering 'these psychological phenomena and symptoms as if they had intention and purpose granting to the unconscious knowledge or foreknowledge' (Jung, 1957/1969, CW 8, para 175).

Personal and cultural transformations

We exist in an era immersed in the Western culture of narcissism, as Christopher Lasch (1979) in the mid-twentieth century highlighted. The current magnitude of uncertainties and transitions makes blatant these challenging times. This applies to everyone as we are all entangled in one way or another in states of consciousness and unconsciousness. The culture of narcissism appears worldwide.

Jungian analytical psychology and thought considers broadly the psychic wounds of narcissism and the effects on people's lives to access healing within the personality. Narcissism can bring us to a sensitive and deep reflection on the nature of these wounds and psychological repair. Hope emerges from the conundrum of those caught in the throes of narcissism, whether it is about themselves, a partner or the effects from a narcissistic parent. This includes attending to the culture of narcissism while the primary focus is understanding the individual psychological situations. As Stein says,

> The transformation of consciousness means overcoming the habitual patterns of thought that become locked into place by routine and repetition, the largely unconscious patterns of behaviour and attitude engrained by family and collective culture, and the rigid psychological formations created by life experiences.
> (2019, p. 6)

Self-reflection and fascination with self are necessary for growth and development, to a point including, not excluding others.

'The myth deals with the human drive for self-knowledge and self-realization ... implies the possibility of transcending the narrower forms of narcissistic problems' (Jacoby, 1990, p. 29). Narcissus and his exclusion of Echo poignantly illustrates the struggle for this type of person to connect and to love. Narcissism is the love of an image, but one unrecognisable as himself. In the myth both Narcissus and

Echo die from lack of love and the failure to unite or change. Echo symbolises the feminine in us all, her body and psyche as the rejected object, pining after what cannot happen.

Narcissism is a study in self-deception compounded by apprehensions of exploring the unconscious. Although the narcissist would prefer it, perfection is not possible in human life. The narcissistic insistence on sameness becomes a defence against feelings of inferiority and shame. For the narcissist the blues of depression, self-loathing and desperation occur with the smallest signs of imperfection. To fall short of the ideal of greatness and to experience this in themselves is debilitating, yet it brings them into the reality of what they can have. Entitlement is an attempt to mitigate the disappointment, compensate with feelings of grandeur and sidestep the losses learned from early emotional betrayals continuing through life. Narcissists are fragile, or feel they are. The defensive impenetrability signifies the lack of connection with the self and its ramifications reverberate clinically, personally and culturally.

There is a timelessness to the issues while the narcissist finds themselves in a state of self-dissatisfaction, pining after something they cannot possess. However, the narcissist hides this with a show, deceptively marvellous and mesmerising, while their inside remains vacant and unknown. Reality is fraught with anguish, panic, absence, void and melancholia, all consciously unacknowledged but present, nonetheless.

The narcissistic mirror is distorted, and the narcissist cannot find themselves in its reflection. The idealised persona is constructed to hide what is considered the shadow with its existing cracks threatening to open, like an anticipated earthquake one does everything to avoid. The feeling of fraudulence and living on illusions is based on the avoidance of being intimately known. This person struggles to establish an integrated sense of 'I'. Yet, the overriding question within this personality remains, if I am not seen as exceptional, what am I?

Although we are interested in narcissism, this topic contains a conundrum, seductive in gaining attention as many people face this personality type or a form of it in relationships within themselves and others. The subsequent and various interpretations and roots link to updated viewpoints of this personality aspect and trait. Psychological growth and creativity increase from understanding its intricate and paradoxical dynamics.

Narcissistic demand for love

Knowledge enriches the fabric of the psyche. This writing highlights Jungian analytic perspectives with its in-depth approach so necessary for our times. To expand Jungian thought and align its paradigm with other psychoanalytic perspectives challenges the singularity the narcissist hides behind. The information gains layers and complexity from the cross-disciplinary, generative meanings weaving through these multiple threads.

We need to know ourselves well enough to perceive our own demand for love, for attention; only in this way will we be able to receive our own gifts, which will be the balm to treat the wounds inflicted by another or by ourselves, the other within us.

(Rubini, 2020, p. 69)

A narcissist inhabits the world yet feels fragmentary, wearing a façade, a personality beneath which parts are hiding, desiring, yearning for a certain love but unable to attain it. To live with consciousness is to own but not be ruled by narcissistic aspects and to be conscious of them. It requires an effort to mediate between the body and the mind and find the movement, unity and connection through encountering differences. How hard it is for the narcissist to accept all their parts, including the shadows, and cherish them without façades but with persona reality.

It is an uncomfortable path to the Self but full of rewards. This is an investigation of the disconnect and dissociations from how we perform as the authentic people we are, opening a pathway toward more conscious and coherent selves. Narcissism is a complex and enigmatic subject. Lying deep beneath our personal and literal histories, vaster regions of the psyche beckon the ego to awaken into the fields of the imaginal. This engages our personal and collective narratives as we examine the myth behind narcissism and where we fit or not. We are made of many, not one, as listening and responding to the voice of Echo illustrates, by reaching out rather than remaining in the singularity of Narcissus. To love self and others is a task of our times and concerns our being in the world. Tapping into the unconscious invites its entering consciousness and facilitating transformation. 'In loving the individual goes beyond [themself], beyond the narcissistic' (Badiou, 2009, p. 12).

Searching for a deeper understanding of life means following the symbolic language touching the heart and soul. 'Love is a quest for truth' (Badiou, 2009, p. 22). We are changed from the unconscious movement to consciousness to cohere the self and engage with the world, accepting and valuing pluralities. The emphasis is on the growth potential of the narcissist, should they proceed to the entry point of the psyche. The possibility of repair suggests we can recover what has been lost and set about integrating what has been refused and not understood.

Endings are also beginnings entailing the possibility of opening new horizons. Narcissism carries a transformational possibility along with its challenges. It requires going back to move forwards, relooking at what has happened with the idea of repair and the alteration to widen rather than shut down. This creates the freedom for creativity, internal confidence and solidity of connection to the Self.

A slice of a woman's dream ended with the following phrase: *I am more than me*. She realises she is more than the career strivings, the ego achievements as she yearns for love in relationship and wants to express new creative endeavours. She longs to expand her world yet has retained the narcissistic enclosure – internal isolation and intimacy compromised and never fully grasped, received or met. Yet what this means we can only imagine as the future unfolds from what is unknown, germinating at the dream moment. For her, it means a promise and hope of intimacy and a movement from singularity to inclusiveness of the other, both inner and outer. Acknowledging the urge for transformation embedded in the narcissistic aspects of the personality is a gateway through the agony, absence and loss to find aliveness, curiosity and potential within the love of self and others. 'Love ... is of fundamental importance in human life and ... of far greater significance than the individual suspects' (Jung, 1912/1969, CW 7, para. 423).

References

Badiou, A. (2009). *In praise of love*. The New Press.
Britton, R. (2015). *Between mind and brain*. Routledge.
Hillman, J. (1975). *Re-Visioning psychology*. Harper & Row.
Jacoby, M. (1990). *Individuation and narcissism: The psychology of self in Jung and Kohut*. Routledge.
Jung, C. G. (1912/1969). New paths in psychology. In *Two essays on analytical psychology* (Vol. 7). Princeton University Press.
Jung, C. G. (1946/1966). The psychology of the transference. *The Practice of Psychotherapy* (Vol. 16). Princeton University Press.
Jung, C. G. (1957/1969). The transcendent function. In *The structure and dynamics of the psyche* (Vol. 8). Princeton University Press. Jung, C. G. *Liber Novus*.
Jung C. G. (1989). *Nietzsche's Zarathustra: Notes from the seminars given in 1934–1939*. (J. L. Jarrett, Ed.). Routledge.
Jung, C. G. (2009). *The red book: Liber novus*. W. W. Norton & Co.
Lasch, C. (1979). *Culture of narcissism: American life in an age of diminishing expectations*. W. W. Norton & Co.
Rubini, R. (2020). Psychic wounds, Jung and narcissism. *Junguiana*, 38(1), 57–72.
Stein, M. (2019). Psychological individuation and spiritual enlightenment: some comparisons and points of contact. *Journal of Analytical Psychology*, 64(1), 6–22.

Index

abject/abjection 134–136
Abraham, K. 98
anima and animus 92–95
Arendt, H. 6
'as-if' personality 26–29, 63–66, 103–105, 140
Astor, J. 119
authenticity 50–52

beliefs 184–185
belonging: and attachment 151; and identity 162; recognition of 155
Berry, P. 123
Bion, W. 29, 34
Bisagni, F. 53
blackness, as starting gate 168–169
body 169–170; abjection 136–137; and emotions 48, 174; and feelings 68; loss 88–90; and mind 68, 70–71, 91, 103, 112, 187; and psyche 68, 72, 76, 156, 184; and subjective self 74
Bollas, C. 53, 85
boredom 51, 57
Borges, J. L. 144
Britton, R. 13, 64, 100, 103, 104

circumambulation 7
Cixous, H. 69, 83, 85–87
clinical narcissism 104
collective unconscious 8
Colman, W. 172
consciousness 47, 53, 66, 93–95, 117, 132, 158, 185
conundrum 12–15
crime dream 138, 140

cultural complexes 12, 151–153, 156
cultural exclusion 150–152
cultural identifications 152
culture of narcissism 12, 18, 185

deadness 59, 73–74, 111, 131, 169, 176–179
death, life narcissism and 106–108, 111, 113
de Beauvoir, S. 50, 51
deception 54
defences 32; dissociative 118; narcissistic 9, 18, 58, 60; self 24, 125, 149
defensive avoidance of distressing memories 32
demon lover: clinical example 107–112; parental absences, effects of 112–115
depression 54, 106, 107, 110–111, 124, 183
Derrida, J. 34
desire *see* emotion, desire and
destructive (death) narcissism 39, 100, 106–115, 140
detachment 106, 171, 176
Deutsch, H. 26, 64, 98, 103
disenchantment 36–38
disillusionments 26, 61, 64, 162, 165
dissociation 125, 171, 173
dissociative defences 118
distress 65, 143
Doolittle, H. 83
dreams 37, 72–73, 114–115, 118, 123, 142–143, 147, 154, 157, 161, 165, 172, 173, 176; anima in 95; being stuck in 105; committing a crime 137–138; on

escaping 108–109; on robbing 55–56; woman emerging out of a stone wall 74–75

Echo 82–86, 88–89, 123, 135, 181, 182, 185–186; myth of 8, 15, 19, 23, 69, 71, 73
ego 5, 36, 43, 52, 78, 122, 124, 127, 129, 137, 175, 182
ego consciousness, and unconscious 156, 171, 178
ego-libido 99
Eigen, M. 169
Ellis, A. 98
emotional neglect 13
emotion, desire and 34–48; being envied 42–46; disenchantment 36–38; envy and rage 38–42; impact on personality 37; libido 35–36; in psyche exploration 36; sadism 46–47; transformative 47–48
empathy 102
emptiness 26, 48, 73–74; 'as-if' personality 63–66; authenticity 50–52; and boredom 50–66; and envy 38, 40; fear of being inadequate 61–63; grandiosity 52–53; and loneliness 15; melancholia 53–54; within narcissist 57; predictable analysis 54–59; puer and puella 59–61; representing potential of fulfilment 59; and soullessness 127
envy: being the object of 42–46; destructive forces of 34; devouring aspect of 43; disguised expressions 44; on identity and relationships 44–46; rage and 38–42, 102; sadism and 46–47
Eros, offence to 92–95

false self 9, 13, 98, 102–103, 128
fantasies 31–32, 104
fearlessness 6
fear of being inadequate 61–63
feminine 76–77, 88–89, 92–94, 118, 120
Fordham, M. 123, 125, 169
fragility: of 40, 45, 51, 54, 60, 106; self-attack and 173–174
Freud, S. 13, 28, 97, 99–100, 117, 169
Fröbe-Kapteyn, O. 94

galvanometer, Jung and 70
Glissant, É. 5
Gogol, N. 162
grandiosity 52–53, 63, 101–102, 106; characteristics of 22; and idealisation 103; narcissistic 52, 122; and omnipotence 47
Green, A. 13–14, 98, 106–107, 110–114, 146–147, 155, 158–159, 171, 176; *see also* demon lover
Griffin, S. 161

healthy narcissism 21–22
Hera 88
Heraclitus 29
Hillman, J. 5, 20, 92, 95, 183
Hughes, T. 75
human love 126
Humbert, E. 119

identity 93, 107, 152, 156, 162; self-identity 27, 28, 126–128, 177
illness, as metaphor for the self 34–35
image 76, 118
individuation, Jungian process of 2, 6, 17, 19, 36, 48, 60, 94, 119, 127, 140, 147–148, 150, 174
inflated consciousness 47, 124
initiation 123
intimacy 4, 11, 19, 25, 38, 60, 82–95, 131, 138, 167, 182

Jacoby, M. 52, 119, 123, 127
James, W. 50
Jung, C. G. 13, 15, 23, 36, 43, 73, 84, 148–151, 182, 185; anima and animus 93, 95; artistic yearning and primordial image 75; body and 70; *Collected Works* 71, 107; collective unconscious 8, 132; complexes and 15, 74, 141; on consciousness 66, 117; consequences of inflated consciousness 47; on desire and love 38; on dreams 137; on ego and persona 27; eternal child in psyche 121; on fantasies 31; future attitudes and unconscious 166; on importance of psychic balance for individuals and

society 106; individuation and 2, 6, 17, 19, 36, 48, 60, 94, 119, 127, 147, 150, 155, 174; on 'inner emptiness' 173; on libido 35–36; on love 131, 133; on memory and unconscious 35; mythology and archetypal symbolism 118; on natural urge of life 34; negative capability and 29; psyche as natural phenomenon 59, 74; *The Red Book* 183; rejection of Freud's views on narcissism 117; repetition 85; on self 5–6, 19, 51, 85, 95, 119, 127, 179; self-confidence and 118; on shadow 56, 120, 136, 155, 174–175; on symbolic reality 57; transcendent function and 156–157; transference and 159; on unconscious 32, 75, 166, 173; on wholeness 37, 120, 183
Jung, E. 94

Keats, J. 29
Kernberg, O. 101–102
Kimbles, S. 153
Klein, M. 46
Kohut, H. 101, 102, 123
Kristeva, J. 4, 13, 62, 131, 134–136
Kunitz, S. 146

Lasch, C. 12, 185
libidinal narcissism 100
libido 35–36
life narcissism 106–115
loneliness 160
love 20–21, 24, 32, 37, 38, 43, 50, 60, 87, 89, 100, 132–134, 162, 182; and consciousness 132; and hate 46; knowledge of 86; loss of 53; mythology and psychology of 132; and narcissism 144, 182–184; narcissistic demand for 186–188; of self/other 118, 134; shadows of 131–144; transformative potential of 122–126; transgressive power 47–48; *see also* self-love
Love and Saint Augustine (Arendt) 6

masculine 92–94
melancholia 28, 53–54, 133; of nigredo 170–173

melancholic loss, defined 28
memory 32, 35, 132
Meredith-Owen, W. 40
Metamorphosis 1, 3
mind: and body 68, 70–71, 91, 103, 112, 187; fascist state of 53
'Mirror' (Plath) 68, 75
mirrored body 71–73
mirror image 25–26, 75–80; and Sylvia Plath 75–80
Mizen, R. 71
mythology of living 8

Nacke, P. 98
narcissism 1–2, 11, 19, 97, 131; of aggression and rejection 127; and 'as-if' personality 27; basic psychoanalytic concept of 98–99; case example 9–11, 90–92, 105–106; character/personality 90, 98, 119, 122, 124–126, 155, 167; concept of 3–4, 8, 98; as conundrum 12–16; cultural impact 12, 19; description 20–21; detachment from true self 128; development from early deficient dynamics 102; development of 19; and empathy 102; and false self 102–103; forms of 100; Freud's view 99–100; Hillman on 5; in historical and transcultural perspective 127; Humbert's explanation of 119; impenetrability in relationships 111; in Jungian thought 117–129; Jung's perspective vs. Freud's theory 117; Kernberg's view 101–102; kinds of 99; Kristeva defining 135; later theorists on 100–103; libidinal 100; and love 144, 182–184; medium of illusion 112; misconceptions about 19; as multifaceted experience 6; narcissistic destruction 58; narcissistic types, thin-skinned/thick-skinned 100–101, 104; origins of 18; paradox of 11; as part of emotional development 184; primary 28, 99; problems and symptoms of 125; psychic wounds of 23; as psychodynamic function 126; psychological complexity of 98; search for admiration and idealisation 137; and

search for what is lost 36; secondary 99; and self 119; in self-deception 23, 186; and self-states 53; therapeutic and analytical challenge 22–25; as trait of personality 17; transformative potential of 102; vagaries of 17–32; Winnicott's view 102–103; *see also individual entries*
narcissistic defences 9, 18, 58, 60
narcissistic fantasies 31–32
narcissistic injury 112
narcissistic intrigue 11–12
narcissistic withdrawal 111, 114
Narcissus 1, 5, 8, 10, 19, 20, 22, 23, 25, 69, 70, 73, 82, 85–88, 123, 135, 181, 185–186
negative capability, concept of 29–31
negative narcissism 111
negative primal relationship 18
Neumann, E. 18
nigredo 166–168, 174, 177; melancholia of 170–173
Nussbaum, M. 83

openness 22, 34, 41, 126
otherness: alterity and 25; conscious of 28; dimensions of 134; diversity and 11; eliminating 13, 95; engaging with 63; in love relationships 132; sameness and 127
Ovid 1, 3, 8

painful experiences 34
parental absences, effects of 112–115
perfect image, lure of 70–71
personal and cultural transformations 185–186
personal complex 152–156
Phillips, A. 30, 87, 105, 132
philoxenia 151
The Picture of Dorian Gray (Wilde) 65
Plath, S. 68; and mirror image 75–80; self-flagellation 77
positive narcissism 111
primary narcissism 28, 99
Proner, B. 40, 41
Proust, M. 2, 19, 133

psyche 12, 15, 17, 36, 47, 59, 68, 72–74, 79, 92, 95, 114, 119, 121, 133, 155–158, 162, 172, 178, 186
psychical holes 106
psychic retreat 64, 87, 101, 150, 161, 172
psychic wounds 23, 45, 141–142, 185
psychotherapy 178
puer and puella 59–61, 120–122
putrefaction *see* nigredo

rage, envy and 38–42, 102
repetition 84–85, 90
repression 32, 36, 89, 93
Riviere, J. 64
Rosenfeld, H. 13, 97–98, 100–101
Rustin, M. 100

sadism 46–47, 113
Samuels, A. 149
Schwartz-Salant, N. 23, 119, 123–126
secondary narcissism 99
self 2, 13, 24, 34, 41, 47, 74, 79, 83, 102, 119, 127, 162, 169, 174, 179; analytical bridge to 146–162; concept of 6; core 45; defences of 24, 125, 149; denial of 48, 89; discovery of 161; and ego 5, 46, 52, 85, 117, 118, 124, 129, 175; finding 36, 65; fragility of 40, 45, 51, 54, 60, 106, 122, 133; idealised 141; and identity formation 89; illusions of 127; love of 118; and others 4, 6, 11, 17, 22, 23, 27, 28, 31, 34–35, 40, 57, 98, 126, 132, 147, 148, 152, 156, 158, 166, 182; and persona 144; physical/psychological 70, 89; psychic texture of 19; psychology 102; relationship to 95; sense of 79, 101; silencing of 88; subjective experience of 91; true 103, 143; wounded 44
self-attack, fragility and 173–174
self-belonging 74
self-cohesion 133
self-confidence 118
self-consciousness 28
self-deception 20, 23, 57, 65, 186
self-disillusionment 19

self-esteem 27, 46, 52, 99, 103, 126
self-exploration 55
self-hatred, and envy 41–42
self-identity 27, 28, 126–128, 177
self-love 4, 6, 18, 22, 23, 48, 53, 117, 118, 134, 135, 162
self-recognition 126
self-reflection 10, 12, 43, 62, 97, 118, 121, 125, 153, 185
self-representation 133
self-talk 68
self-value 5
shadows 56, 120, 121, 133, 136, 155, 174–176; of love in relationship 131–144
shame 3, 9, 22, 23, 28, 40, 46, 48, 69, 126, 182, 186
Shorter, B. 148
social media 14, 19, 27, 70
Solomon, H. 64, 103
soul image and its projection 117
spontaneity 22, 153
Steiner, J. 13, 87, 100
subpersonalities 74

symbolic reality 57
symbolism (mirror) 76, 78; *see also* mirror image
symbols 159

threshold experiences 121
Time Regained (Proust) 2
transcendent function 156–159
transferences 23, 126, 135, 148, 155, 158–161, 167
true self 103, 143

violence 71, 102, 124
von Franz, M. L. 122, 123

wholeness 37, 120, 183
Wilde, O. 65
Winnicott, D. 13, 102–103, 113
'Womanliness as Masquerade' (Riviere) 64
Woolf, V. 68

Zeus 88